Nathan Frank

The Bankrupt Act of 1867

As Embodied in the Revised Statutes, Consolidated with its Amendments

Nathan Frank

The Bankrupt Act of 1867

As Embodied in the Revised Statutes. Consolidated with its Amendments

ISBN/EAN: 9783337123697

Printed in Europe, USA, Canada, Australia, Japan

Cover: Foto ©Suzi / pixelio.de

More available books at **www.hansebooks.com**

THE
BANKRUPT ACT

OF 1867,

AS EMBODIED IN THE

REVISED STATUTES,

CONSOLIDATED WITH ITS AMENDMENTS,

INCLUDING ALL SUBSEQUENT

AMENDATORY AND SUPPLEMENTAL ACTS.

THIRD EDITION, WITH NOTES.

COMPILED, WITH THE RULES AND INDEX, BY

NATHAN FRANK,
OF THE ST. LOUIS BAR.

ST. LOUIS:
THE CENTRAL LAW JOURNAL.
1877.

Entered according to Act of Congress, in the year 1877, by
NATHAN FRANK,
In the office of the Librarian of Congress at Washington.

MAYNARD AND TEDFORD, PRINTERS.

PREFACE TO THE THIRD EDITION.

The previous editions of this work exhibited the bankrupt act *as it should be read*, by a consolidation of the Act of March 2, 1867, with its amendments. Since those editions were published, the Revised Statutes of the United States have appeared. The object of this edition is to exhibit the laws relating to bankruptcy as they *should now be read*, by consolidating with the title "Bankruptcy" in the Revised Statutes of the United States, all subsequent amendatory and supplemental acts, and placing the numbers of the sections of the Revised Statutes, with which they correspond. The Author has endeavored to collect the decisions which construe and expound the law as it now stands, with particular reference to the adjudications upon the amendatory acts, which it is hoped will be of some assistance to the practitioner. The General Orders promulgated by the Supreme Court have been added, with a Table of Contents. The entire work has been carefully indexed.

St. Louis, October, 1877.

TABLE OF CASES CITED.

Abbe, In re 2 N. B. R. 75, p. 76, n. 177.
Adams v. Boston R. R. Co., 4 N. B. R. 314, p 77, n. 181.
Alabama R. R. Co. v. Jones, 5 N. B. R. 97, p. 26, n. 55; p. 77, n. 181.
Alexander, In re, 3 N. B. R. 29, p. 7, n. 11; p. 8, n. 16.
Alton v. Robinett, 9 N. B. R. 74, p. 73, n. 171.
Am. Plate Glass Ins. Co. In re, 12 N. B. R. 56, p. 46, n. 93.
Anderson, In re, 9 N. B. R. 360, p. 4, n. 5.
Anderson, In re, 12 N. B. R. 502, p. 50, n. 105.
Angell, In re, 10 N. B. R. 73; s. C. 1 Cent. L. J. 363; 6 Ch. L. N. 341, p. 24, n. 45.
Asten, In re, 14 N. B. R. 7, p. 62, n. 137.
Augustine Ass. v. McFarland, 13 N. B. R. 7, p. 4, n. 5.
Austin v. O'Reilly, 12 N. B. R. 329, p. 49, n. 101.

B

Badenheim, In re, 15 N. B. R. 370, p. 35, n. 69.
Baer, In re, 14 N. B. R. 97, p. 36, n. 77.
Bailey, In re, 15 N. B. R. 48, p. 16, n. 28.
Bailey, In re, 2 Woods 222, p. 46, n. 92.
Bailey v. Loeb, 2 Woods 578, p. 47, n. 97.
Bailey v. Wier, 12 N. B. R. 24; s. C. 21 Wall. 342, p. 41, n. 86.
Baker, In re, 14 N. B. R. 433, p. 84, n. 187; p. 86, n. 189.
Bakewell, In re, 4 N. B. R. 619, p. 59, n. 126.
Balch Ex parte, 13 N. B. R. 160, p. 46, n. 94.
Baldwin v. Rapplee, 5 N. B. R. 19, p. 6, n. 9; p. 7, n. 13.
Bank of Columbia v. Overstreet, 13 N. B. R. 154; s. C. 10 Bush, 148, p. 36, n. 69.
Barker v. Smith, 12 N. B. R. 474, p. 85, n. 187.
Barman, In re, 14 N. B. R. 125, p. 84, n. 187.
Barnard v. Norwich & Worcester R. R., 14 N. B. R. 469, p. 35, n. 68.
Barnes, In re, 1 Lowell 560, p. 56, n. 122.
Barnes v. United States, 12 N. B. R. 526, p. 45, n. 90.
Barnett v. Highblower, 10 N. B. R. 157, p. 24, n. 45.

Barnewell v. Jones, 14 N. B. R. 278, p. 84, n. 186; p. 86, n. 190.
Barrett, In re, 2 N. B. R. 533, p. 33, n. 65.
Barron v. Morris, 14 N. B. R, 371, p. 6, n. 9; p. 8, n. 14.
Barston v. Peckham, 5 N. B. R. 72, p. 6, n. 6.
Bartholow v. Bean, 18 Wall. 635; s. C. 1 Cent. L. J. 166, p. 84, n. 185.
Batchelder v. Putnam, 13 N. B. [R. 404; s. C. 54 N. H. 84, p. 36, n. 69.
Beal, In re, 2 N. B. R. 587, p. 67, n. 154; p. 68, n. 157.
Bean, In re, 14 N. B. R. 182, p. 51, n. 110.
Beardsley, In re, 1 N. B. R. 304, p. 67, n. 153, 154.
Bechet, In re, 12 N. B. R. 201, s. C. 2 Woods 173, p. 63, n. 139, 143.
Beckerford, In re, 1 Dill. 45, p. 38, n. 78.
Belden, In re, 2 N. B. R. 42, p. 67, § 5110.
Bellamy, In re, 1 Ben. 390, p. 40, n. 84.
Bennett, In re, 2 N. B. R. 181, p. 37, n. 70.
Bennett, In re, 12 N. B. R. 257, p. 35, n. 68.
Bennett, In re, 12 N. B. R. 181, p. 75, n. 174.
Bennett v. Goldthwait, 109 Mass. 494, p. 72, n. 168.
Bergeron, In re, 12 N. B. R. 385, p. 23, n. 37; p. 27, n. 59.
Bigelow, In re, 2 Ben. 480, p. 48, n. 103.
Bill v. Beckwith, 2 N. B. R. 241, p. 43, n. 89.
Black v. Blazo, 13 N. B. R. 195; s. C. 117 Mass. 17, p. 73, n. 170.
Black v. McClelland, 12 N. B. R. 481, p. 45, n. 92.
Blair v. Allen, 3 Dill. 101, p. 6, n. 10.
Blodgett, In re, 5 N. B. R. 472, p. 34, n. 66.
Bloss, In re, 4 N. B. R. 147, p. 46, n. 92.
Blue Ridge Co., In re, 13 N. B. R. 315, p. 49, n. 102.
Blum v. Ellis, 76 N. C. 293, p. 3, n. 2; p. 49, n. 103.
Blum v. Ellis, 13 N. B. R. 345; s. C. 73 N. C. 293.; p. 72, n. 167.
Bolander v. Gentry, 36 Cal. 105, p. 25, n. 53.
Bontelle, In re, 2 N. B. R. 129, p. 69, n. 160.
Booth, In re, 14 N. B. R. 232, p. 57, n. 126.

TABLE OF CASES CITED.

Booth v. Brooks, 12 N. B. R. 398, p. 84, n. 186; p. 87, n. 195.
Boothroyd, In re, 14 N. B. R. 230, p. 37, n. 74; p. 38, n. 76.
Boston, Hartford & Erie R. R., In re, 9 Blatch. 101; s. c. 6 N. B. R. 209, p. 27, n. 59; p. 33, n. 65.
Bowie, In re, 1 N. B. R. 628, p. 4, u. 5.
Bowman v. Harding, 4 N. B. R. 20; s. c. 58 Me. 559, p. 36, n. 69.
Bracken v. Johnston, 15 N. B. R. 108, p. 35, n. 69.
Bradbury v. Galloway, 12 N. B. R. 299; s. c. 3 Sawy. 346, p. 84, n. 186; p. 88, 196.
Brady v. Otis, 14 N. B. R. 345, p. 35, u. 67.
Braley v. Boomer, 12 N. B. R. 303; s. c. 116 Mass. 527, p. 36, n. 69.
Brandon Mfg. Co. v. Frazer, 13 N. B. R. 352; s. c. 47 Vt. 88, p. 72, n. 168.
Bratton v. Anderson, 14 N. B. R. 99, p. 66, n. 150.
Breck, In re, 12 N. B. R. 215, p. 47, n. 97.
Brett v. Carter, 14 N. B. R. 301, p. 85, u. 187.
Briggs, In re, 3 N. B. R. 638, p. 25, n. 53.
Brigham v. Claflin, 7 N. B. R. 412, p. 4, u. 5; p. 87, n. 195.
Brightman, In re, 15 N. B. R. 213, p. 67, n. 152.
Brinkman, In re, 7 N. B. R. 421, p. 4, n. 5.
Broich, In re, 15 N. B. R. 11, p. 23, n. 37, 39, 40; p, 24, n. 43; p. 27, u. 59; p. 50, u. 105.
Brook v. McCracken, 10 N. B. R. 461; s. c. 8. P. L. R. 102; s. c. 7 Ch. L. N. 10, p. 84, n. 186.
Brookmire v. Bean, 12 N. B. R. 217; s. c. 3 Dill. 136, p. 46, n. 92.
Brown v. Gibbons, 13 N. B. R. 407; s. c. 37 Ia. 665; p. 49, n. 102a; p. 50, u. 106.
Browne, In re, 12 N. B. R. 529, p. 47, n. 96.
Brunquest In re, 14 N. B. R. 529, p. 49, u. 100.
Bryan Mining Co., In re, 4 N. B. R. 144; s. c. 4 N. B. R. 394, p. 77, n. 182.
Buchanan v. Smith, 16 Wall. 277, p. 84, u. 185
Buckman v. Goss, 13 N. B. R. 337, p. 85, u. 188.
Buckner v. Jewell, 14 N. B. R. 287, p. 57, n. 124.
Bunste In re, 5 N. B. R. 82, § 5114, p. 70.
Burbank v. Bigelow, 14 N. B. R. 445; s. c. 92 U. S. 179, p. 4, u. 3; p. 6, n. 6, 8.
Burch, In re, 10 N. B. R. 150, p. 24, n. 48.
Burke, In re, 15 N. B. R. 40, p. 11, n, 21.
Burnell, In re, 14 N. B. R. 498, p. 79, n. 184.

Burper v. Sparhawk, 4 N. B. R. 685; s. c. 108 Mass. 111, p. 73, n. 170,
Burr v. Hopkins, 12 N. B. R. 211, p. 53, n. 118.
Burt, In re, 1 Dill. 439, p. 21, n. 32.
Bush v. Lester, 15 N. B. R. 36; s. c. 55 Ga. 579, p. 35, n. 68; p. 37, n. 71; p. 38, u. 78; p. 49, n. 102a.
Butterfield, In re, 14 N. B. R. 147, p. 69, n. 160.
Butterfield, In re, 14 N. B. R. 195, p. 56, n. 122.
Buxbaum, In re, 13 N. B. R. 478, p. 69, u. 160.

C

California R. R., In re, 3 Sawy. 240, p. 77, n. 181.
Canby v. McLear, 13 N. B. R. 22, p. 53, n. 117.
Carpenter v. Turrell, 100 Mass. 450, p. 36, n. 69.
Carrier, In re, 13 N. B. R. 208, p. 24, n. 45.
Chamberlaines, In re, 12 N. B. R. 230, p. 40, n. 83.
Chamberlain v. Mfg Co., 118 Mass. 532, p. 66, n. 150.
Chase In re, 14 N. B. R. 139, 157, p. 58, n. 128.
Christly, In re. 10 N. B. R. 268, p. 56, n. 122.
Citizens' Bank v. Ober, 13 N. B. R. 328, p. 42, n. 88.
City Bank, In re, 6 N. B. R. 71, p. 48, n. 99.
Claflin v. Houseman, 15 N. B. R. 49; s. c. 93 U. S. 130, p. 87, n. 193,
Clairmont, In re, 1 N. D. R. 270, p. 33, u. 65.
Clapp, In re, 14 N. B. R. 191, p. 63, n. 140.
Clark, In re, 3 N. B. R. 491, p. 39, n. 80.
Clinton v. Mayo, 12 N. B. R. 41, p. 27, u. 57, 59.
Coan Carriage Co. In re, 12 N. B. R. 203, p. 40, n. 83.
Cobb In re, ⏐ N. B. R. 414, p. 37, n. 72.
Cocks In re, 3 Ben. 260, p. 68, n. 157.
Coit v. Robinson, 9 N. B. R. 289, s. c., 19 Wall. 274, p. 8, n. 16, 17; p. 9, n. 19.
Coleman, In re, 7 Blatch. 192, p. 7, n. 11.
Collier, In re, 12 N. B. R. 266, p. 76, n. 175.
Collins, In re, 12 N. B. R. 379, p. 35, u. 68; p. 85, n. 187.
Colwell, In re, 15 N. B. R. 92, p. 57, n. 125.
Commercial Bulletin Co., In re, 2 Woods, 220, p. 47, n. 97.
Compton v. Conklin, 15 N. B. R. 417, p. 76, n. 177.
Comstock, In re, 10 N. B. R. 451, p. 8, n. 16.
Comstock, In re, 13 N. B. R. 193, p. 54, n. 118.

TABLE OF CASES CITED.   vii

Comstock, In re, 8 Ch. L. N. 418, p. 24, n. 45.
Cone, In re, 2 Ben. 502, p. 25, n. 48.
Conro v. Crane, 94 U. S., p. 8, n. 15.
Cook v. Rogers, 13 N. B. R. 97, p. 86, n. 190.
Cornwall In re, 6 N. B. R. 305, p. 45, n. 91.
Cote In re, 14 N. B. R. 503, p. 68, n. 157.
Crajon v. Carmichael, 11 N. B. R. 511; s. C. 2 Dill. 519, p. 84, n. 187.
Cram In re, 1 N. B. R. 504, p. 50, n. 105.
Cramer In re, 13 N. B. R. 225, p. 53, n. 118.
Crawford In re, 5 N. B. R. 361, p. 46, n. 94.
Cragin v. Thompson, 12 N. B. R. 81, p. 86, n. 190.
Cretiew, In re, 5 N. B. R. 423, p. 66, n. 155.
Crump v. Chapman, 15 N. B. R. 571, p. 87, n. 194.
Cummings v. Clegg, 14 N. B. R. 49; s. C. 52 Ga. 605, p. 37, n. 78.
Cunningham v. Cady, 13 N. B. R. 526, p. 22, n. 33.
Currier, In re, 13 N. B. R. 68, p. 22, n. 34; p. 23, n. 37, 42; p. 53, n. 115.
Cutter v. Dingee, 14 N. B. R. 294, p. 89, n. 80

D

Darby, In re, 4 N. B. R. 211, 309, p. 59, n. 129.
Daubman v. White, 12 N. B. R. 436; s. C. 48 Cal. 439, p. 87, n. 193, 194.
Davidson, In re, 4 Ben. 10 p. 53, n. 115.
Davis v. Anderson, 6 N. B. R. 145, p. 40, n. 84; p. 41, n. 86.
Davis, In re, 2 N. B. R. 391, p. 49, n. 103.
Davis v. R. R. Co., 13 N. B. R. 258, p. 49, n. 102.
Dean, In re, 1 N. B. R. 249, p. 57, n. 123; p. 79, n. 134.
Deckert, In re, 10 N. B. R. 2, p. 38, n. 78.
Derby, In re, 12 N. B. R. 241, p. 70, n. 161.
Detroit Car Works, In re, 14 N. B. R. 243, p. 77, n. 183.
Devoe, In re, 2 N. B. R. 27, p. 66, n. 151.
Dibble, In re, 3 Ben. 354, p. 42, n. 87.
Dickerson v. Spaulding, 15 N. B. R. 312, p. 36, n. 69.
Dillard, In re, 9 N. B. R. 8, p. 38, n. 78.
Dingee v. Becker, 9 N. B. R. 508, p. 65, n. 149.
Dow, In re, 6 N. B. R. 10, p. 40, n. 82.
Dow, In re, 14 N. B. R. 307, p. 48, n. 98; p. 49, n. 101.
Drake, In re, 14 N. B. R., 150, p. 57, n. 123.
Drisco, In re, 14 N. B. R. 551; s. C. N. B. R. 112, p. 71, n. 163.
Duerson, In re, 13 N. B. R. 183, p. 37, n. 73.
Duncan, In re, 14 N. B. R. 18, p. 24, n. 46; p. 26, n. 56.

Dunkerson, In re, 12 N. B. R. 413, p. 50, n. 105; 12 N. B. R. 391, p. 76, n. 175.
Dutcher v. Wright, 15 Alb. L. J. 100; p. 14, n. 26.

E

Eastman v. Hibbard, 13 N. B. R. 360, p. 72, n. 167.
Ebersole v. Adams, 13 N. B. R. 141, p. 86 n. 190.
Eldridge, In re, 4 N. B. R. 498, p. 40, n. 82; 12 N. B. R. 540, p. 45, n. 91, 92; p. 49, n. 100.
Ellis, In re, 1 N. B. R. 555, p. 35, n. 69.
Exchange Bank v. Harris, 14 N. B. R. 512; s. C., 3 Cent. L. J. 768, p. 84, n. 187.
Eyster v. Gaff, 13 N. B. R. 546; s. C., 91 U. S. 521, p. 4, n. 3.

F

Farnsworth, In re, 14 N. B. R. 148, p. 48, n. 98.
Farrar v. Walker. 13 N. B. R. 82, p. 77, n. 180.
Farrin v. Crawford, 2 N. B. R. 602, p. 22, n. 32.
Fendley, In re, 10 N. B. R. 250, p. 6, n. 6.
Fernberg, In re, 2 N. B. R. 353, p. 33, § 5036.
Filligin v. Thornton, 12 N. B. R. 92, p. 4, n. 5.
Fireman's Ins. Co., In re, 8 N. B. R. 123; s. C., 3 Biss. 46!, p. 49, n. 100.
First, In re, 3 Cent. L. J. 51, p. 90, n. 206.
Flanders v. Abbey, 6 Biss. 16, p. 86, n. 192.
Flannagan v. Pearson, 14 N. B. R. 37, p. 66, n. 150; p. 71, n. 164.
Foote, In re, 12 N. B. R. 337, p. 76, n. 175.
Foster v. Ames, 2 N. B. R. 455. p. 43, n. 89.
Foster v. Hackley, 2 N. B. R. 406, p. 25, n. 53.
Foster v. Inglee, 13 N. B. R. 239, p. 58, n. 127.
Fowler v. Dillon, 12 N. B. R. 308, p. 3, n. 2.
Fox v. Gardiner, 12 N. B. R. 137, p. 86, n. 191.
Fraley v. Kelly, 67 N. C. 78, p. 72, n. 166.
Francke, In re, 10 N. B. R. 488. p. 70, n. 161.
Freeman v. Fort, 14 N. B. R. 46; s. C., 52 Ga. 371, p. 4, n. 5.
Frisbie, In re, 13 N. B. R. 349, p. 53, n. 117.
Frizelle, In re, 5 N. B. R. 122, p. 49, n. 106
Frost, In re, 11 N. B. R. 69, p. 23, n. 39.
Frost v. Hotchkiss, 14 N. B. R. 443, p. 4, n. 4.

Frostman v. Hicks. 15 N. B. R. 41, p. 66, n. 150.
Funkenstein, In re, 14 N. B. R. 213, p. 26, n. 56.

G

Gainey, In re, 2 N. B. R. 525, p. 37, n. 72.
Gallison, In re, 5 N. B. R. 353, p. 46, n. 92.
Galtman v. Honea, 12 N. B. R. 493, p. 85, n. 187, 188.
Gates v. American, 14 N. B. R. 141, p. 38. n. 79.
Gay, In re, 2 N. B. R. 358. p. 68, n. 156.
Gibson v. Dobie. 14 N. B. R. 156, p. 85, n. 188.
Gibson v. Warden, 14 Wall. 214, p. 84, n. 187.
Gies, In re, 12 N. B. R. 179, p. 58, n. 127.
Globe Ins. Co. v. Cleveland Ins. Co., 14 N. B. R. 311, p. 22, n. 32; p. 86, n. 190.
Gold Mining Co., In re, 15 N. B. R. 545, p. 35, n. 68.
Goldschmidt, In re, 3 N. B. R. 165, p. 21, n. 32.
Goodrich v. Hunton, 2 Woods, 137, p. 72, n. 168.
Goodrich v. Wilson, 14 N. B. R. 555; s. c., 119 Mass. 429, p. 4, n. 3.
Graves, In re, 2 Ben. 100, p. 42, n. 87.
Greeley v. Scott, 12 N. B. R. 248, p. 38, n. 75.
Green, In re, 15 N. B. R. 198, p. 46, n 92.
Green Pond R. R. Co., In re, 13 N. B. R. 118, p. 21, n. 30; p. 23, n. 39.
Griffin, In re, 9 N. B. R. 254, p. 37, n. 71.
Griffith, In re, 3 N. B. R. 731, p. 40, n. 82.
Griffiths, In re, 10 N. B. R. 456, p. 70, n. 161.
Gunike, In re, 4 N. B. R. 92, p. 70, n. 162.

H

Haber v. Clayburg, 4 Cent. L. J. 342, p. 66, n. 150.
Hadley, In re, 12 N. B. R. 366, p. 22, n. 32, 33; p. 23, n. 35, 37; p. 25, n. 54.
Haggerton v. Morrison, 59 Mo. 324, p. 66, n. 150.
Halcy, In re, 2 N. B. R. 36, p. 50. n. 107.
Hall, In re, 1 Dill. 586, p. 22, n. 32.
Hall, In re, 15 N. B. R. 81, p. 23, n. 37.
Hall v. Allen, 12 Wall. 452, p. 9, n. 19.
Hamhright, In re, 2 N. B. R. 498, p. 36, n. 69.
Hamburger, In re, 12 N. B. R. 277, p. 47, n. 97.
Hamilton v. Bryant, 14 N. B. R. 479, p. 36, n. 69.

Hamlin v. Pettibone, 10 N. B. R. 172; s. c. 1 Cent. L. J. 404; s. c. 6 Biss. 167, p. 84, n. 186.
Handell, In re, 15 N. B. R. 71, p. 58, n. 127.
Handlin, In re, 12 N. B. R. 49; s. c. 2 Cent. L. J. 264, p. 38, n. 76.
Hanibel, In re, 15 N. B. R. 236, p. 22, n. 33.
Hanson v. Herrick, 100 Mass. 323, p. 25, n. 53.
Hapgood In re, 14 N. B. R. 495, p. 40, n. 82.
Harden, In re, 1 N. B. R. 395, p. 45, n. 91
Hardy v. Bininger, 4 N. B. R. 262, p. 21, n. 32.
Hasbrouck, In re, 1 Ben. 402, p. 11, n. 21.
Haskell, In re, 4 N. B. R. 558, p. 13, n. 25.
Haskill v. Frye, 14 N. B. R. 525, p. 3, n. 2; p. 87, n. 195.
Hatch v. Seeley, 13 N. B. R. 380, p. 35, n. 69; p. 49. n. 101.
Hatcher v. Jones, 14 N. B. R. 387, p. 37, n. 73.
Hatje, In re, 12 N. B. R. 548, p. 23, n. 40; p. 27, n. 59; p. 46, n. 92.
Hawkins v. Hastings, 1 Dill. 453, p. 7, n. 11.
Haworth v. Travis, 13 N. B. R. 145; s. c. 67 Ill. 301, p. 37, n. 73.
Hayes v. Dickinson. 15 N. B. R.3 50, p. 35, n. 68.
Heard v. Jones, 15 N. B. R. 402, p. 49, n. 103.
Heffron, In re, 10 N. B. R. 213; s. c. 6 Ch. L. N. 358, p. 23, n. 35.
Henkelman v. Smith, 12 N. B. R. 121, p. 35, n. 69; p. 36, n. 69.
Henly v. Lanier, 15 N. B. R. 280, p. 72, n. 166.
Hercules Mutual Life Ins. Society, 6 N. B. R. 338, p. 22, n. 32, 33.
Herndon v. Howard, 4 N. B. R. 212; s. c. 9 Wall. 664, p. 39, n. 80; p. 40, n. 81.
Herpich, In re, 15 N. B. R. 426, p. 85, n. 188.
Herrman, In re, 4 Ben. 126, p. 52, n. 114.
Hester, In re, 5 N. B. R. 285, p. 37, n. 71.
Hewett v. Norton, 13 N. B. R. 276, p. 39, n. 80.
Hill, In re, 1 Ben. 321, p. 32, n. 64; p. 56, n. 122.
Hill, In re, 1 N. B. R. 16, 275, 431, p. 67, n. 154.
Hinsdale, In re, 12 N. B. R. 480, p. 60, n. 129.
Hiscock v. Jaycox, 12 N. B. R. 507, p. 76, n. 176.
Hitchcock v. Rollo, 4 N. B. R. 690; s. c. 3 Biss. 276, p. 48, n. 99.

… TABLE OF CASES CITED. ix

Hobson v. Markson. 1 Dill. 421, p. 86, n. 190.
Holland, In re, 12 N. B. R. 403, p. 25, n. 51.
Holmes, In re, 12 N. B. R. 86, p. 62, n. 137.
Holmes, In re, 14 N. B. R. 209, p. 67, n. 152.
Holmes, In re, 14 N. B. R. 493, p. 58, n. 127.
Holyoke v. Adams, 13 N. B. R. 413, p. 38, n. 69.
Home Ins. Co. v. Hollis, 14 N. B. R. 337, p. 39, n. 80.
Hoover v. Wise, 14 N. B. R. 264; s. c., 91 U. S. 308; s. c., 3 Cent. L. J. 276, p. 85, n. 187.
Hoppock, In re, 2 Ben. 478, p. 28, n. 63.
Houseberger, In re, 2 Ben. 504, p. 58, n. 127.
Hubbard's Case, 1 N. B. R. 679; s. c., 1 Lowell, 190, p. 52, n. 111.
Hudgins v. Lane, 11 N. B. R. 462, p. 76, n. 177.
Hufnagel, In re, 12 N. B. R. 554, p. 35, n. 67; p. 47, n. 97; p. 49, n. 103.
Humble v. Carson, 6 N. B. R. 84, p. 72, n. 166.
Hunt, In re, 5 N. B. R. 433, p. 37, n. 70, 71.
Hurst, In re, 13 N. B. R. 455, p. 62, n. 136.
Hurst v. Teft, 13 N. B. R. 108, p. 9, n. 18.
Husseman, In re, 2 N. B. R. 437, p. 25, n. 53; p. 67, n. 154.
Hyman, In re, 3 Ben. 28, p. 11, n. 21.
Hymes, In re, 10 N. B. R. 434, p. 23, n. 37; p. 24, n. 47.

I

Independent Ins. Co., In re, 6 N. B. R. 169, p. 21, n. 30.
Iron Mt. Co., In re, 9 Blatch. 320, p. 3, n. 2.
Irving, In re, 14 N. B. R. 289, p. 25, n. 49, 50.
Israel, In re, 12 N. B. R. 204, p. 23, n. 42.
Ives v. Tregent, 14 N. B. R. 60; s. c., 29 Mich. 390, p. 4, n. 5.

J

Jack, In re, 13 N. B. R. 296, p. 22, n. 32; p. 27, n. 59; p. 35, n. 69.
Jackson, In re, 14 N. B. R. 449, p. 51, n. 110; p. 52, n. 114.
Jackson v. McCulloch, 13 N. B. R. 233, p. 86, n. 189, 190.
Janeway, In re, 4 N. B. R. 100, p. 40, n. 83.
Jaycox, In re, 13 N. B. R. 122, p. 46, n. 92.
Jenkins v. Armour, 14 N. B. R. 276, p. 48, n. 96.

Johnson v. Bishop, 1 Woolw. 324, p. 3, n. 2.
Johnson v. Price, 13 N. B. R. 523, p. 3, n. 2; p. 6, n. 6.
Johnson v. Rogers, 15 N. B. R. 2, p. 49, n. 101.
Johnson v. Worden, 13 N. B. R. 335; s. c., 47 Vt. 457, p. 71, n. 184.
Johnston, In re, 14 N. B. R. 569, p. 54, n. 118.
Joliet Iron Co., In re, 10 N. B. R. 60, p. 23, n. 86.
Jones, In re, 2 N. B. R. 59, p. 60, n. 129.
Jones, In re, 12 N. B. R. 48, p. 70, n. 161.
Jones, In re, 13 N. B. R. 286, p. 68, n. 155.
Jones v. Russell, 49 Ga. 460, p. 71, n. 164.
Jordan, In re, 8 N. B. R. 180, p. 38, n. 78.
Jordan, In re, 10 N. B. R. 427, p. 38, n. 78.
Jordan v. Downey, 12 N. B. R. 427; s. c., 40 Md. 401, p. 86, n. 193.

K

Kaiser v. Richardson, 14 N. B. R. 391, p. 86, n. 69.
Kean, In re, 8 N. B. R. 367, p. 38, n. 78.
Keefer, In re, 4 N. B. R. 389, p. 67, n. 153.
Keller, In re, 10 N. B. R. 419, p. 23, n. 36.
Kemmerer v. Tool, 12 N. B. R. 334; s. c. 78 Penn. St. 147, p. 85, n. 187.
King, In re, 10 N. B. R. 568, p. 70, n. 161.
King v. Loudon, 14 N. B. R. 383; s. c. 53, Ga. 64, p. 35, n. 69.
Kingsley, In re, 1 N. B. R. 329, p. 45, n. 91.
Kline v. Bauendahl, 12 N. B. R. 575; s. c., 6 N. Y. sup 546, p. 39, n. 80.
Knapp v. Anderson, 15 N. B. R. 316, p. 72, n. 168.
Knickerbocker Ins. Co. v. Comstock, 8 N. B. R. 145; s. c. 16 Wall. 258, p. 7, n. 12.
Knight, In re, 8 N. B. R. 436, p. 75, n. 175.
Knight v. Cheney, 5 N. B. R. 305, p. 6, n. 8; p. 43, n. 89.
Knoepfel, In re, 1 Ben. 330, p. 56, n. 122.
Krogman, In re, 5 N. B. R. 116, p. 41, n. 86.
Kyler, In re, 2 Ben. 414, p. 52, n. 113.

L

L. J. Ship Canal R. R. & Iron Co., In re, 10 N. B. R. 76, p. 51, n. 109.
Lake Sup. Ship Canal R. R. Co., In re, 7 N. B. R. 376, 389, p. 52, n. 114.
Lamb v. Brown, 12 N. B. R. 522, p. 72, n. 166.
Lammer, In re, 14 N. B. R. 460, p. 38, n. 75.
Lamp Co. v. Brass Co., 13 N. B. R. 385, p. 66, n. 150.

TABLE OF CASES CITED.

Lanz, In re, 14 N. B. R. 159, p. 22, n. 32.
Langdon, In re, 13 N. B. R. 60, p. 62, n. 136.
Langley v. Perry, 2 N. B. R. 596, p. 22, n. 32.
Lansing v. Manton, 14 N. B. R. 126, p. 3, n. 2.
Lathrop v. Drake, 13 N. B. R. 472; s. c. 91 U. S. 518, p. 6, n. 2; p. 6, n. 6.
Lavender v. Gosnell, 12 N. B. R. 282, p. 86, n. 190.
Leach v. Green, 12 N. B. R. 376; s. c. 116 Mass. 534, p. 39, n. 80.
Leavenworth Bank, In re, 14 N. B. R. 82, 92, p. 90, n. 206.
Leavenworth Sav. Bank, In re, 14 N. B. R. 82, 92; 3 Cent. L. J. 207, p. 77, n. 180, 183.
Lee, In re, 14 N. B. R. 89, p. 53, n. 116.
Leighton, In re, 5 N. B. R. 95, p. 21, n. 31.
Leighton v. Harwood, 12 N. B. R. 360; s. c. 111 Mass. 67, p. 41, n. 85.
Leland, In re, 5 N. B. R. 222, p. 76, n. 177, 178.
Lesynsky, In re, 3 Ben. 487, p. 150 66, n.
Levin, In re, 14 N. B. R. 385, p. 69, n. 160.
Levy, In re, 1 Ben. 496, p. 13, n. 24, 25.
Lewis, In re, 4 Ben. 67, p. 54. n. 118.
Lewis, In re, 14 N. B. R. 144, p. 62, n. 136.
Lewis v. United States, 14 N. B. R. 64, p. 58, n. 127.
Lightner v. First Nat. Bank, 15 N. B. R. 69; s. c., 82 Penn. 301, p. 55, n. 119.
Little v. Alexander, 12 N. B. R. 134; s. c., 21 Wall. 500, p. 85, n. 186.
Lloyd, In re, 15 N. B. R. 257, p. 23, n. 36.
Longstreth v. Pennock, 42 N. B. R. 95; s. c. 20 Wall. 575, p. 47, n. 96.
Lowenstein, In re, 13 N. B. R. 479; s. c., 3 Dill. 145, p. 67, n. 152; p. 70, n. 161.
Lytle, In re, 14 N. B. R. 457, p. 63, n. 145.

M

McDermot Bolt Co., In re, 3 Ben. 369, p. 22, n. 32.
McDonald, In re, 14 N. B. R. 477, p. 52, n. 113a; p. 72, n. 166.
McDowell, In re, 6 Biss. 193, p. 63, n. 141.
McDuffee, In re, 14 N. B. R. 336, p. 50, n. 108.
McEwen, In re, 12 N. B. R. 11; s. c. 6 Biss. 294, p. 75, n. 175.
McGrath, In re, 5 N. B. R. 254, p. 47, n. 97.
McKay v. Funk, 13 N. B. R. 334; s. c. 87 Iowa, 661, p. 49, n. 102a.
McKibben, In re, 12 N. B. R. 97, p. 22, n. 83.
McKinsey v. Harding, 4 N. B. R. 86, p. 52, n. 113.

McLean, In re, 15 N. B. R. 333, p. 75, n. 175.
McLean v. Brown, 4 N. B. R. 585, p. 22, n. 33.
McNaughton, In re, 8 N. B. R. 44, p. 22, n. 33.
MacDonald v. Moore, 15 N. B. R. 26, p. 49. n. 101.
Macintire, In re, 1 Ben. 277, p. 13, n. 23.
Machad, In re, 2 N. B. R. 352, p. 70, n. 162.
Mackay, In re, 4 N. B. R. 66, p. 68, n. 156.
Magie, In re, 2 Ben. 369, p. 15, n. 27.
Major, In re, 14 N. B. R. 71, p. 33, n. 65; p. 42, n. 88.
Mann, In re, 14 N. B. R. 572, p. 23, n. 36.
March v. Heaton, 2 N. B. R. 180, p. 3, n. 2.
Marioneaux, In re, 13 N. B. R. 222, p. 73, n. 171a.
Markson v. Heaney, 1 Dill. 497, 511, p. 3, n. 2; p. 8, n. 18; p. 43, n. 89.
Markson v. Haney, 19 N. B. R. 484; s. c., 47 Ind. 31, p. 50, n. 106.
Marshall v. Knox, 8 N. B. R. 97; s. c., 16 Wall. 555, p. 9, n. 19.
Marter, In re, 12 N. B. R. 185, p. 3, n. 2; p. 6, n. 6; p. 22, n. 32; p. 86, n. 190.
Martin, In re, 13 N. B. R. 397, p. 37, n. 73.
Marvin, In re, 1 Dill. 178, p. 21, n. 30.
Marvin v. Chambers, 12 N. B. R. 77, p. 85, n. 187.
Mason v. Warthen, 14 N. B. R. 346, p. 36, n. 69.
Mason Organ Co. v. Bancroft, 4 Cent. L. J. 295, p. 63, n. 144.
Maxwell v. Faxton, 4 N. B. R. 210, p. 66, n. 150.
May v. Howe, 4 N. B. R. 677; s. c., 108 Mass. 502, p. 73, n. 170, 171.
Maybin, In re, 13 N. B. R. 468, p. 56, n. 121.
Mayer v. Hellman, 13 N. B. R. 440; s. c., 91 U. S. 496, p. 86, n. 190.
Mays v. Fritton, 11 N. B. R. 229; s. c.. 20 Wall. 414, p. 4, n. 5.
Mead v. Thompson, 8 N. B. R. 529; s. c., 15 Wall. 638, p. 9, n. 19.
Meader v. Sharp, 14 N. B. R. 492; s. c., 54 Ga. 125, p. 71, n. 164.
Mendelsohn, In re, 12 N. B. R. 533; s. c., 3 Sawy. 342, p. 22. n. 32; p. 27, n. 59.
Merchants Ins. Co., 6 N. B. R. 43, p. 21, n. 30.
Merritt v. Glidden, 39 Cal. 559, p. 72, n. 166.
Metcalf, In re. 2 Ben. 78, p. 68, n. 150.
Metz, In re, 6 Ben. 571, p. 47, n. 97.
Meyer v. Crystal Lake Works, 14 N. B. R. 9, p. 4, n. 5.

TABLE OF CASES CITED.

Michaels v. Post, 12 N. B. R. 152; s. c., 21 Wall. 398, p. 23, n. 42; p. 25, n. 61.
Michener v. Payson, 13 N. B. R. 49, p. 40, n. 81; p. 77, n. 180.
Migel, In re, 2 N. B. R. 481, p. 65, n. 149; p. 66, n. 150.
Miller v. McKenzie, 13 N. B. R. 496, p. 68, n. 140.
Miller v. O'kain, 14 N. B. R. 145, p. 65, n. 149.
Milwain, In re, 12 N. B. R. 358, p. 52, n. 114.
Minon v. Van Nostrand, 4 N. B. R. 108, p. 66, n. 151.
Montgomery, In re, 12 N. B. R. 321, p. 84, n. 186; p. 88, n. 197.
Montgomery v. Bucyrus Machine Works, 14 N. B. R. 193; 92 U. S. 257, p. 35, n. 68.
Moran v. Bogert, 14 N. B. R. 393, p. 42, n. 88.
Morford, In re, 1 Ben. 264, p. 17, n. 29.
Morgan v. Thornhill, 5 N. B. R. 1; s. c. 11 Wall. 65, p. 6, n. 6; p. 8, n. 16, 17; p. 9, n. 19.
Morris, In re, 11 N. B. R. 443, p. 62, n. 137
Morris, in re, 12 N. B. R. 170, p. 62, n. 133, 134.
Morse, In re, 13 N. B. R. 376; p. 75, n. 175.
Muller v. Bretano, 3 N. B. R. 329, p. 25, n. 53.
Munson v. Boston, Hartford and Erie R. R., 14 N. B. R. 173; s. c. 120 Mass. 80, p. 36, n. 69; p. 66, n. 150.
Murphy, In re, 10 N. B. R. 43; p. 21, n. 30.
Mutual Building Society, In re, 15 N. B. R. 44, p. 55, n. 119.

N

Nat. Bank v. Conway, 14 N. B. R 175, 513, p. 84, n. 187.
Nat. Bank v. Iron Co., 5 N. B. R. 491, p. 25, n. 52.
Nebe, In re, 11 N. B. R. 289, p. 50, n. 108.
Needham, In re, 2 N. B. R. 387, p. 67, n. 153.
New Lamp Co. v. Ausonia Co., 13 N. B. R. 385; s. c. 91 U. S. 656; p. 77, n. 179, 180.
Newman, In re, 2 N. B. R. 302, p. 68, n. 156.
Nichols v. Eaton, 13 N. B. R. 421; s. c. 91 U. S. 716, p. 35, n. 68.
Noesen, In re, 12 N. B. R. 422, p. 23, n. 41; p. 45, n. 91.
Noonan v. Orton, 12 N. B. R. 405; s. c. 84 Wis. 259, p. 39, n. 80.
North rn Iron Co., In re, 14 N. B. R. 359, p. 52, n. 114.
Norton v. De La Villebeuve, 13 N. B. R. 304, p. 41, n. 86.

Norton's Assignee v. Boyd, 8 Howard, 426, p. 4, n. 5.
Noyes, In re, 6 N. B. R. 277, p. 11, n. 21.
Nudd v. Burrows, 13 N. B. R. 289, p. 85, n. 188; p. 86, n. 189.

O

O'Bannon, In re, 2 N. B. R. 15, p. 67, n. 154; p. 68, n. 157.
Ohear, In re, 10 N. B. R. 153; s. c., 1 Cent. L. J. 362, p. 24. n. 45.
Odell v. Wootten, 4 N. B. R. 183; s. c., 88 Ga. 224, p. 72, n. 166.
O'Farrel, In re, 3 Ben. 191, p. 70, n. 162.
Olcott v. MacLeans, 14 N. B. R. 379, p. 85, n. 188.
Oregon Printing Co., In re, 13 N. B. R. 503, p. 24, n. 44.
Oregon Pub. Co., In re, 14 N. B. R. 394; s. c., 3 Sawy. 614, p. 8, n. 16; p. 77, n. 182, 183; p. 90, n. 206.
Orne, In re, 1 Ben. 361, p. 45, n. 92.
Orne, In re, 1 Ben. 420, p. 11, n. 21; p. 17, n. 29.
Owens, In re, 12 N. B. R. 516, p. 37, n. 73; p. 38, n. 78.
Owsley v. Cobin, 15 N. B. R. 489, p. 71, n. 164.
Oxford Iron Co. Slv. after, 14 N. B. R. 380, p. 84, n. 186.

P

Paddock, In re, 6 N. B. R. 132, p. 46, n. 92.
Palmer, In re, 14 N. B. R. 437, p. 68, n. 158; p. 69, n. 159; p. 70, § 5114.
Parsons v. Topliff, 14 N. B. R. 547, p. 85, n. 189.
Patterson In re, 1 Ben. 448 p. 13, n. 24.
Patterson In re 1 Ben. 508, p. 10, n. 20.
Pattison v. Wilbur, 12 N. B. R. 193, p. 72, n. 165; s. c., 10 R. I. 448, p. 72, n. 168.
Payne v. Able, 4 N. B. R. 220, p. 72, n. 166.
Payne v. Solomon, 14 N. B. R. 162, p. 27, n. 59.
Payson v. Coffin, 5 Cent. L. J. 220, p. 41, n. 86.
Pease In re, 13 N. B. R. 168, p. 76, n. 175.
Peebles, In re, 13 N. B. R. 149, p. 49, n. 101, 104.
Peiper v. Harmer, 5 N. B. R. 252, p. 41, n. 86.
Penn, In re, 5 N. B. R. 30, p. 75, n. 172; p. 76, n. 178.
People v. Brennan, 12 N. B. R. 567; s. c. 6 N. Y. Sup, 120, p. 3, n. 2.
Perkins, In re, 10 N. B. R. 529, p. 70, n. 161.
Perkins v. Gay, 3 N. B. R. 772, p. 73, n. 171.
Phelps, In re, 1 N. B. R. 525, p. 33, n. 65.

xii   TABLE OF CASES CITED.

Phelps v. Sellick, 8 N. B. R. 390, p. 4, n. 5; p. 49, n. 100.
Phillips, In re, 14 N. B. R. 219, p. 50, n. 108.
Phillips v. Bowdoin, 14 N. B. R. 43; s. c. 52 Ga. 545, p. 72, n. 167.
Pickering, In re, 10 N. B. R. 208, p. 24, n. 45.
Pickett v. McGavick, 14 N. B. R. 236, p. 73, n. 171.
Price, In re, 3 N. B. R. 258, p. 21, n. 32.
Pitt, In re, 14 N. B. R. 59, p. 75, n. 174.
Place, In re, 4 N. B. R. 541, p. 7, n. 11.
Platt v. Parker, 13 N. B. R. 14, p. 72, n. 166.
Pool v. McDonald, 15 N. B. R. 560, p. 63, n. 118.
Port Huron Dock Co., In re, 14 N. B. R. 253, p. 51, n. 109, 110.
Potter v. Coggeshall, 4 N. B. R. 73, p. 40, n. 82.
Powell, In re, 2 N. B. R. 45, p. 33, n. 65; p. 56, n. 122.
Pratt, In re, 6 N. B. R. 276, p. 21, n. 30.
Pratt v. Curtis, 6 N. B. R. 139, p. 38, n. 79.
Price, In re, 3 Dill. 514, p. 23, n. 38.
Pierce, In re, 4 N. B. R. 406, p. 34, n. 86.
Pulver, In re, 1 Ben. 381, p. 32, n. 64.
Pupke, In re, 1 Ben. 342, p. 27, n. 57.

R

Raffauff, In re, 6 Ch. L. N. 341; s. c., 1 Cent. L. J. 364, n; s. c., 10 N. B. R. 69, p. 24, n. 45.
Rainsford, In re, 5 N. B. R. 381, p. 67, n. 154.
Randall, In re, 3 N. B. R. 18; s. c., Deady, 594, p. 21, n. 32; p. 22, 33.
Rankin v. Florida R. R. Co., 1 N. B. R. 647, p. 77, n 181.
Rankin v. Nat. Bank, 14 N. B. R. 4, p. 85, n. 188.
Ratcliffe, In re, 1 N. B. R. 400, p. 17, n. 29.
Rathborne, In re, 1 N. B. R. 294, 324, 536, p. 67, n. 154.
Ray, In re, 1 N. B. R. 203, p. 45, n. 91.
Ray, In re, 2 Ben. 53, p. 52, n. 113.
Ray v. Brigham, 12 N. B. R. 145; s. c., 23 Wall. 128, p. 49, n. 102.
Ray v. Lapham, 27 Ohio St. Con. 452, p. 73, n. 170.
Ray v. Wight, 14 N. B. R. 563; s. c., 119 Mass. 426, p. 36, n. 69.
Reed, In re, 12 N. B. R. 390, p. 51, n. 109; p. 68, n. 156.
Reiman, In re, 13 N. B. R. 128, p. 62, n. 130, 136, 137.
Reitz v. The People, 72 Ill. 435, p. 46, n. 93.
Rice v. Grafton Mills, 13 N. B. R. 209; s. c., 117 Mass. 220, p. 86, n. 183.

Richardson, In re, 2 N. B. R. 202, p. 3, n. 2.
Richardson, In re, 2 Ben. 517, p. 66, n. 150.
Richter, In re, 1 Dill. 544, p. 53, n. 116.
Riorden, In re, 14 N. B. R. 332, p. 53, n. 116.
Robinson, In re, 6 Blatchf. 253, p. 65, n. 149.
Robinson v. Wilson, 14 N. B. R. 565; s. c., 15 Kan. 595, p. 36, n. 69.
Rockett, Ex parte, 15 N. B. R. 95, p. 58, n. 127.
Rollins v. Twitchell, 14 N. B. R. 20, p. 48. n. 99.
Rosenburg, In re, 3 Ben. 14, p. 66, n. 150.
Rosenthal, In re, 10 N. B. R. 191; s. c. 1 Cent. L. J. 364 n.; s. c. 6 Ch. L. N. 342, p. 24, n. 45.
Rowe v. Page, 13 N. B. R. 366; s. c. 54 N. H. 190, p. 86, n. 190.
Ruddick v. Billings, 1 Woolw. 332, p. 7, n. 12; p. 8, n. 16.
Russell v. Owen, 15 N. B. R. 322; s. c. 61 Mo. 185, p. 4, n. 3.
Ryan, In re, 6 N. B. R. 235, p. 42, n. 88.

S

Sabin, In re, 12 N. B. R. 142, p. 49, n. 100.
Sacchi, In re, 10 Blatch. 29, p. 3, n. 2.
Sampson v. Burton, 4 N. B. R. 1, p. 39, n. 80; p. 66, n. 150.
Sandusky v. First Nat. Bank, 12 N. B. R. 176; s. c. 23 Wall. 289, p. 8, n. 16; p. 9, n. 19.
Sanford v. Sanford, 12 N. B. R. 565; s. c. 58 N. Y. 67, p. 39, n. 80.
Sanger v. Upton, 13 N. B. R. 226; s. c. 91 U. S. 56, p. 3, n. 2.
Sargeant, In re, 13 N. B. R. 144, p. 22, n. 33; p. 23, n. 35.
Saunders, In re, 13 N. B. R. 164, p. 33, n. 65; p. 51, n. 110; p. 52, n. 112.
Sauthoff, In re, 14 N. B. R. 364, p. 49, n. 104.
Sawyer, In re, 14 N. B. R. 241, p. 63, n. 146.
Sawyer v. Hoag, 9 N. B. R. 145; s. c. 17 Wall. 610, p. 48, n. 98.
Sawyer v. Turpin, 13 N. B. R. 271; s. c. 91 U. S. 114, p. 84, n. 187.
Scammon, in re, 10 N. B. R. 67, p. 23, n. 36.
Scammon, In re, 7 Ch. L. N. 42, p. 24, n. 47.
Scammon v. Kimball, 13 N. B. R. 445, p. 48, n. 98.
Scheiffer, In re, 2 N. B. R. 591, p. 33, n. 65.
Schick, In re, 2 Ben. 5, p. 22, n. 32.
Schuman v. Fleckenstein, 15 N. B. R. 224, p. 87, n. 193.

TABLE OF CASES CITED.

Scott, In re, 15 N. B. R. 73; s. c., 4 Cent. L. J. 29, p. 62, n. 132; p. 63, u. 140.
Scott v. Kelly, 12 N. B. R. 96, p. 4, n. 3, 5.
Scrafford, In re, 4 Cent. L. J. 19, p. 22, n. 40.
Scull, In re, 10 N. B. R. 153; s. c., 10 Alb. L. J. 214, p. 84, n. 185.
Scull, In re, 10 N. B. R. 166, p. 23, n. 38.
Sectional Dock Co., In re, 3 Dill. 83, p. 75, n. 174.
Sedgwick v. Casey, 4 N. B. R. 496, p. 41, n. 86.
Sedgwick v. Place, 3 Ben. 360, p. 42, § 5060.
Seymour, In re, 1 Ben, 348, p. 66, n. 150.
Seymour v. Street, 5 Neb. 85, p. 73, n. 170.
Shearman v. Bingham, 7 N. B. R. 490, p. 3, n. 2.
Sholdon, In re, 12 N. B. R. 13, p. 70, n. 161.
Sheppard, In re, 1 N. B. R. 439, p. 45, n. 91; p. 50, n. 107.
Sherwood, In re, 1 N. B. R. 344, p. 79, n. 184.
Shields, In re, 15 N. B. R. 532; s. c., 4 Cent. L. J. 537, p. 63, n. 140.
Shryock v. Bashore, 13 N. B. R. 481, p. 86, n. 190.
Shurtleff v. Thompson, 12 N. B. R. 524; s. c., 63 Me. 118, p. 72, n. 169.
Sigsby v. Willis, 3 Ben. 371, p. 46, n. 93.
Simmons, In re, 10 N. B. R. 254; s. c., 1 Cent. L. J. 440, p. 23, n. 35.
Sims v. Jacobson, 51 Ala. 186, p. 35, n. 69.
Singer v. Sloan, 12 N. B. R. 208; s. c., 3 Dill. 110, p. 84, n. 186; p. 87, n. 105.
Slafter v. Sugar Co., 13 N. B. R. 520, p. 84, n. 186.
Sloan, In re, 12 N. B. R. 59, p. 67, n. 152.
Sloan v. Lewis, 12 N. B. R. 173; s. c., 22 Wall. 150, p. 28, n. 61; p. 45, n. 92.
Smith, In re, 3 N. B. R. 377 p. 21, n. 32.
Smith, In re, 5 N. B. R. 20, p. 67, n. 153, p. 69, n. 160.
Smith, In re, 9 N. B. R. 401, p. 38. n. 78.
Smith, In re, 13 N. B. R. 258, p. 87, n. 154.
Smith, In re, 13 N. B. R. 500, p. 75, n. 175.
Smith, In re, 14 N. B. R. 295, p. 38, n. 78.
Smith, In re, 14 N. B. R. 432, p. 54, n. 118.
Smith v. Eagle, 14 N. B. R. 481, p. 63, n. 140, 142.
Smith v. Mason, 6 N. B. R. 1; s. c., 14 Wall. 419, p. 3, n. 2; p. 4, § 4973; p. 8, n. 6; p. 9, n. 19.
Smith v. Ramsey, 27 Ohio St. Com. 339, p. 73, n. 170.
Smith v. Vodges, 13 N. B. R. 433, p. 85, n. 187.

Soloman, In re, 2 N. B. R. 285, p. 68, n. 158.
Soldier's Business Co., In re. 3 Ben. 204, p. 40, n. 82.
Solis, In re, 4 Ben. 143, p. 53, n. 117.
Son, In re, 1 N. B. R. 310, p. 55, n. 120.
Spades, In re, 13 N. B. R. 72, p. 62, n. 131, 132, 134; p. 63, n. 148.
Sparhawk v. Drexel, 12 N. B. R. 450, p. 49, n. 101; p. 86, n. 190.
Sparhawk v. Richards, 13 N. B. R. 74, p. 84, n. 187.
Speyer, In re, 6 N. B. R. 255, p. 11, n. 21.
Spicer v. Ward, 3 N. B. R. 512, p. 21, n. 32.
Spillman, In re, 13 N. B. R. 214, p. 62, n. 131, 132.
Stafford, In re, 13 N. B. R. 378, p. 11, n. 21.
Steadman, In re, 8 N. B. R. 319, p. 3, n. 2.
Steinman, In re, 6 Ch. L. N. 338, p. 24, n. 47.
Stevens, In re, 4 N. B. R. 367, p. 52, n. 114.
Stevens, In re, 5 N. B. R. 112, p. 75, n. 174; p. 78, n. 177.
Stevens, In re, 5 N. B. R. 298, p. 36, n. 69; p. 39, n. 71.
Stevens v. Bank, 101 Mass. 109, p. 72, n. 168.
Stevenson v. McLaren, 14 N. B. R. 403, p. 25, n. 53; p. 28, n. 62.
Stewart, In re, 13 N. B. R. 295, p. 38, n. 76
Stokes, In re, 1 N. D. R. 489. p. 34, n. 66.
Stokes v. Mason, 12 N. B. R. 498; s. c. 10 R. I. 261, p. 46, n. 92; p. 71, n. 164.
Stoll v. Wilson, 14 N. B. R. 571, s. c. 38 N. J. (Law) 198, p. 72, n. 168.
Strauss, In re, 2 N. B. R. 48, p. 50, n. 107.
Sutherland v. Davis, 10 N. B. R. 424, p. 3, n. 2.
Sweatt v. Boston, Hartford and Erie R. R. 5 N. B. R. 234, p. 3, n. 1; p. 77, n. 181.

T

Thompson, In re, 13 N. B. R. 300, p. 35, n. 68; p. 85, n. 187.
Thornton, In re, 2 N. B. R. 189, p. 37, n. 70.
Thornton v. Hogan, 63 Mo. 143, p. 49, n. 100.
Thurman v. Andrews, 13 N. B. R. 157, p. 72, n. 166.
Tinker v. Vandyke, 11 N. B. R. 308; s. c. 14 N. B. R. 112, p. 84, n. 186; p. 87, n. 195.
Todd v. Barton, 13 N. B. R. 197, p. 66, n. 150.
Tonkin. In re, 4 N. B. R. 52, p. 53, n. 116.
Tonne, In re, 13 N. B. R. 170, p. 37, n. 73; p. 38, n. 76.

TABLE OF CASES CITED.

Tooker, In re, 14 N. B. R. 35, p. 63, n. 145.
Trafton, In re, 14 N. B. R. 507, p. 62, n. 135, 137; p. 63, n. 139.
Treadwell v. Holloway, 12 N. B. R. 61; s. c. 46 Cal. 547, p. 71, n. 164.
Trim, In re, 5 N. B. R. 23, p. 47, n. 96.
Trimble v. Williamson, 14 N. B. R. 53; s. c. 49 Ala. 525, p. 35, n. 68.
Triplett v. Hanley, 1 Dill. 217, p. 56, n. 127.
Troy Woolen Co., In re, 8 Blatch. 465, p. 42, n. 68.
Tyler, In re, 4 N. B. R. 104, p. 68, n. 157.

U

Ulrich, In re, 3 Ben. 355, p. 27, n. 56.
Union Pac. R. R. Co., In re, 10 N. B. R. 178, p. 21, n. 32.
United States v. Bayer, 13 N. B. R. 88; s. c. 3 Cent. L. J. 11, p. 90, n. 203, 205.
United States v. Black, 12 N. B. R. 340, p. 90, n. 204.
United States v. Block, 15 N. B. R. 325; p. 89, n. 200.
United States v. Clark, 4 N. B. R. 59, p. 89, n. 201, 203.
United States v. Geary, 4 N. B. R. 535, p. 89, n. 203.
United States v. Herron, 20 Wall. 251, p. 72, n. 167.
United States v. Lewis, 13 N. B. R. 33, p. 56, n. 128.
United States v. Penn, 13 N. B. R. 464, p. 69, n. 202, 203.
United States v. Prescott, 4 N. B. R. 112, p. 89, n. 203.
United States v. Pusey, 6 N. B. R. 284, p. 89, n. 199.
United States v. Rob Roy, 13 N. B. R. 35, p. 72, n. 167.
United States v. Rob Roy, 13 N. B. R. 235, p. 47, n. 95.
United States v. Smith, 13 N. B. R. 61, p. 89, n. 201, p. 90, n. 203.
Usher v. Pease, 12 N. B. R. 305; s. c. 116 Mass. 440, p. 25, n. 51.

V

Valk, In re, 3 Ben. 431, p. 66, n. 151.
Valliant v. Childress, 11 N. B. R. 317; s. c., 21 Wall. 642, p. 36, n. 69.
Van Auken, In re, 14 N. B. R. 425, p. 62, n. 134, 136, p. 63, n. 143.
Van Nostrand v. Carr, 30 Md. 128, p. 86, n. 190.
Vogel, In re, 7 Blatch. 18, p. 35, n. 67.
Voight v. Lewis, 14 N. B. R. 543, p. 40, n. 83.

Von Hein v. Elkus, 15 N. B. R. 194, p. 86, n. 190.
Voorhees v. Frisbie, 8 N. B. R. 152, p. 87, n. 195.

W

Wald, In re, 12 N. B. R. 491, p. 62, n. 134.
Walford, In re, 4 Ben. 9, p. 12, n. 22.
Walker v. Siegel, 12 N. B. R. 394; s. c., 2 Cent. L. J. 508, p. 35, n. 68.
Walker v. Towner, 5 Cent. L. J. 208, p. 41, n. 86.
Wallace, In re, 12 N. B. R. 191, p. 75, n. 173.
Walshee, In re, 2 Woods, 225, p. 62, n. 138.
Warner v. Cronkhite, 13 N. B. R. 52; s. c., 6 Biss. 453, p. 71, n. 164.
Warner v. Garber, 15 N. B. R. 409, p. 84, n. 186.
Warren Sav. Bank v. Palmer, 10 N. B. R. 239; s. c., 6 Ch. L. N. 386, p. 24, n. 47.
Washington Ins. Co., In re, 2 Ben. 292, p. 26, n. 55.
Watrous, In re, 14 N. B. R. 258, p. 51, n. 110.
Watts, In re, 3 Ben. 166, p. 17, n. 29.
Webb v. Sacks, 15 N. B. R. 166, p. 85, n. 188.
Weber Furniture Co., In re, 13 N. B. R. 529, p. 62, n. 138, p. 63, n. 147.
Weeks, In re, 13 N. B. R. 263, p. 46, n. 94; p. 49, n. 101.
Weitzel, In re, 14 N. B. R. 466; s. c., 3 Cent. L. J. 557, p. 21, n. 30.
Welch, In re, 5 N. B. R. 348, p. 37, n. 76.
Whipple, In re, 11 N. B. R. 524, p. 62, n. 138.
White v. Jones, 6 N. B. R. 175, p. 40, n. 83.
Whitney, In re, 14 N. B. R. 1, p. 68, n. 156.
Wicks v. Perkins, 13 N. B. R. 280, p. 49, n. 100, 102, 102a.
Wielarski, In re, 4 N. B. R. 390, p. 15, n. 27.
Wiener, In re, 14 N. B. R. 218, p. 52, n. 111.
Wilkins v. Davis, 15 N. B. R. 60, p. 75, n. 174; p. 76, n. 177.
Williams, In re, 2 N. B. R. 229, p. 46, n. 92.
Williams, In re, 14 N. B. R. 132, p. 22, n. 32.
Williams v. Butcher, 12 N. B. R. 143, p. 72, n. 166.
Williams v. Harkins, 15 N. B. R. 34; s. c., 55 Ga. 172, p. 48, n. 92.
Wills v. Claflin, 13 N. B. R. 437; s. c., 92 U. S. 135, p. 27, n. 60.
Wilson, In re, 8 N. B. R 396, p. 22, n. 33.

TABLE OF CASES CITED.

Wilson, In re, 13 N. B. R. 253, p. 70, n. 161.
Wilson v. City Bank, 17 Wall. 473, p. 84, n. 185.
Wilt v. Stickney, 15 N. B. R. 23, p. 41, n. 86.
Winkens, In re, 2 N. B. R. 349, p. 76, n. 177.
Winship v. Phillips, 14 N. B. R. 50; s. c. 52 Ga. 593, p. 72, n. 167.
Wiswall v. Campbell, 15 N. B. R. 421, p. 6, n. 9; s. c. 93 U. S. 347, p. 8, n. 15.
Witt v. Hereth, 13 N. B. R. 106, p. 86, n. 189.
Wood v. Bailey, 12 N. B. R. 132; s. c. 21 Wall. 640, p. 7, n. 11.
Woodford, In re, 13 N. B. R. 575, p. 22, n. 34; p. 23, n. 37.
Woodward, In re, 12 N. B. R. 297, p. 54, n. 118.

Woolsey v. Cade, 15 N. B. R. 236; s. c. 4 Cent. L. J. 202, p. 71, n. 164.
Worthington, In re, 14 N. B. R. 388, p. 3, n. 2; s. c. 390, p. 49, n. 101.
Wright, In re, 8 N. B. R. 430; s. c. 3 Biss. 359, p. 38, n. 75.
Wright, In re, 2 Ben. 509, p. 65. n. 149.
Wylie v. Breck, 2 Woods, 673, p. 47. n. 97.
Wynne, In re, 4 N. B. R. 23, p. 47, n. 96; p. 84, n. 187.

Y

York, In re, 4 N. B. R. 497, p. 7, n. 11.

Z

Zinn, In re, 4 N.B. R. 370; s. c. 4. N. B.R. 436, p. 33, n. 65.

REVISED STATUTES OF THE UNITED STATES, TITLE, BANKRUPTCY.

CHAPTER ONE.

COURTS OF BANKRUPTCY, THEIR JURISDICTION, ORGANIZATION AND POWERS.

SECTION
- 4972. *As Amended.*—Courts of Bankruptcy; Scope of their Jurisdiction; what Assets or Debts may be collected in State Courts.
  - NOTE 1.—Original Jurisdiction of Courts of Bankruptcy.
  - 2.—Of such Jurisdiction in General.
  - 3.—Such Jurisdiction Concurrent with, but not Exclusive of, State Courts.
  - 4.—Jurisdiction of Bankrupt Courts, held under the Revised Statutes, Exclusive.
  - 5.—Cases holding that such Jurisdiction is not Exclusive.
- 4973. Courts of Bankruptcy to be always Open; Power of Judges in Term Time and Vacation; Contempt.
- 4974. Such Court may sit at any Place in District.
- 4975. Power of such Courts to compel Obedience.
- 4976. Powers of Circuit Judge during Absence, Sickness or Disability of District Judge.
- 4977. Powers of the Supreme Court for the District of Columbia.
- 4978. *As Amended.*—Powers of the District Courts for the Territories.

SECTION
- 4979. *As Amended.*—Concurrent Jurisdiction of Circuit Courts of Actions between Assignees and Persons claiming Adverse Interests.
  - NOTE 6.—Construction of Original Act.
  - 7.—Amendatory Act of June 8, 1872, construed.
  - 8.—Citizenship of Parties.
- 4980. Appeals and Writs of Error from District to Circuit Courts.
  - NOTE 9.—As to Appeals.
  - 10.—As to Writs of Error.
- 4981. Conditions upon which Appeals and Writs of Error are Granted; Notice, Bond, etc.
  - NOTE 11.—This Statute Construed.
  - 12.—Construed as to Writs of Error.
- 4982. Appeals, when to be entered.
  - NOTE 13.—This Provision Directory merely.
- 4983. Waiver of Appeal.
- 4984. Appeal from Decision rejecting Claim.
  - NOTE 14.—What must be Filed.
- 4985. Judgment of Circuit Court Conclusive; Costs of Appeal.
  - NOTE 15.—Judgment rejecting Claim not Reviewable.
- 4986. Power of General Superintendence conferred on Circuit Court.

§ 4972.]   Courts of Bankruptcy.

SECTION		SECTION	
	NOTE 16.—This section Construed.	5002.	Powers of Registers when so acting; may summon Witnesses; require Production of Books, etc.
	17.—This Jurisdiction final.		
	18.—Practice under this Section.		
4987.	Superintendence of Supreme Courts of Territories.	5003.	Evidence in Bankruptcy Proceedings, how taken; Attendance of Witnesses; Production of Books and Papers.
4988.	Power of District Judge in District not in any Organized Circuit.		
		5004.	Depositions; Register may administer Oaths.
4989.	Appeal and Writ of Error to Supreme Court; Limit of Jurisdiction.	5005.	Compulsory attendance of Witnesses; entitled to Protection; liable for Contempt.
	NOTE 19.—This section Construed.	5006.	Contempt in Proceedings before Register.
4990.	*As Amended.*—General Orders in Bankruptcy; Supreme Court may prescribe in what Cases.		NOTE 22.—Committed by Bankrupt's Wife.
4991.	Commencement of Proceedings; what deemed to be.	5007.	Registers may act for each other.
	NOTE 20.—This section Construed.	5008.	Fees of Registers; by whom paid.
4992.	Records; Dockets; Copies; Evidence.		NOTE 23.—Same Subject.
		5009.	Contested Issues to be decided by Judge.
4993.	Registers in Bankruptcy; Appointment of.		NOTE 24.—Law and Fact.
4994.	Who Eligible to Office of.	5010.	Opinion of Judge may be taken in Case Certified.
4995.	Bond and Oath of Register.		
4996.	Restrictions upon Registers.		NOTE 25.—But not on Fictitious Case.
4997.	Removal of Registers.		
4998.	Powers of Registers.	5011.	Agreed Cases; Judgments upon, to be final, when; Agreements in Special Cases.
	NOTE 21.—The same Subject.		
4999.	Limitations upon Powers of Registers.	5012.	Penalties against Judges and Officers.
5000.	Registers to keep Memoranda of Proceedings.	5013.	Meaning of Terms and Computation of Time.
5001.	Registers to attend at Place directed by Judge.		NOTE 26.—Computation of Time.

ORIGINAL ACT OF 1867, § 1; R. S. § 4972, AS AMENDED.—The jurisdiction conferred upon the district courts as courts of bankruptcy shall extend: 1, to all cases and controversies arising between the bankrupt and any creditor or creditors who shall claim any debt or demand under the bankruptcy; 2, to the collection of all the assets of the bankrupt; 3, to the ascertainment and liquidation of the liens and other specific claims thereon; 4, to the adjustment of the various priorities and conflicting interests of all parties; 5, to the marshaling and disposition of the different funds and assets, so as to secure the rights of all parties and due distribution of the assets among all the creditors; 6, to all acts, matters, and things to be done under and in virtue of the bankruptcy, until the final distribution and settlement of

COURTS OF BANKRUPTCY; Scope of jurisdiction.

[§ 4972.]   Courts of Bankruptcy.   [Notes 1-3.

the estate of the bankrupt, and the close of the proceedings in bankruptcy. [*Provided*, that the court having charge of the estate of any bankrupt may direct that any of the legal assets or debts of the bankrupt, as contradistinguished from equitable demands, shall, when such debt does not exceed five hundred dollars, be collected in the courts of the state where such bankrupt resides, having jurisdiction of claims of such nature and amount.][1]

What assets or debts collected in state courts.

NOTE 1. *Original Jurisdiction.*—The United States District Court has original jurisdiction in all matters and proceedings in bankruptcy. Sweatt v. Boston, Hartford & Erie R. R., 5 N. B. R. 234. The first paragraph of the original act of March 2, 1867, corresponds with subdivision 18, of § 563 of the Revised Statutes, which reads thus: "The district courts are constituted courts of bankruptcy, and shall have in their respective districts original jurisdiction in all matters and proceedings in bankruptcy."

2. *In General.*—A proceeding in bankruptcy is, in its nature and objects, a general creditor's bill. As a court of equity with jurisdiction over "all cases and controversies between the bankrupt and his creditors," etc., the bankrupt court has the same power as a state court of equity, to restrain the enforcement of a judgment at law recovered against a bankrupt for an improper amount. Fowler v. Dillon, 13 N. B. R. 308. It is within the general equity powers of a court of bankruptcy, after an adjudication and before the selection of an assignee, to appoint a receiver for the temporary care and custody of the estate. Lansing v. Manton, 14 N. B. R. 128. Such receiver has no power to bring suit in his own name to recover the value of property conveyed by the bankrupt in fraud of the bankrupt law. Until an assignee is appointed, the legal title to the assets is in the bankrupt, and it is not only the right, but the duty of the bankrupt to bring suit for the protection and preservation of the property. Ibid.; Sutherland v. Davis, 10 N. B. R. 424; *Re* Steadman, 8 N. B. R. 319; March v. Heaton, 2 N. B. R. 180. The district court has power to restrain a holder of a mortgage or other lien from proceeding in a state court to enforce the same. *Re* Iron Mt. Co., 9 Blatch. 320; *Re* Sacchi, 10 Blatch. 29. See Johnson v. Bishop, 1 Woolw. 324; Blum v. Ellis, 76 N. C. 293. Where a party who is proceeded against by a summary proceeding, where the proper form of proceeding is a bill in equity, consents to a reference of the case for hearing before a register, he thereby gives the district court jurisdiction over his person, and can not, in a collateral action, impeach its decree. People v. Brennan, 12 N. B. R. 567; s. c., 6 N. Y. Sup. 120. An order of the district court directing an assignee to collect unpaid subscription on stock is conclusive upon his right to sue. He may sue at law for unpaid subscriptions to stock. Ibid.; Sanger v. Upton, 13 N. B. R. 226; s. c., 91 U. S. 56. District courts, as well as circuit courts, have jurisdiction of suits at law or in equity, brought by an assignee claiming an adverse interest touching any property or rights of property of the bankrupt, transferable to or vested in such assignee. Haskill v. Frye, 14 N. B. R. 525; Smith v. Mason, 6 N. B. R. 1; s. c., 14 Wall. 419. The district court can not determine the validity of the title of a party holding adversely to the bankrupt's assignee, by a summary proceeding. *Re* Marter, 12 N. B. R. 185. But if the party submits, voluntarily, his claims to the court, it can. *Re* Worthington, 14 N. B. R. 388. Section 4979 was not intended to limit the jurisdiction of the district court conferred by this section. Johnson v. Price, 13 N. B. R. 523. Jurisdiction is limited to cases pending in the district court of the district where the jurisdiction is invoked. *Re* Richardson, 2 N. B. R. 202. A careful discussion of this question may be found in Markson v. Heaney, 1 Dill. 497. But see the more recent interpretation in Shearman v. Bingham, 7 N. B. R. 490; Lathrop v. Drake, 13 N. B. R. 473; s. c., 91 U. S. 516.

3. *Concurrent with, but not Exclusive of State Courts.*—If the Bankrupt Act has,

(1) Act of June 22, 1874, § 2.

for certain purposes, conferred a jurisdiction for the benefit of assignees on the circuit and district courts, it is concurrent with, and does not divest that of the state courts. Eyster v. Gaff, 13 N. B. R. 546; s. c., 91 U. S. 521; Burbank v. Bigelow, 14 N. B. R. 445; s. c., 92 U. S. 179. A state court has jurisdiction of an action brought by an assignee to recover money paid to a creditor as a preference. Goodrich v. Wilson, 14 N. B. R. 555; s. c., 119 Mass. 429. See § 5128 and note, post. Assignee may collect assets in state courts. Russel v. Owen, 15 N. B. R. 322; s. c., 61 Mo. 185. The commencement of proceedings in bankruptcy does not affect the jurisdiction of a state court over a proceeding then pending to foreclose a mortgage, and a sale thereunder will pass a valid title, although the assignee is not made a party thereto. Eyster v. Gaff, 13 N. B. R. 546; s. c., 3 Cent. L. J. 250; s. c., 91 U. S. 521. Where an assignee submits himself and his rights to the jurisdiction of the state court, he can not, after judgment, object to the power of the state court to act in the premises. Scott v. Kelly, 12 N. B. R. 96.

4. *Exclusive under the Revised Statutes.*—Under the Revised Statutes a state court has no jurisdiction of a suit by an assignee in bankruptcy to recover property alleged to have been conveyed by the bankrupt in fraud of the act. The Revised Statutes took away the jurisdiction, although passed after suit was begun. Frost v. Hotchkiss, 14 N. B. R. 443. See § 711, subdivision 6 Rev. Stat. U. S.

5. *Have not Exclusive Jurisdiction.*—See Augustine Ass. v. McFarland, 13 N. B. R. 7; Re Bowie, 1 N. B. R. 628; Norton's Assignee v. Boyd, 3 Howard, 426; Mays v. Fritton, 11 N. B. R. 229; s. c., 20 Wall. 414; Scott v. Kelly, 12 N. B. R. 96. Contra, Phelps v. Sellick, 8 N. B. R. 390; Re Anderson, 9 N. B. R. 360; Brigham v. Claflin, 7 N. B. R. 412; Re Brinkman, 7 N. B. R. 421. An assignee in bankruptcy may be sued in a state court for trover of property sold by him as assignee in bankruptcy, and which he refuses to deliver up, if the bankrupt court has not taken any action in the matter. Ives v. Tregent, 14 N. B. R. 60; s. c., 29 Mich. 390. A state court will not grant an injunction restraining a party from applying for the benefit of the bankrupt law. Fillingin v. Thornton, 12 N. B. R. 92. A state court will not surrender its jurisdiction over the property in the custody of receivers of an insolvent firm, appointed by it, and which firm has subsequently been adjudged bankrupt, and turn it over to the assignee in bankruptcy, on a mere motion of the assignee. Freeman v. Fort, 14 N. B. R. 46; s. c., 59 Ga. 071. Regular proceedings for that purpose must be instituted in the bankrupt court. Ibid. But see Meyer v. Crystal Lake Works, 14 N. B. R. 9.

IBID. § 1; R. S. § 4973.—The district courts shall be always open for the transaction of business in the exercise of their jurisdiction as courts of bankruptcy; and their powers and jurisdiction as such courts shall be exercised as well in vacation as in term time; and a judge sitting at chambers shall have the same powers and jurisdiction, including the power of keeping order and of punishing any contempt of his authority, as when sitting in court.[1]

Courts always open; Power of Judges in term time and vacation; Contempt.

IBID. § 1; R. S. 4974.—A district court may sit for the transaction of business in bankruptcy, at any place within the district, of which place and of the time of commencing session the court shall have given notice, as well as at the places designated by law for holding sessions of such court.

Court may sit at any place in district.

IBID. § 1; R. S. § 4975.—The district courts as courts of bankruptcy shall have full authority to compel obedience to all orders and decrees passed by them in bankruptcy, by process of contempt and other remedial process, to the same

Power of district court to compel obedience.

(1) Smith v. Mason, 6 N. B. R. 1; s. c., 14 Wall. 419.

BANKRUPT LAW.

§§ 4976–4979. Concurrent Jurisdiction.

extent that the circuit courts now have in any suit pending therein in equity.

ACT JUNE 30, 1870, § 2; R. S. § 4976.—In case of a vacancy in the office of district judge in any district, or in case any district judge shall, from sickness, absence, or other disability, be unable to act, the circuit judge of the circuit in which such district is included may make, during such disability or vacancy, all necessary rules and orders preparatory to the final hearing of all causes in bankruptcy, and cause the same to be entered or issued, as the case may require, by the clerk of the district court. *Powers of circuit judge during sickness, absence, or disability of district judge.*

ORIGINAL ACT OF MARCH 2, 1867, § 49; R. S. § 4977.—The same jurisdiction, power and authority which are hereby conferred upon the district courts in cases of bankruptcy are also conferred upon the Supreme Court of the District of Columbia, when the bankrupt resides in that district. *Powers of the supreme court of the District of Columbia.*

IBID. § 49; R. S. § 4978, AS AMENDED.—The same jurisdiction, power and authority which are hereby conferred upon the district courts in cases of bankruptcy, are also conferred upon [district][1] courts of the several territories when the bankrupt resides in either of the territories, [subject to the general superintendence and jurisdiction conferred upon circuit courts by section two[2] of said act.][3] This jurisdiction may be exercised, upon petitions regularly filed in such courts, by either of the justices thereof while holding the district court in the district in which the petitioner or the alleged bankrupt resides.[4] *Powers of the district courts for Territories.*

IBID. § 2, AS AMENDED BY ACT OF JUNE 8, 1872; R. S. § 4979, AS AMENDED.—The several circuit courts shall have, within each district, concurrent jurisdiction with the district court [of any district,][5] whether the powers and jurisdiction of a circuit court have been conferred on such district court or not, of all suits at law or in equity, brought by an assignee in bankruptcy against any person claiming an adverse interest, [or owing any debt to such bankrupt],[5] or by any such person against an assignee, touching any property or rights of the bankrupt transferable to or vested in such assignee. *CONCURRENT JURISDICTION: Of actions between assignees and persons claiming adverse interests.*

(1) So amended by Act of June 22, 1874, § 16. The original reading was "supreme."
(2) See § 4986, post.
(3) So amended by Act of June 22, 1874, § 16. These amendments were made to the original act of 1867, by name, and the words "said act," in the last clause, refer to the Act of 1867.
(4) Act of June 30, 1870, ch. 177, § 1.
(5) So amended in effect by the Act of June 22, 1874. The original act, as amended by the Act of June 22, 1874, reads as follows, the amendments of 1874 being indicated by the words in brackets: "Said circuit courts shall also have concurrent jurisdiction with the district courts of [any] district of all suits at law or in equity which may or shall be brought by the assignee in bankruptcy against any person claiming an adverse interest [or owing any

§§ 4970–4980.]   Concurrent Jurisdiction—Appeals—Writs of Error.   [Notes 6–10.

6. *Construction of Original Act.*—Controversies, in order that they may be cognizable hereunder, must have respect to some property, or rights of property, of the bankrupt, transferable to or vested in his assignee; and the suit, whether at law or in equity, must be in the name of one of the two parties described therein and against the other. Morgan v. Thornhill, 5 N. B. R. 11; s. c., 11 Wall. 65; Smith v. Mason, 6 N. B. R. 1; 14 Wall. 419; Knight v. Cheney, 5 N. B. R. 305. Proceedings hereunder must be plenary. Barston v. Peckham, 5 N. B. R. 72; *Re* Marter, 12 N. B. R. 185, and cases *supra.* Circuit courts of the United States have concurrent jurisdiction with district courts of suits brought by an assignee appointed in another district. Lathrop v. Drake, 13 N. B. R. 472; s. c., 91 U. S. 516; Burbank v. Bigelow, 14 N. B. R. 445. The circuit court has no jurisdiction of a bill filed by creditors before the appointment of an assignee, to restrain a chattel mortgagee from selling the goods of the bankrupt. *Semble,* that the district court has such jurisdiction. Johnson v. Price, 13 N. B. R. 523. The district court has such jurisdiction by a summary proceeding, it seems. *Re* Fendley, 10 N. B. R. 250.

7. *Amendatory Act of June* 8, 1872, *Construed.*—This amendment removed any ambiguity that may have existed, but did not thereby impress a more restricted meaning upon the language of the original act than was due to it by a fair judicial construction. Lathrop v. Drake, 13 N. B. R. 472; s. c., 91 U. S. 516. For an elaborate discussion of the jurisdiction of circuit courts, see 7 Am. Law Reg. 641.

8. *Citizenship of Parties.*—Whenever state courts have jurisdiction over controversies between the assignee and third parties, the circuit courts have it independently of the bankrupt law, if the proper citizenship of the parties exists. Burbank v. Bigelow, 14 N. B. R. 445; s. c., 92 U. S. 179.

ORIGINAL ACT OF 1867, § 8; R. S. § 4980.—Appeals may be taken from the district to the circuit courts in all cases in equity, and writs of error from the circuit courts to the district courts may be allowed in cases at law, arising under or authorized by this title, when the debt or damages claimed amount to more than five hundred dollars; and any supposed creditor, whose claim is wholly or in part rejected, or an assignee who is dissatisfied with the allowance of a claim, may appeal from the decision of the district court to the circuit court for the same district.

APPEALS AND WRITS OF ERROR: From district to circuit courts.

9. *An Appeal* to the circuit court lies in a suit by an assignee to set aside a claim and lien for it on the bankrupt's property. Barron v. Morris, 14 N. B. R. 371. Also from a decision allowing or rejecting a claim. Wiswall v. Campbell, 15 N. B. R. 421. A compliance with rule twenty-six, in relation to the time of *filing* an appeal, is not necessary to give the circuit court jurisdiction. Ibid.; Baldwin v. Rapplee, 5 N. B. R. 19. The rule is merely directory. Ibid.

10. *Writ of Error.*—None will lie from the circuit court to the district court, where the case is tried before the district court without a jury. Blair v. Allen, 3 Dill. 101.

debt to such bankrupt], or by such person against such assignee, touching any property or rights of property of said bankrupt transferable to or vested in such assignee." The word "any" was substituted for the words "the same" in the original act. The amendatory act of June 8, 1872, which the revisers designed to embody in the above section, read as follows: "That the powers and jurisdiction granted to the several circuit courts of the United States, or any justice thereof, by section two of an act entitled 'An act to establish a uniform system of bankruptcy throughout the United States,' approved March 2d, 1867, may be exercised in any district in which the powers or jurisdiction of a circuit court have been or may be conferred on the district court for such district, as if no such powers or jurisdiction had been conferred on such district court; it being the true intent and meaning of said act that the system of bankruptcy thereby established shall be uniform throughout the United States.

§§ 4981–4084.]   Appeals and Writs of Error.   [Notes 11-14.

IBID. § 8; R. S. § 4981.—No appeal shall be allowed in any case from the district to the circuit court, unless it is claimed, and notice given thereof to the clerk of the district court, to be entered with the record of the proceedings, and also to the assignee or creditor, as the case may be, *Conditions of appeals and writs of error: Notice, bond, etc.* or to the defeated party in equity, within ten days after the entry of the decree or decision appealed from; nor unless the appellant at the time of claiming the same shall give bond in the manner required in cases of appeals in suits in equity; nor shall any writ of error be allowed unless the party claiming it shall comply with the provisions of law regulating the granting of such writs.

11. *Construction.*—Appeals from the district to the circuit court will be dismissed, unless notice is given to the opposite party within ten days after the entry of the decree appealed from. Wood v. Bailey, 12 N. B. R. 132; s. c., 21 Wall. 640. *Re* York, 4 N. B. R. 479; *Re* Place, 4 N. B. R. 541; Hawkins v. Hastings, 1 Dill. 453. "Defeated party" in this section must be construed to mean opposite party. Ibid. In computing the time, Sunday is to be counted, except when the last day would fall on Sunday, then Sunday is to be excluded. *Re* York, 4 N. B. R. 479. The circuit court has no jurisdiction of the appeal, unless these requirements are complied with. The regulation of appeals is a regulation of jurisdiction. *Re* Alexander, 3 N. B. R. 29; *Re* Coleman, 7 Blatch. 192.

12. *Writs of Error* are governed by the requirements of this section. Knickerbocker Ins. Co. v. Comstock, 8 N. B. R. 145; s. c., 16 Wall. 258. On writ of error no question of fact can be re-examined. Ruddick v. Billings, 1 Woolw. 332.

IBID. § 8; R. S. § 4982.—Such appeal shall be entered at the term of the circuit court, which shall be held within the district next after the expiration of ten days from the time of claiming the same. *Appeals, when entered.*

13. *Directory.*—This is merely directory. The time for entering the appeal may be enlarged by agreement. Baldwin v. Rapplee, 5 N. B. R. 19.

IBID. § 8; R. S. § 4983.—If the appellant, in writing, waives his appeal before any decision thereon, proceedings may be had in the district court as if no appeal had been taken. *Waiver of appeal.*

IBID. § 24; R. S. § 4984.—A supposed creditor who takes an appeal to the circuit court from the decision of the district court, rejecting his claim in whole or in part, shall, upon entering his appeal in the circuit court, file in the *Appeal from decision rejecting claim.* clerk's office thereof a statement in writing of his claim, setting forth the same, substantially, as in a declaration for the same cause of action at law, and the assignee shall plead or answer thereto in like manner, and like proceeding shall thereupon be had in the pleadings, trial and determination of the cause, as in actions at law commenced and prosecuted, in the usual manner, in the courts of the United States, except that no execution shall be awarded against the assignee for the amount of a debt found due to the creditor.

14. *What must be Filed.*— What is required to be filed within ten days from the time of taking an appeal, is the appeal, containing a statement of the appellant's claim

§§ 4985-4986.]   Appeals and Writs of Error.   [Notes 15-18.

and a brief account of what has been done in the district court, and the grounds of appeal. The transcript of the proceedings need not be filed in ten days. Barron v. Morris, 14 N. B. R. 371.

IBID.; R. S. § 4985.—The final judgment of the circuit court, rendered upon any appeal provided for in the preceding section, shall be conclusive, and the list of debts shall, if necessary, be altered to conform thereto. The party prevailing in the suit shall be entitled to costs against the adverse party, to be taxed and recovered as in suits at law; if recovered against the assignee, they shall be allowed out of the estate.

Judgment of circuit court conclusive: Costs of appeal.

15. *Judgment Rejecting Claims not Reviewable.*—The judgment of the circuit court rejecting a claim presented by a supposed creditor of the estate of a bankrupt is not reviewable in the United States Supreme Court on error. Wiswall v. Campbell, 93 U. S. 347; Conro v. Crane, 94 U. S. After the decision of the Register on the validity of a creditor's claim, the district court may order further testimony to be taken before passing on the register's decision. Wiswall v. Campbell, *supra*.

ORIGINAL ACT OF 1867, § 2, AS AMENDED BY ACT OF JUNE 8, 1872; R. S. § 4986.—The circuit court for each district shall have a general superintendence and jurisdiction of all cases and questions arising in the district court for such district when sitting as a court of bankruptcy, whether the powers and jurisdiction of a circuit court have been conferred on such district court or not; and except when special provision is otherwise made, may, upon bill, petition, or other proper process, of any party aggrieved, hear and determine the case as in a court of equity; and the powers and jurisdiction hereby granted may be exercised either by the court in term time, or in vacation, by the circuit justice or by the circuit judge of the circuit.[1]

Power of general superintendence conferred on circuit court.

16. *Construed.*—The construction which gives due effect to all parts of this act relating to revisory jurisdiction, is that which, on the one hand, excludes from the category of general superintendence and jurisdiction of the circuit court the appellate jurisdiction defined by section 4980; and, on the other, brings within that category all decisions of the district court or the district judge at chambers, which can not be reviewed upon appeal or writ of error under the provisions of that section. Re Alexander, 3 N. B. R. 29; Coit v. Robinson, 9 N. B. R. 289; s. c., 19 Wall. 274; Morgan v. Thornhill, 5 N. B. R. 1; s. c., 11 Wall. 65. A proceeding in bankruptcy, from the time of its institution to the final settlement of the estate, is one suit. The adjudication on a petition is reviewable by the circuit court. Sandusky v. First Nat. Bank, 12 N. B. R. 176; s. c., 23 Wall. 289; Re Comstock, 10 N. B. R. 451; Re Oregon Pub. Co., 14 N. B. R. 394; s. c., 3 Sawy. 614. A stay of proceedings during review is in the discretion of the circuit court. Re Oregon Pub. Co., *supra*. Order granting or refusing a discharge is reviewable by petition. Ruddick v. Billings, 1 Woolw. 330.

17. *Final.*—The jurisdiction or superintendence of the circuit court, under this section, is final. Morgan v. Thornhill, 5 N. B. R. 1; s. c., 11 Wall. 65; Coit v. Robinson, 9 N. B. R. 289; s. c., 19 Wall. 274.

18. *Practice on Review.*—The circuit judge has power at chambers, though outside of the geographical district, to entertain and act upon a petition for review. Markson v. Heaney, 1 Dill. 511. The practice under this section is informal and irregular. The supreme court has promulgated no rules to govern the practice, nor have the

(1) See § 4979 and note.

§§ 4987–4990.]   Appeals—Writs of Error—Orders in Bankruptcy.   [Note 18–19.

circuit courts (with one exception) made any rules to regulate it. A summary order of the district court should be brought for review to the circuit court by a simple petition. Hurst v. Teft, 13 N. B. R. 108.

AMENDATORY ACT OF JUNE 30, 1870, § 1; R. S. § 4987.—The several supreme courts of the territories shall have the same general superintendence and jurisdiction over the acts and decisions of the justices thereof in cases of bankruptcy as is conferred on the circuit courts over proceedings in the district courts.[1]   *Superintendence by supreme courts of territories.*

ORIGINAL ACT OF 1867, § 49; R. S. 4988.—In districts which are not within any organized circuit of the United States, the power and jurisdiction of a circuit court in bankruptcy may be exercised by the district judge.   *Power of district judge not in any organized circuit.*

IBID. § 9; R. S. § 4989.—No appeal or writ of error shall be allowed in any case arising under this title from the circuit courts to the supreme court, unless the matter in dispute in such case exceeds two thousand dollars.   *Appeal and writ of error to Supreme Court.*

19. *Construction.*—No appeal lies to the supreme court from a decree of the circuit court rendered in the exercise of the supervisory jurisdiction conferred upon that court by section 4986; and it seems that the amount involved is immaterial. Morgan v. Thornhill, 5 N. B. R. 1; s. c., 11 Wall. 65; Hall v. Allen, 12 Wall. 452; Smith v. Mason, 6 N. B. R. 1; s. c., 14 Wall. 430; Mead v. Thompson, 8 N. B. R. 529; s. c., 15 Wall. 638; Marshall v. Knox, 8 N. B. R. 97; s. c., 16 Wall. 556. Cases arising under section 4979, where the amount is sufficient, are within this section, and, as such, when the case has proceeded to final judgment or decree, may be removed to the supreme court by writ of error or appeal. Coit v. Robinson, 9 N. B. R. 289; s. c., 19 Wall. 274. No appeal lies to the supreme court from a decision on an application to set aside an adjudication of bankruptcy. Sandusky v. First Nat. Bank, 12 N. B. R. 176; s. c., 23 Wall. 289.

IBID. § 10, AS AMENDED; R. S. § 4990, AS AMENDED.—The general orders in bankruptcy heretofore adopted by the justices of the supreme court, as now existing, may be followed in proceedings under this title; and the justices may, from time to time, subject to the provisions of this title, rescind or vary any of those general orders, and may frame, rescind, or vary other general orders, for the following purposes: 1. For regulating the practice and procedure of the district courts in bankruptcy, and the forms of petitions, orders, and other proceedings to be used in such courts in all matters under this title; 2, for regulating the duties of the various officers of such courts; 3, for regulating the fees payable and the charges and costs to be allowed [except such as are established by this title or by law],[2] with respect to all proceedings in bankruptcy before such courts, not exceed-   *GENERAL ORDERS IN BANKRUPTCY: Supreme court may prescribe, in what cases.*

---

(1) See § 4978. The act of April 14, 1876, 19 Stat. 33, provided for the transfer from the supreme to the district courts of the territories, of all cases in bankruptcy commenced in the former courts prior to the act of June 22, 1874.

(2) The words in brackets read, in the original act, "except such as are established by this act or by law." These words were, by the act of June 22, 1874, § 18, *repealed*.

§§ 4990–4995.]   Commencement of Proceedings—Records—Registers.   [Note 20.

ing the rate of fees now allowed by law for similar services in other proceedings; 4, for regulating the practice and procedure upon appeals; 5, for regulating the filing, custody, and inspection of records; 6, and generally for carrying the provisions of this title into effect; all such general orders shall, from time to time, be reported to Congress, with such suggestions as the justices may think proper.

IBID. § 38; R. S. § 4991. — The filing of the petition for an adjudication in bankruptcy, either by a debtor in his own behalf, or by any creditor against a debtor, shall be deemed to be the comencement of proceedings in bankruptcy.

COMMENCEMENT OF PROCEEDINGS: What deemed to be.

20. *Construed.*—*Re* Patterson, 1 Ben. 508. In the original act, the following words appeared after the word "debtor:" "Upon which an order may be issued by the court or by a register, in the manner prescribed by section four." It was held that the words "may be issued" should be read "shall be issued." Ibid.

IBID. § 38; R. S. § 4992. — The proceedings in all cases of bankruptcy shall be deemed matters of record, but the same shall not be required to be recorded at large, but shall be carefully filed, kept, and numbered in the office of the clerk of the court, and a docket only, or short memorandum thereof, kept in books to be provided for that purpose, which shall be open to public inspection. Copies of such records, duly certified under the seal of the court, shall in all cases be presumptive evidence of the facts therein stated.

RECORDS: Dockets: Copies: Evidence.

IBID. §§ 3, 5; R. S. § 4993. — Each district judge shall appoint, upon the nomination and recommendation of the chief justice of the supreme court, one or more registers in bankruptcy, when any vacancy occurs in such office, to assist him in the performance of his duties, under this title, unless he shall deem the continuance of the particular office unnecessary.

REGISTERS IN BANKRUPTCY: Appointment of.

IBID.; R. S. § 4994.— No person shall be eligible for appointment as register in bankruptcy, unless he is a counselor of the district court for the district in which he is appointed, or of some one of the courts of record of the state in which he resides.

Who is eligible.

IBID.; R. S. § 4995.—Before entering upon the duties of his office, every person appointed a register in bankruptcy shall give a bond to the United States, for the faithful discharge of the duties of his office, in a sum not less than one thousand dollars, to be fixed by the district judge, with sureties satisfactory to such judge; and he shall, in open court, take and subscribe the oath prescribed in section seventeen hundred and fifty-six, title, "PROVISIONS APPLICABLE TO SEVERAL CLASSES OF OFFICERS," and also an oath that he will not, during his continuance in office, be, directly or indirectly, interested in or benefited by the fees or emoluments arising

Bond: Oath.

§§ 4996–5000.]   Registers in Bankruptcy.   [Note 21.

from any suit or matter pending in bankruptcy, in either the district or circuit court in his district.

IBID. § 4; R. S. § 4996.—No register shall be of counsel or attorney, either in or out of court, in any suit or matter pending in bankruptcy in either the circuit or district court of his district, nor in an appeal therefrom; nor shall he be executor, administrator, guardian, commissioner, appraiser, divider, or assignee of, or upon any estate within the jurisdiction of either of those courts as courts of bankruptcy, nor shall he be interested in the fees or emoluments arising from any such trusts. Restrictions upon registers.

IBID. § 5; R. S. § 4997.—Registers are subject to removal from office by the judge of the district court. Removal of registers.

IBID. § 4; R. S. § 4998.—Every register in bankruptcy has power: 1, to make adjudication of bankruptcy in cases unopposed; 2, to receive the surrender of any bankrupt; 3, to administer oaths in all proceedings before him; 4, to hold and preside at meetings of creditors; 5, to take proof of debts; 6, to make all computations of dividends, and all orders of distribution; 7, to furnish the assignee with a certified copy of such orders, and of the schedules of creditors and assets filed in each case; 8, to audit and pass accounts of assignees; 9, to grant protection; 10, to pass the last examination of any bankrupt in cases whenever the assignee or a creditor do not oppose; 11, to sit in chambers and dispatch there such part of the administrative business of the court and such uncontested matters as shall be defined in general rules and orders, or as the district judge shall in any particular matter direct. Powers of registers.

21. *Powers of Registers.*—Registers may hear and determine all uncontested petitions filed by attorneys against the assignee to compel the payment of their fees and disbursements. *Re* Stafford, 13 N. B. R. 378. General Order No. 5 gives the register power to act on all uncontested orders concerning the winding up of the bankrupt's estate which are not specifically required to be made by the court. Ibid.; *Re* Noyes, 6 N. B. R. 277. Register may make an order to compel a bankrupt to pay over funds belonging to his estate to his assignee, and a disobedience of such an order is a contempt. *Re* Speyer, 6 N. B. R. 255. In voluntary cases, he is authorized to receive surrender of estate and keep safely until assignee is chosen. *Re* Hasbrouck, 1 Ben. 402. As to his duty with reference to passing on sufficiency of schedule, see *Re* Orne, 1 Ben. 420. He may designate newspapers in which notice of sale shall be published. *Re* Burke, 15 N. B. R. 40. Proceedings before him are under his control. *Re* Hyman, 3 Ben. 28.

IBID. R. S. § 4999.—No register shall have power to commit for contempt, or to make adjudications of bankruptcy when opposed, or to decide upon the allowance or suspension of an order of discharge. Limitations upon powers of registers.

IBID. R. S. § 5000.— Every register shall make short memoranda of his proceedings in each case in which he acts, in a docket to be kept by him for that purpose, and shall forthwith, as the proceedings are taken, forward to the clerk of the district court a certified copy of these Registers to keep memoranda of proceedings.

[§§ 5001-5006.]   Evidence—Depositions—Witnesses—Contempt.   [Note 22.

memoranda, which shall be entered by the clerk in the proper minute-book, to be kept in his office.

IBID. § 5; R. S. § 5001.—The judge of the district court may direct a register to attend at any place within the district, for the purpose of hearing such voluntary applications under this title as may not be opposed, of attending any meeting of creditors, or receiving any proof of debts, and, generally, for the prosecution of any proceedings under this title.

Registers to attend at place directed by judge.

IBID. R. S. § 5002.—Every register, so acting, shall have and exercise all powers, except the power of commitment, vested in the district court for the summoning and examination of persons or witnesses, and for requiring the production of books, papers and documents.

Powers when so acting.

IBID. § 38; R. S. § 5003.—Evidence or examination in any of the proceedings under this title may be taken before the court, or a register in bankruptcy, viva voce or in writing, before a commissioner of the circuit court, or by affidavit, or on commission, and the court may direct a reference to a register in bankruptcy, or other suitable person, to take and certify such examination, and may compel the attendance of witnesses, the production of books and papers, and the giving of testimony, in the same manner as in suits in equity in the circuit court.

Evidence; how taken; Attendance of witnesses; Books, papers, etc.

IBID. § 5, AS AMENDED BY ACT OF JULY 27, 1868, § 3; R. S. § 5004.—All depositions of persons and witnesses taken before a register, and all acts done by him, shall be reduced to writing, and be signed by him, and shall be filed in the clerk's office as part of the proceedings. He shall have power to administer oaths in all cases and in relation to all matters in which oaths may be administered by commissioners of circuit courts.

Depositions: Register may administer oaths.

IBID. § 7; R. S. § 5005.—Parties and witnesses summoned before a register shall be bound to attend in pursuance of such summons at the place and time designated therein, and shall be entitled to protection, and be liable to process of contempt in like manner as parties and witnesses are now liable thereto in case of default in attendance under any writ of subpœna.

Parties and witnesses must attend; Contempt.

IBID.; R. S. § 5006.—Whenever any person examined before a register refuses or declines to answer, or to swear to or sign his examination when taken, the register shall refer the matter to the judge, who shall have power to order the person so acting to pay the costs thereby occasioned, and to punish him for contempt, if such person be compellable by law to answer such question or to sign such examination.

Contempt before register.

22. *Bankrupt's Wife* is punishable. *Re* Woolford, 4 Ben. 9.

§§ 5007-5012.]   Fees—Contested Issues—Agreed Cases—Penalties.   [Notes 23-25.

IBID. § 4; R. S. § 5007.—Any register may act in the place of any other register appointed by and for the same district court. Registers may act for each other.

IBID.; R. S. § 5008.—The fees of registers, as established by law, or by rules and orders framed pursuant to law, shall be paid to them by the parties for whom the services may be rendered. Their fees: By whom paid.

23. *Register's Fees.*—*Re* Macintire, 1 Ben. 277.

IBID.; R. S. § 5009.—In all matters where an issue of fact or of law is raised and contested by any party to the proceedings before any register, he shall cause the question or issue to be stated by the opposing parties in writing, and he shall adjourn the same into court for decision by the judge. Contested issues to be decided by judge.

24. *Law and Fact.*—What is question of law and what of fact. See *Re* Patterson, 1 Ben. 448; *Re* Levy, 1 Ben. 496.

IBID. § 6; R. S. § 5010.—Any party shall, during the proceedings before a register, be at liberty to take the opinion of the district judge upon any point or matter arising in the course of such proceedings, or upon the result of such proceedings, which shall be stated by the register in the shape of a short certificate to the judge, who shall sign the same if he approve thereof; and such certificate, so signed, shall be binding on all the parties to the proceeding; but every such certificate may be discharged or varied by the judge at chambers or in open court. Opinion of judge: May be taken on case certified.

25. The "*Point or Matter*" must arise "during" or "in the course of" the proceedings, and the court will not decide mere abstract questions which do not so arise. *Re* Haskell, 4 N. B. R. 558; *Re* Levy, 1 Ben. 496.

IBID.; R. S. § 5011.—In any proceedings within the jurisdiction of the court under this title, the parties concerned, or submitting to such jurisdiction, may at any stage of the proceedings, by consent, state any questions in a special case for the opinion of the court, and the judgment of the court shall be final, unless it is agreed and stated in the special case that either party may appeal, if, in such case, an appeal is allowed by this title. The parties may also, if they think fit, agree that, upon the questions raised by such special case being finally decided, a sum of money, fixed by the parties, or to be ascertained by the court, or in such manner as the court may direct, or any property, or the amount of any disputed debt or claim, shall be paid, delivered, or transferred by one of such parties to the other of them, either with or without costs. Agreed cases: Judgments, when final: Agreeements in special cases.

IBID. § 45; R. S. § 5012.—If any judge, register, clerk, marshal, messenger, assignee, or any other officer of the several courts of bankruptcy, shall, for anything done or pretended to be done under this title, or under color of doing anything thereunder, willfully demand or take, or appoint or allow any person whatever to take for him, or on his account, or for or on Penalties against judges and officers.

account of any other person, or in trust for him or for any other person, any fee, emolument, gratuity, sum of money, or anything of value whatever, other than is allowed by law, such person shall forfeit and pay a sum not less than three hundred dollars and not more than five hundred dollars, and be imprisoned not exceeding three years.

IBID. § 48; R. S. § 5013.—In this title the word "assignee," and the word "creditor," shall include the plural also; and the word "messenger" shall include his assistant or assistants, except in the provision for the fees of that officer.

Meaning of terms and computation of time.

The word "marshal" shall include the marshal's deputies; the word "person" shall also include "corporation"; and the word "oath" shall include "affirmation." And in all cases in which any particular number of days is prescribed by this title, or shall be mentioned in any rule or order of court, or general order which shall at any time be made under this title, for the doing of any act, or for any other purpose, the same shall be reckoned, in the absence of any expression to the contrary, exclusive of the first and inclusive of the last day, unless the last day shall fall on a Sunday, Christmas day, or on any day appointed by the President of the United States as a day of public fast or thanksgiving, or on the Fourth of July, in which case the time shall be reckoned exclusive of that day also.

26. *In computing Time* in a suit to recover a preference, the day of filing petition in bankruptcy is to be excluded. Dutcher v. Wright, 15 Alb. L. J. 100.

CHAPTER TWO.

VOLUNTARY BANKRUPTCY.

SECTION
5014. Commencement of Proceedings; who may petition; Petition.
    NOTE 27.—This section construed.
5015. Schedule of debts.
5016. *As Amended.*—Inventory and valuation.

SECTION
5017. Oath to Schedule and Inventory.
    NOTE 28.—Oath; Notary.
5018. Oath of allegiance.
5019. *As Amended.*—Warrant to marshal; Notice to Creditors.
5020. Bankrupt may correct schedule.
    NOTE 29.—Construed; Additions to Schedule.

ORIGINAL ACT OF 1867, § 11; R. S. § 5014.—If any person residing within the jurisdiction of the United States, and owing debts provable in bankruptcy exceeding the amount of three hundred dollars, shall apply by petition addressed to the judge of the judicial district in which such debtor has resided or carried on business for the six months next preceding the time of filing such petition, or for the longest period during such six months, setting forth his place of residence, his inability to pay all his debts in full, his willingness to surrender all his estate and effects for the benefit of his creditors, and his desire to obtain a discharge from his debts, and shall annex to his petition a schedule and inventory, in compliance with the next two sections, the filing of such petition shall be an act of bankruptcy, and such petitioner shall be adjudged a bankrupt. *[marginal: Commencement of Proceedings; Who may petition; Petition.]*

27. *Construed.*—*Re* Magie, 2 Ben. 369. A person can not file a petition for adjudication as a voluntary bankrupt, where a petition for adjudication is still pending, filed by the debtor without any discharge or discontinuance. *Re* Wielarski, 4 N. B. R. 390. A lunatic may, through his guardian, apply for the benefits of the bankrupt law. See *post*, § 5021, note.

IBID.; R. S. § 5015.—The said schedule must contain a full and true statement of all his debts, exhibiting, as far as possible, to whom each debt is due, the place of residence of each creditor, if known to the debtor, and if not known, the fact that it is not known; also the sum due to each creditor; the nature of each debt or demand, whether founded on written security, oblig- *[marginal: Schedule of debts.]*

§§ 5016–5019.]   Inventory—Schedule-Oath—Warrant.   [Note 28.

tion, or contract, or otherwise; the true cause and consideration of the indebtedness in each case, and the place where such indebtedness accrued; and also a statement of any existing mortgage, pledge, lien, judgment or collateral or other security given for the payment of the same.

IBID.; R. S. § 5016, AS AMENDED.—The said inventory must contain an accurate statement [and valuation]¹ of all the petitioner's estate, both real and personal, assignable under this title, describing the same and stating where it is situated, and whether there are any, and, if so, what incumbrances thereon.

Inventory and valuation.

IBID.; R. S. § 5017.—The schedule and inventory must be verified by the oath of the petitioner, which may be taken either before the district judge, or before a register, or before a commissioner of the circuit court.

Oath to schedule and inventory.

28. *Oath—Notary.*—A bankrupt may swear to his schedule before a notary public. *Re* Bailey, 15 N. B. R. 48.

IBID.; R. S. § 5018.—Every citizen of the United States petitioning to be declared bankrupt shall, on filing his petition, and before any proceedings thereon, take and subscribe an oath of allegiance and fidelity to the United States, which oath may be taken before either of the officers mentioned in the preceding section, and shall be filed and recorded with the proceedings in bankruptcy.

Oath of allegiance.

IBID.; R. S. § 5019, AS AMENDED.— Upon the filing of such petition, schedule and inventory, the judge or register shall forthwith, if he is satisfied that the debts due from the petitioner exceed three hundred dollars, issue a warrant, to be signed by such judge or register, directed to the marshal for the district, authorizing him forthwith, as messenger, to publish notices in such newspapers [as the marshal shall select, not exceeding two];² to serve written or printed notice, by mail or personally, on all creditors upon the schedule filed with the debtor's petition, or whose names may be given to him in addition by the debtor; and to give such personal or other notice to any persons concerned as the warrant specifies. [But whenever the creditors of the bankrupt are so numerous as to make any notice now required by law, to them, by mail or otherwise, a great and disproportionate expense to the estate, the court

Warrant: Notice; Service and publication of.

---

(1) So amended by Act of June 22, 1874, § 15. The word "statement" read "inventory," in the original act, and the words "and valuation" were interpolated by the Act of 1874, (which, in terms, amended the original act), after the word "inventory"; so that now, to give the exact value of the amendment, it would be necessary to read the text "inventory and valuation."

(2) So amended by Act June 22, 1874, § 5. The words "as the marshal shall select, not exceeding two," are inserted in place of the words of the original act and of the Revised Statutes, "as the warrant specifies," which are stricken out.

§ 5020.]   Notice—Publication—Correction of Schedule.   [Note 29

may, in lieu thereof, in its discretion, order such notice to be given by publication, in a newspaper or newspapers, to all such creditors whose claims, as reported, do not exceed the sums, respectively, of fifty dollars.]²

IBID. § 26; R. S. § 5020.—Every bankrupt shall be at liberty, from time to time, upon oath, to amend and correct his schedule of creditors and property, so that the same shall conform to the facts. *Bankrupt may correct schedule.*

29. *Construed.*—*Re* Orne, 1 Ben. 420; *Re* Morford, 1 Ben. 264; *Re* Watts, 3 Ben. 166. Material additions to schedule not allowable after first meeting of creditors, except upon such conditions as may prevent injustice. *Re* Ratcliff, 1 N. B. R. 400.

(2) So amended by Act June 22, 1874, § 5.

Involuntary Bankruptcy.

CHAPTER THREE.

INVOLUNTARY BANKRUPTCY.

SECTION
5021. *As Amended.*—Involuntary Bankruptcy; what shall be deemed Acts of Bankruptcy; Number and Amount of Creditors; Petition, Limitation; Voluntary Assignment no Bar to Discharge; embraces what Cases; Proceedings with Reference to Number and Amount of Creditors; Recovery of Property, etc., fraudulently conveyed; Disability of Fraudulent Conveyee; Verification of Petition; what Creditors reckoned.
 NOTE 30.—Who can not commit an Act of Bankruptcy.
 31.—Where Petition to be filed.
 32.—What an Act of Bankruptcy. (1) Assignment under State Laws. (2) Suspension of Payment of Commercial Paper. (3) Preferences.
 33.—Practice; Pleading.
 34.—Claims may be Purchased.
 35.—Creditor joining can not withdraw.
 36.—Sufficiency of Number joining in Petition.
 37.—What Creditors to be reckoned.
 38.—Partnership Cases.
 39.—Secured Creditors not reckoned.
 40.—Attaching Creditors not reckoned.
 41.—Debts barred by Limitation.

SECTION
 42.—Preferred Creditors.
 43.—Interest.
 44.—Burden of Proof; Evidence.
 45.—Whether Amendments of 1874 are Retroactive.
 46.—Sufficiency of Number a Jurisdictional Fact.
 47.—Denial of Requisite Number.
5022. Prior Acts of Bankruptcy.
5023. Repealed.
5024. Debtor ordered to show Cause; Injunction; Arrest; Provisional Order of Seizure.
 NOTE 48.—Sufficient Grounds.
 49.—Jurisdiction of State Court.
 50.—Injunction.
 51.—Arrest.
 52.—Provisional Assignee; Receiver.
 53.—Executing Warrant of Seizure.
 54.—Separate Petition.
5025. *As Amended.*—Service of Order to show Cause; Number and Amount of Creditors.
 NOTE 55.—"If the Debtor can not be found."
 56.—Number and Amount of Creditors.
5026. *As Amended.*—Petition summarily heard, or tried by Jury; Judgment for Respondent, when; Discontinuance; Failure of Petitioning Creditor to Appear, what.

[§ 5021.] Involuntary Bankruptcy.

SECTION	SECTION
NOTE 57.—Demand for Jury.	NOTE 61.—Conclusiveness of Adjudication.
58.—Effect of Appearance.	5029. Proceedings upon Warrant.
59.—Who may oppose Adjudication.	NOTE 62.—What Property seized.
59a.—Adjudication set aside.	63.—Facts must be Proved.
60.—Proof of Discontinuance.	5030. *As Amended.* Schedule, Inventory and Valuation.
5028.—Adjudication and Warrant.	5031. Proceedings if Debtor has failed to Appear.

ORIGINAL ACT OF 1867, § 39, AS AMENDED; R. S. § 5021, AS AMENDED.[1]— That section thirty-nine of said act of March 2d, 1867, be amended so as to read as follows: *INVOLUNTARY BANKRUPTCY.*

"Sec. 39. That any person residing, and owing debts, as aforesaid, who, after the passage of this act, shall depart from the state, district or territory of which he is an inhabitant, with intent to defraud his creditors; or, being absent, shall, with such intent, remain absent; or shall conceal himself to avoid the service of legal process in any action for the recovery of a debt or demand provable under this act; or shall conceal or remove any of his property to avoid its being attached, taken or sequestered on legal process; or shall make any assignment, gift, sale, conveyance or transfer of his estate, property, rights, or credits, either within the United States or elsewhere, with intent to delay, defraud, or hinder his creditors; or who has been arrested and held in custody under or by virtue of mesne process or execution, issued out of any court of the United States, or of any state, district, or territory, within which such debtor resides, or has property, founded upon a demand in its nature provable against a bankrupt's estate, under this act, and for a sum exceeding one hundred dollars, and such process is remaining in force and not discharged by payment, or in any other manner provided by the law of the United States or of such state, district, or territory, applicable thereto, for a period of twenty days, or has been actually imprisoned for more than twenty days in a civil action founded on contract for the sum of one hundred dollars or upwards; or who, being bankrupt or insolvent, or in contemplation of bankruptcy or insolvency, shall make any payment, gift, grant, sale, conveyance or transfer of money or other property, estate, rights, or credits, or confess judgment, or give any warrant to confess judgment, or procure his property to be taken on legal process, with intent to give a preference to one or more of his creditors, or to any person or persons who are or may be liable for him as indorsers, bail, sureties, or otherwise, or with the intent, by such disposition of his property, to defeat or delay the operation of this act; or who, being a bank, banker, broker, merchant, trader, manufacturer, or miner, has fraudulently stopped payment, or who being a bank, banker, broker, merchant,

What shall be deemed acts of bankruptcy.

(1) So amended by Act of June 22, 1874, § 12.

[§ 5021.]   Acts of Bankruptcy—Number and Amount of Creditors.

trader, manufacturer, or miner, has stopped or suspended and not resumed payment, within a period of forty days, of his commercial paper (made or passed in the course of his business as such), or who, being a bank or banker, shall fail for forty days to pay any depositor upon demand of payment lawfully made, shall be deemed to have committed an act of bankruptcy, and, subject to the conditions hereinafter prescribed, shall be adjudged a bankrupt on the petition of one or more of his creditors, who shall constitute one-fourth thereof, at least, in number, and the aggregate of whose debts provable under this act amounts to at least one-third of the debts so provable. *Provided*, That such petition is brought within six months after such act of bankruptcy shall have been committed. [*Provided*, also, that no voluntary assignment by a debtor or debtors of all his or their property, heretofore or hereafter made in good faith for the benefit of all his or their creditors, ratably and without creating any preference, and valid according to the law of the state where made, shall of itself, in the event of his or their being subsequently adjudicated bankrupts in a proceeding of involuntary bankruptcy, be a bar to the discharge of such debtor or debtors.][1] And the provisions of this section shall apply to all cases of compulsory or involuntary bankruptcy commenced since the first day of December, 1873, as well as to those commenced hereafter. And in all cases commenced since the first day of December, 1873, and prior to the passage of this act, as well as those commenced hereafter, this court shall, if such allegation as to the number or amount of petitioning creditors be denied by the debtor, by a statement in writing to that effect, require him to file in court forthwith a full list of his creditors, with their places of residence and the sums due them respectively, and shall ascertain, upon reasonable notice to the creditors, whether one-fourth in number and one-third in amount thereof, as aforesaid, have petitioned that the debtor be adjudged a bankrupt. But if such debtor shall, on the filing of the petition, admit in writing that the requisite number and amount of creditors have petitioned, the court (if satisfied that the admission was made in good faith) shall so adjudge, which judgment shall be final, and the matter proceed without further steps on that subject. And if it shall appear that such number and amount have not so petitioned, the court shall grant reasonable time, not exceeding, in cases heretofore commenced, twenty days, and, in cases hereafter commenced, ten days, within which other creditors may join in such petition. And if, at the expiration of such time so limited, the number and amount shall comply with the requirements of this section, the matter of bank-

(1) So amended by Act of July 26, 1876.

[§ 5021.]   Fraudulent Conveyances—What Creditors reckoned.   [Notes 30–32.

ruptcy may proceed; but if, at the expiration of such limited time, such number and amount shall not answer the requirements of this section, the proceedings shall be dismissed, and, in cases hereafter commenced, with costs. And if such person shall be adjudged a bankrupt, the assignee may recover back the money or property so paid, conveyed, sold, assigned, or transferred contrary to this act: *Provided*, That the person receiving such payment or conveyance had reasonable cause to believe that the debtor was insolvent and knew[2] that a fraud on this act was intended; and such person, if a creditor, shall not, in cases of actual fraud on his part, be allowed to prove for more than a moiety of his debt; and this limitation on the proof of debts shall apply to cases of voluntary as well as involuntary bankruptcy. And the petition of creditors under this section may be sufficiently verified by the oaths of the first five signers thereof, if so many there be. And if any of said first five signers shall not reside in the district in which such petition is to be filed, the same may be signed and verified by the oath or oaths of the attorney or attorneys, agent or agents, of such signers. And in computing the number of creditors, as aforesaid, who shall join in such petition, creditors whose respective debts do not exceed two hundred and fifty dollars shall not be reckoned. But if there be no creditors whose debts exceed said sum of two hundred and fifty dollars, or if the requisite number of creditors holding debts exceeding two hundred and fifty dollars fail to sign the petition, the creditors having debts of a less amount shall be reckoned for the purposes aforesaid."

Recovery of property, etc., fraudulently conveyed.

Disability of fraudulent conveyee.

Verification of petition.

What creditors reckoned.

30. *Who can Commit an Act of Bankruptcy.*—A person of unsound mind can not. *Re* Marvin, 1 Dill. 178; *Re* Weitzel, 14 N. B. R. 466; s. c., 3 C. L. J. 557. A lunatic may be proceeded against in bankruptcy. *Re* Weitzel, 14 N. B. R. 466. But see *Re* Murphy, 10 N. B. R. 48. A voluntary petition for adjudication may be filed on behalf of a lunatic by his guardian. *Re* Pratt, 6 N. B. R. 276. Where a state court appointed receivers of an insolvent corporation, and a petition was subsequently filed by creditors against the corporation to have it adjudged bankrupt, the court so adjudged. *Re* Independent Ins. Co., 6 N. B. R. 169; *Re* Merchants' Ins. Co., 6 N. B. R. 43; *Re* Green Pond R. R. Co., 13 N. B. R. 118.

31. *Where Petition to be Filed.*—The restrictions in section 5014 as to place where proceedings must be had apply to this section. *Re* Leighton, 5 N. B. R. 95.

32. *What an Act of Bankruptcy*—(1) *Assignment under State Laws.*—A general assignment without preferences, whether made under a statute law of voluntary assignments or at common law for benefit of creditors, is an act of bankruptcy, and is void as against an assignee in bankruptcy, because it is a conveyance which " *defeats the operation of the act.*" *Re* Smith, 3 N. B. R. 377; *Re* Randall, 3 N. B. R. 18; *Re* Goldschmidt, 3 N. B. R. 165; *Re* Pierce & Holbrook, 3 N. B. R. 258; Hardy v. Bininger, 4 N. B. R. 262; *Re* Union Pac. R. R. Co., 10 N. B. R. 178; *Re* Spicer v. Ward, 3 N. B. R. 512; *Re* Burt, 1 Dill. 439. For an elaborate discussion of the question, see Globe Ins. Co. v. Cleve-

(2) In place of the word "knew" the original act read "had reasonable cause to believe."

§ 5021.]   Acts of Bankruptcy—Practice—Purchase of Claims.   [Notes 32–35.

land Ins. Co., 14 N. B. R. 311. *Contra*, Langley v. Perry, 2 N. B. R. 596; Farrin v. Crawford, 2 N. B. R. 602; *Re* Marter, 12 N. B. R. 185. But an assignment which is invalid under the statute laws of the state, is not an act of bankruptcy. *Re* Mendelsohn, 12 N. B. R. 533.

(2). *Suspension of Payment of Commercial Paper.*—The law requires that the person suspending payment of his paper, shall have been a trader at the time of making the note. *Re* Jack, 13 N. B. R. 296. Where a manufacturing firm dissolved, and one partner purchased the other partner's interest in the machinery and business, and gave his notes for the purchase, which notes were negotiated, the holders of which petitioned the payee into bankruptcy, it was held that it was not commercial paper of the manufacturer, made and passed in the course of his business as such. *Re* Lanz, 14 N. B. R. 159. Note given for money borrowed is not commercial paper. *Re* McDermot Bolt Co., 3 Ben. 389. Any person who has fraudulently stopped payment of his debts generally, may be adjudged a bankrupt; it need not necessarily be commercial paper. This is a *dictum* in *Re* Hadley, 12 N. B. R. 366. See also *Re* Hall, 1 Dill. 585; *Re* Hercules Mutual Life Ins. Society, 6 N. B. R. 338.

(3.) *Preferences.*—Allowing fictitious judgments to be entered is *procuring* property to be taken on legal process. *Re* Schick, 2 Ben. 5. Petitioning creditors who hold preferences can not allege the preferences to them as an act of bankruptcy; they are estopped. *Re* Williams, 14 N. B. R. 132. So, also, if they hold a note which the debtor has no chance to pay, for forty days, they are estopped from alleging the non-payment as an act of bankruptcy. Ibid.

33. *Practice—Pleadings.*—A petition will not be dismissed because the depositions in support thereof are defective. Supplemental depositions may be filed on motion. Cunningham v. Cady, 13 N. B. R. 526. When the depositions are defective, an order to show cause will be set aside, but an *alias* order may be issued on supplemental depositions. Cunningham v. Cady, 13 N. B. R. 526. A defective affidavit to a petition may, upon motion, be amended. *Re* Sargent, 13 N. B. R. 144. Where the act of bankruptcy, alleged in the petition, is a fraudulent conveyance, the deposition in support of such allegation must show the fraudulent intent of the debtor. Cunningham v. Cady, 13 N. B. R. 526. A charge in the alternative "that the debtor is insolvent, or in contemplation of bankruptcy," is not sufficient. *Re* Hanibel, 15 N. B. R. 233. The petition in involuntary proceedings for an adjudication need not contain a detailed statement of the petitioner's demand; it should be so far stated that the court may see that it is a provable debt. *Re* Hadley, 12 N. B. R. 366. It is not necessary that proof of the act of bankruptcy charged, should appear in the petition; but it must appear in the *deposition* to the act. *Re* Hadley, 12 N. B. R. 366. Where the act of bankruptcy charged is a payment by way of preference, it is not necessary to allege that it was in fraud of the provisions of the act. Ibid. Depositions to acts of bankruptcy should be made upon the personal knowledge of the deponent. Ibid. The allegation of stoppage may be in two forms: The pleader may set up a general stoppage of payment, without describing any paper, or he may aver the stoppage of a particular piece of commercial paper, and rely upon it as *prima facie* evidence of a general stoppage. *Re* Hadley, 12 N. B. R. 366; McLean v. Brown, 4 N. B. R. 585; *Re* Hercules Mut. Life Ins. Society, 6 N. B. R. 338; *Re* McNaughton, 8 N. B. R. 44; *Re* Wilson, 8 N. B. R. 396. If the stoppage of a particular piece is relied upon, it must be described. *Re* Randall, 3 N. B. R. 18; s. c., Deady, 524. Allegation of sufficiency of number may be amended. *Re* McKibben, 12 N. B. R. 97.

34. *Claims may be Purchased.*—A party may purchase a claim in good faith in order to join in an involuntary petition and make the necessary number. *Re* Woodford, 13 N. B. R. 575. If the sale of a claim is void for fraud or want of consideration, the claim is to be deemed to belong to the assignor. *Re* Woodford, 13 N. B. R. 575. It is not necessary that the larger creditors shall be requested to sign the petition, and refuse, before recourse can be had to the smaller ones. *Re* Currier, 13 N. B. R. 68.

35. *Creditor Joining can not Withdraw.*—Where a creditor in good faith has joined

§ 5021.] Creditors—Number Joining—Who Reckoned—Secured, etc. [Notes 36-43.

in a petition, he can not withdraw. *Re* Sargent, 13 N. B. R. 144; *Re* Heffron, 10 N. B. R. 213; s. c., 6 C. L. N. 358. But if, through misrepresentation or misunderstanding, he may withdraw before adjudication. Ibid. But may not object to amendments which are necessary. Ibid. Where the petition is verified by an agent or attorney, it must appear that the persons for whom the agent or attorney signs, are non-residents of the district, if they are the first five petitioners. *Re* Hadley, 12 N. B. R. 366. His authority must be shown. *Re* Sargent, 13 N. B. R. 144. Where there are less than five signers to the petition, and it is verified by an agent, it is not necessary for such agent to state the residence of his principals as the foundation of his right to act. *Re* Simmons, 10 N. B. R. 254; 1 C. L. J. 440.

36. *Sufficiency of Number Joining in Petition.*—The amendment to section thirty-five (R. S., § 5021), requiring a fixed proportion of creditors to join in a petition for the adjudication of a person a bankrupt, has given rise to much complicated litigation, and has weakened the efficacy of the act. The allegation in an involuntary petition that the petitioners constitute the requisite proportion of creditors need be upon belief only, without charging either information or knowledge. *Re* Mann, 14 N. B. R. 572. But see *Re* Joliet Iron Co., 10 N. B. R. 60; *Re* Scammon, 10 N. B. R. 67; *Re* Scull, 10 N. B. R. 160; *Re* Keeler, 10 N. B. R. 419.

37. *What Creditors to be Reckoned.*—Creditors whose claims are under two hundred and fifty dollars are not to be counted in computing the number who must unite in an involuntary petition, if one-fourth of the creditors whose claims are above that sum join in the petition. *Re* Woodford, 13 N. B. R. 575; *Re* Currier, 13 N. B. R. 3; *Re* Hadley, 12 N. B. R. 366; *Re* Bergeron, 12 N. B. R. 385; *Re* Broich, 15 N. B. R. 1. Contra, *Re* Hymes, 10 N. B. R. 433. In computing the amount or value, all the aims must be reckoned, and the petitioners must constitute one-third of all. *Re* Broich, 15 N. B. R. 11; *Re* Woodford, 13 N. B. R. 575; *Re* Currier, 13 N. B. R. 68; *Re* Hadley, 12 N. B. R. 366. Contra, *Re* Hymes, 10 N. B. R. 434. If one-fourth of all creditors in number, irrespective of amount of their claims, join in the petition, and one-third in amount of the debts, the requirements of the section are fulfilled. *Re* Hall, 15 N. B. R. 31; *Re* Currier, *supra*.

38. *Partnership Cases.*—In an involuntary proceeding against a separate partner, creditors of the partnership are to be counted in ascertaining the number and value. *Re* Lloyd, 15 N. B. R. 257; *Re* Price, 3 Dillon, 514.

39. *Secured Creditors not Reckoned.*—Secured creditors are not to be reckoned in computing the proportion of creditors who must join in an involuntary petition. *Re* Green Pond R. R. Co., 13 N. B. R. 118. "*Debts provable under the act,*" means only unsecured debts. Ibid.; *Re* Frost, 11 N. B. R. 69. If a secured creditor joins in a petition for adjudication in involuntary bankruptcy, he surrenders his security. *Re* Broich, 15 N. B. R. 11. If a creditor holds partial security for his claims, the court will ascertain the value of the security, and the creditor's claim will be computed for the excess over the security, in determining the question whether the requisite number and value of creditors have joined. Ibid.

40. *Attaching Creditors not Reckoned.*—*Re* Scrafford, 4 Cent. L. J. 19, overruling s. c., 14 N. B. R. 184; s. c., 3 Cent. L. J. 252. Contra, *Re* Hatje, 12 N. B. R. 548; *Re* Broich, 15 N. B. R. 11.

41. *Debts barred by Limitation* are to be disregarded. *Re* Noesen, 12 N. B. R. 422.

42. *Preferred Creditors.*—Fraudulently preferred creditors of a debtor may be disregarded in estimating whether the requisite proportion of creditors have joined in a petition for adjudication in bankruptcy. *Re* Israel, 12 N. B. R. 204; *Re* Currier, 13 N. B. R. 68; Michaels v. Post, 12 N. B. R. 152; s. c., 21 Wall. 398. A creditor who was induced to discharge his debtor, without consideration, from the payment of the debt due him, by the fraud of another creditor, may file a petition in bankruptcy against the debtor on such debt. Michael v. Post, 12 N. B. R. 152; s. c., 21 Wall. 398.

43. *Interest.*—In ascertaining the amount of debts joined in the petition for adjudication, interest on the debts should stop on all the claims simultaneously, and,

§§ 5021-5024.]   Evidence—Number and Amount of Creditors.   [Notes 43-47.

for purposes of such an inquiry, interest should stop at the date of the filing of the petition. *Re* Broich, 15 N. B. R. 11.

44. *Burden of Proof—Evidence.*—In a case of involuntary bankruptcy, the burden of proof is upon the petitioning creditors. *Re* Oregon Printing Co., 13 N. B. R. 503. A party is insolvent when he is unable to pay his debts as they become due. *Re* Oregon Printing Co., 13 N. B. R. 503. *Semble*, that if his property, put up upon reasonable notice for sale, where it exists under the circumstances of the case, will bring cash enough to pay his debts, he is not insolvent. Ibid. A petitioning creditor is not required to make full and satisfactory proof of the debtor's insolvency, but may offer proof tending to show his insolvency, and the debtor must then explain the evidence, if possible. *Re* Oregon Printing Co., 13 N. B. R. 503. A solvent debtor may pay any or all of his debts, although proceedings in bankruptcy are pending against him. *Re* Oregon Printing Co., 13 N. B. R. 503. A defense which has been stricken out may be offered in evidence as an admission. *Re* Oregon Printing Co., 13 N. B. R. 503. No particular or specific evidence of intent to prefer is necessary when a payment is made by an insolvent debtor, for the act itself is evidence of the intent. But the law will not presume an intent to prefer when the debtor is not aware of his insolvency; but it is incumbent on him to show that fact. *Re* Oregon Printing Co., 13 N. B. R. 503.

45. *Whether Amendments of 1874 are Retroactive.*—The amendatory and supplemental act of June 22, 1874, applied to all cases commenced since December 1, 1878, upon which no adjudications had been had at the time of the passage of the act. *Re* Obear, 10 N. B. R. 153; s. c., 1 Cent. L. J. 362; *Re* Angell, 10 N. B. R. 73; s. c., 1 Cent. L. J. 363; s. c., 6 Ch. L. N. 341; *Re* Raffauff, 6 Ch. L. N. 341; s. c., 1 Cent. L. J. 364, note; s. c. 10 N. B. R. 60; Re Rosenthal, 10 N. B. R. 191; s. c., 1 Cent. L. J. 364, note; s. c., 6 Ch. L. N. 342; *Re* Pickering, 10 N. B. R. 208; Barnett v. Highblower, 10 N. B. R. 157; *Re* Comstock, 6 C. L. N. 413. The following authorities maintain that Congress could not have passed an act which would have had the effect of disturbing adjudications already made: *Re* Comstock, *supra;* *Re* Angell, *supra;* *Re* Raffauff, *supra;* *Re* Pickering, *supra.* An adjudication entered on the 22d of June, 1874, might be set aside on the motion of the debtor, if the provisions of the act passed on that day were not complied with. *Re* Carrier, 10 N. B. R. 208.

46. *Sufficiency of Number a Jurisdictional Fact.*—A *prima facie* case must be made by the petition as to the number and value of creditors, this being a material and substantial fact, before the court can acquire jurisdiction to grant an order to show cause. Re Burch, 10 N. B. R. 150. *Contra, Re* Duncan, 14 N. B. R. 18.

47. *Denial of Requisite Number.*—The debtor's denial that the requisite number have joined in the petition, must be verified. *Re* Steinman, 6 Ch. L. N. 338; *Re* Hymes, 10 N. B. R. 434. The list of creditors filed by the debtor should be verified, in like manner, by the debtor's oath. Ibid. Where petitions were filed against an alleged debtor, and the debtor had made a denial and had demanded a jury trial, and had since filed a demurrer, he was required to file a list of his creditors, and of the amount of their claims. Warren Sav. Bank v. Palmer, 10 N. B. R. 239; s. c., 6 Ch. L. N. 366; *Re* Scammon, 7 Ch. L. N. 42.

R. S. § 5022.—Any act of bankruptcy committed since the second day of March, 1867, may be the foundation of an adjudication of involuntary bankruptcy, upon a petition filed within the time prescribed by law, equally with one committed hereafter.

Prior acts of bankruptcy.

R. S. § 5023.—[Repealed by Act of June 22, 1874, § 12, *supra.*]

ORIGINAL ACT OF 1867, § 40; R. S. § 5024.—Upon the filing of the petition authorized by the preceding section,[1] if it appears that suffi-

(1) This refers to § 5021, as amended.

§ 5024.]   Debtor to show Cause—Injunction—Provisional Warrant.   [Notes 48-54.]

cient grounds exist therefor, the court shall direct the entry of an order requiring the debtor to appear and show cause, at a court of bankruptcy to be holden at a time to be specified in the order, not less than five days from the service thereof, why the prayer of the petition should not be granted. The court may also, by injunction, restrain the debtor, and any other person, in the mean time, from making any transfer or disposition of any part of the debtor's property not excepted by this title from the operation thereof and from any interference therewith; and if it shall appear that there is probable cause for believing that the debtor is about to leave the district, or to remove or conceal his goods and chattels or his evidence of property, or to make any fraudulent conveyance or disposition thereof, the court may issue a warrant to the marshal of the district, commanding him to arrest and safely keep the alleged debtor, unless he shall give bail to the satisfaction of the court for his appearance from time to time, as required by the court, until its decision upon the petition, or until its further order, and forthwith to take possession provisionally of all the property and effects of the debtor, and safely keep the same until the further order of the court. *Debtor ordered to show cause; Injunction; Arrest; Provisional warrant of seizure.*

48. *What are Sufficient Grounds.*—See *Re* Cone, 2 Ben. 502.

49. *Jurisdiction of State Court.*—The mere filing of a petition in involuntary bankruptcy does not divest the state court of an action to foreclose a mortgage instituted before such filing; and, in the absence of an injunction, a party is not liable for selling the property under a decree of foreclosure made in that action. *Re* Irving, 14 N. B. R. 289.

50. *Injunction.*—An injunction granted restraining a person from interfering with the debtor's property "in the meantime, and until the hearing and decision upon the petition, and until further order of the court," ceases to operate after the debtor is adjudged a bankrupt. *Re* Irving, 14 N. B. R. 289.

51. *Arrest.*—This section authorizes the court, upon the filing of the petition in bankruptcy, to issue a warrant for the arrest of the debtor for his appearance. Usher v. Pease, 12 N. B. R. 305; S. C., 116 Mass. 440. No arrest can be made under the warrant after an adjudication is had. Ibid. No authority is conferred by this section to direct the seizure of property, except such as belongs to and is in the possession of the debtor. Where property is supposed to have been conveyed by the debtor in fraud of the act, this court will enjoin the purchaser from disposing of the same until the assignee has had reasonable time for asserting his rights. *Re* Holland, 12 N. B. R. 403.

52. *Provisional Assignee—Receiver.*—A provisional assignee should not be appointed, or a warrant of seizure issued, upon the filing of a petition in bankruptcy, unless the court is satisfied that it is necessary for the protection of the property, and that it will enure to the benefit of the creditors. National Bank v. Iron Co., 5 N. B. R. 491.

53. *Executing Warrants of Seizure.*—A marshal is justified under a warrant of seizure in seizing property transferred by the debtor before the commencement of proceedings, by a transfer which is void under the bankrupt law. Stevenson v. McLaren, 14 N. B. R. 403. Section 35 of the law makes transfers absolutely *void*, which defeat the operation of the act. Ibid. See Bolander v. Gentry, 36 Cal. 105; Hanson v. Herrick, 100 Mass. 323; Foster v. Hackley, 2 N. B. R. 406; *Re* Husaman, 2 N. B. R. 437; Muller v. Bretano, 3 N. B. R. 329; *Re* Briggs, 3 N. B. R. 638.

54. *Separate Petition.*—Where a warrant of seizure and of arrest is prayed for, it should be by a separate petition. *Re* Hadley, 12 N. B. R. 366.

§§ 5025–5026.] Order to Show Cause—Number and Amount—Hearing. [Notes 55–56.

IBID.; R. S. § 5025, AS AMENDED.—A copy of the petition and order to show cause shall be served on the debtor by delivering the same to him personally, or leaving the same at his last or usual place of abode; or, if the debtor can not be found, and his place of residence can not be ascertained, service shall be made by publication in such manner as the judge may direct. No further proceedings, unless the debtor appears and consents thereto, shall be had until proof has been given, to the satisfaction of the court, of such service or publication; and if such proof is not given on the return day of such order, the proceedings shall be adjourned and an order made that the notice be forthwith so served or published. [And if, on the return day of the order to show cause as aforesaid, the court shall be satisfied that the requirement of section thirty-nine of said act as to the number and amount of petitioning creditors has been complied with, or if, within the time provided for in section thirty-nine of this act, creditors sufficient in number and amount shall sign such petition so as to make a total of one-fourth in number of the creditors, and one-third in the amount of the provable debts against the bankrupt, as provided in said section, the court shall so adjudge, which judgment shall be final; otherwise it shall dismiss the proceedings, and, in cases hereinafter commenced, with costs.][1]

Service or publication of order to show cause.

Number and amount of creditors.

55. "*If the Debtor can not be Found*" means "if he can not be found within the jurisdiction of court." The marshal can not serve the order to show cause out of his district. Alabama R. R. v. Jones, 5 N. B. R. 97. A corporation which is dissolved and in the hands of a receiver, 'can not be found,' and service must be made by publication. *Re* Washington Ins. Co., 2 Ben. 292.

56. *Number and Amount of Creditors.*—The allegation that the one-fourth in number of creditors and one-third in value, have joined in the petition in compulsory proceedings, is not a jurisdictional fact, and the judgment of the court is final on that subject in the absence of fraud and bad faith. The fact that the debtor co-operated with the creditors in getting a sufficient number to join in the petition, is no evidence of collusion. *Re* Duncan, 14 N. B. R. 18; *Re* Funkenstein, 14 N. B. R. 213. *Contra*, see note 56, *supra*.

IBID. §§ 41, 42; R. S. § 5026, AS AMENDED.—On such return day or adjourned day, if the notice has been duly served or published, or is waived by the appearance and consent of the debtor, the court shall proceed summarily to hear the allegations of the petitioner and debtor, and may adjourn the proceedings from time to time, on good cause shown, and shall, if the debtor on the same day so demands, in writing, order a trial by jury at the first term of the court at which a jury shall be in attendance, to ascertain the fact of the alleged bankruptcy. [Or, at the election of the debtor, the court may, in its discretion, award a *venire facias* to the marshal of the district, returnable within ten days before him for the trial of the facts set forth.

Petition summarily heard.

Or tried by jury.

(1) So amended by act of June 22, 1874, § 13.

§ 5026.]   Proceedings upon Creditors' Petition.   [Notes b7-60.

in the petition, at which time the trial shall be had, unless adjourned
for cause. And unless, upon such hearing or trial, it
shall appear to the satisfaction of said court, or of the *Judgment for respondent, when.*
jury, as the case may be, that the facts set forth in said
petition are true, or if it shall appear that the debtor has paid and satisfied all liens upon his property, in case the existence of such liens
was the sole ground of the proceeding, the proceeding shall be dismissed, and the respondent shall recover costs; and all proceedings in
bankruptcy may be discontinued on reasonable notice
and hearing, with the approval of the court, and upon *Discontinuance.*
the assent, in writing, of such debtor, and not less than one-half of his
creditors in number and amount; or, in case all the creditors and such
debtors assent thereto, such discontinuance shall be ordered and entered; and all parties shall be remitted, in either case, to the same
rights and duties existing at the date of the filing of the petition for
bankruptcy, except so far as such estate shall have been already administered and disposed of. And the court shall have power to make all
needful orders and decrees to carry the foregoing provision into effect.][1]
If the petitioning creditor does not appear and proceed
on the return day, or adjourned day, the court may, *Failure of petitioning creditor to appear, what.*
upon the petition of any other creditor, to the required
amount, proceed to adjudicate on such petition without requiring a new service or publication of notice to the debtor.

57. *Demand for Jury.*—Must be made on the return day of the order to show cause.
Clinton v. Mayo, 12 N. B. R. 41; *Re* Pupke, 1 Ben. 342.

58. *Appearance* waives all irregularities in the service of process, and confers jurisdiction so far as the person is concerned. *Re* Ulrich, 3 Ben. 355.

59. *Who may Oppose Adjudication—Grounds of Opposition.*—Any creditor who is
able to satisfy the court that his purpose is a meritorious one, ought to be allowed to
intervene and oppose the adjudication of bankruptcy. *Re* Jack, 13 N. B. R. 296; *Re*
Boston, Hartford & Erie R. R., 9 Blatch. 101; s. c., 6 N. B. R. 209. This intervention
may be on grounds going to the merits of the petition, as well as to the question of
requisite proportion of creditors petitioning. Ibid. *Re* Williams, 14 N. B. R. 132;
Re Bergeron, 12 N. B. R. 385. Attaching creditors may intervene and oppose adjudication, on the ground that requisite proportion of creditors have not joined in the
petition. *Re* Hatje, 12 N. B. R. 548; *Re* Jack, 13 N. B. R. 296; *Re* Broich, 15 N. B. R. 11;
Re Mendelsohn, 12 N. B. R. 533; s. c., 3 Sawy. 342. But creditors whose debts are of
doubtful validity, proof of which is postponed as provided by § 5083, can not intervene. Clinton v. Mayo, 12 N. B. R. 41. But a fraudulent vendee of the bankrupt's
property may. Payne v. Solomon, 14 N. B. R. 162.

59a. *Adjudication set Aside.*—An attaching creditor may move to set aside an adjudication in bankruptcy improperly or irregularly entered. *Re* Bergeron, 12 N. B. R.
385. A finding of the court as to the sufficiency of creditors in number and amount
would be binding in a collateral proceeding, yet it is a *quasi* jurisdictional allegation, and an adjudication should be opened where there appears a want of a proper
number. *Re* Bergeron, 12 N. B. R. 385.

60. *Discontinuance, Proof of.*—When an adjudication of bankruptcy is proved, the
party who alleges that the proceedings have been dismissed must prove the time of
dismissal. Wills v. Claflin, 13 N. B. R. 437; s. c., 92 U. S. 135.

(1) So amended by act of June 22, 1874, § 14.

§§ 5028-5031.]   Adjudication—Warrant—Schedule, Inventory, etc.   [Notes 61-63.

R. S. § 5027.—[Repealed by the Act of June 22, 1874, § 14.]

IBID. § 42; R. S. § 5028.—If upon the hearing or trial the facts set forth in the petition are found to be true, or if upon default made by the debtor to appear pursuant to the order, due proof of service thereof is made, the court shall adjudge the debtor to be a bankrupt, and shall forthwith issue a warrant to take possession of his estate.

Adjudication and warrant.

61. *Adjudication Conclusive.*—An adjudication in bankruptcy regularly made can not be assailed in a collateral proceeding. The decree is conclusive, unless when it is called into question by the court where it was entered. Michaels v. Post, 12 N. B. R. 152; s. c., 21 Wall. 398; Sloan v. Lewis, 12 N. B. R. 173; s. c., 22 Wall. 150. Notice by proper form of pleading must be given. Sloan v. Lewis, *supra*.

IBID. § 42; R. S. § 5029.—The warrant shall be directed, and the property of the debtor shall be taken thereon, and shall be assigned and distributed in the same manner and with similar proceedings to those hereinbefore provided for the taking possession, assignment, and distribution of the property of the debtor upon his own petition.

Proceedings upon warrant.

62. *What Property Seized.*—There is no difference in respect to what property the marshal is justified in seizing between the provisional and the final warrant. Stevenson v. McLaren, 14 N. B. R. 403.

63. *Facts must be Proved.*—Petitioners must prove facts alleged in their petition. *Re* Hoppock, 2 Ben. 478.

IBID. § 42; R. S. § 5030, AS AMENDED.—The order of adjudication of bankruptcy shall require the bankrupt forthwith, or within such number of days not exceeding five after the date of the order or notice thereof, as shall by the order be prescribed, to make and deliver, or transmit by mail, postpaid, to the messenger, a schedule of the creditors and an inventory [and valuation]¹ of his estate in the form and verified in the manner required of a petitioning debtor.

Schedule, inventory and valuation.

IBID.; R. S. § 5031.—If the debtor has failed to appear in person, or by attorney, a certified copy of the adjudication shall be forthwith served on him by delivery or publication in the manner provided for the service of the order to show cause; and if the bankrupt is absent or can not be found, such schedule and inventory shall be prepared by the messenger and the assignee from the best information they can obtain.

Proceedings if debtor has failed to appear.

(1) So amended by Act of June 22, 1874, § 15.

BANKRUPT LAW. 29

Proceedings to Realize the Estate for Creditors.

CHAPTER FOUR

PROCEEDINGS TO REALIZE THE ESTATE FOR CREDITORS.

SECTION
5032. What the Notice to Creditors shall state.
5033. First Meeting of Creditors; Marshal's Return.
    NOTE 64.—This section Construed.
5034. Assignee, how chosen; who chosen Assignee.
    NOTE 65.—Election of Assignee; Eligibility; Qualification.
5035. Who can not Vote for or be chosen Assignee.
5036. Bond of Assignee; Failing to give, removed.
5037. Assignee liable for Contempt.
5038. Resignation of Assignee.
5039. Removal of Assignee.
    NOTE 66.—The Same Subject.
5040. Effect of Resignation or Removal.
5041. Vacancies, how Filled.
5042. Estate vested in Remaining Assignee.
5043. Conveyance to new Assignee; Court to make Orders.
5044. Assignment; relates back; vests estate; dissolves Attachments.
    NOTE 67.—Assignment not Acknowledged; Relates Back.
    68.—What Assignee takes; Effect of Equities, Judgments, etc.
    69.—Effect of Assignment upon Attachments.
5045. What Property exempt in Hands of Bankrupt; Exemption, how to Operate.

SECTION
    NOTE 70.—What is Exempt.
    71.—No Title to Exempt Property passes to Assignee.
    72.—Setting apart Exempt Property.
    73.—Exemption extends to what Property; how Affected by Judgments, Liens, etc.
    74.—Homesteads purchased in Fraud of Creditors.
    75.—Physical Character of Homestead.
    76.—Partners not entitled to Exemptions out of Partnership Estate.
    77.—Statute Laws existing in 1871 govern.
    78.—Constitutionality of this Statute.
5046. What Property vests in Assignee.
    NOTE 79.—Property Conveyed in Fraud of Creditors etc.
5047. Assignee may recover Debts; be admitted to Pending Suits; defend Actions.
    NOTE 80.—Decisions under this Section; Rights of Assignee, Bankrupt, etc.
5048. Suits not to abate by Death or Removal.
5049. Copy of Assignment Conclusive Evidence of Title.
    NOTE 81.—This section Construed; Exemplification of Part of Record.

Proceedings to Realize the Estate for Creditors.

SECTION
5050. Bankrupt's Books of Account.
5051. Debtor must Execute Instruments.
5052. Certain Mortgages not Invalidated.
    NOTE 82.—This section Construed.
5053. Trust Property.
    NOTE 83.—Identity of Trust Property.
5054. Notice of Appointment of Assignee and Recording of Assignment.
    NOTE 84.—Construction of this Section.
5055. Assignee to demand all Assigned Estate.
5056. Notice prior to Suit against Assignee.
    NOTE 85.—Seizure by Assignee of Property of Stranger.
5057. Suits to be brought within two years; Rights barred not Revived hereby.
    NOTE 86.—Applies to Suits brought by Assignee.
5058. *Superseded.*
5059. Assignee to Deposit Money and keep Effects Separate from his Own.
5060. Temporary Investment of Money.
5061. Assignee may submit Controversies to Arbitration; may settle Controversies.
    NOTE 87.—Arbitration; Composition of Doubtful Claim.
5061a. Assignee may carry on Business, when.
5062. Assignee may make Sales, but Court may make order as to Time, Place, etc.
    NOTE 88.—Assignee's Sales.
5063. Sale of Disputed Property.
    NOTE 89.—Sale of Disputed Property.
5064. Sale of Uncollectible Assets.
5065. Sale of Perishable Property.
5065a. Assignee's Sales to be at Auction; Notice of, how Published; Supervisory Power of Court; Sales on Credit.
5065b. Assignee to keep Accounts; Penalties against; Punishment of Persons combining with; Re-

SECTION
    ports of; to account for all Interest, Benefits, etc.; Affidavit and Examination of; Penalty against, for False-Swearing.
5066. Assignee may Discharge Liens, Perform Conditional Contracts, etc.
5067. Debts and Proofs of Claims; what Debts Provable; Demands for Conversion of Chattels; Unliquidated Damages.
    NOTE 90.—Debts due the United States.
    91.—Statutes of Limitation.
    92.—What are Provable Debts.
5068. Contingent Debts and Liabilities.
    NOTE 93.—The same Subject.
5069. Liability of Bankrupt as Drawer, Endorser, etc.
    NOTE 94.—The same Subject.
5070. Sureties for Bankrupt.
    NOTE 95.—Bond to return Property.
5071. Debts Falling due at Stated Periods.
    NOTE 96.—Rent; Landlord's Lien.
    97.—Occupation by Assignee of Leased Premises.
5072. No other Debts Provable.
5073. *As Amended.*—Set-offs.
    NOTE 98.—Set-off; Claim of Stockholder; of Bailee.
    99.—Claim Purchased or Transferred.
5074. Mixed Liabilities.
5075. Secured Debts; Value of Security exceeding Debt, what.
    NOTE 100.—Practice when Debt secured.
    101.—Who are Lien Creditors.
    102.—Sale of Incumbered Property.
    103.—Sale at Request of Creditor.
    104.—Marshalling Securities.
    105.—What not Secured.
    106.—Action in State Court to enforce Lien stayed.
5076. Debts Provable before what Officer.

BANKRUPT LAW. 31

Proceedings to Realize the Estate for Creditors.

SECTION
- NOTE 107.—Cases.
- 5076a. Notary may take Proof of Debts.
  - NOTE 108.—Power of Notaries; Use of Seal.
- 5077. Claims, how Verified.
  - NOTE 109.—Proof must show what.
- 5078. Oath, by whom Made; Corporations; other Evidence received.
  - NOTE 110.—Who may make Proof.
- 5079. Oath, before whom Taken; how Transmitted; Creditors in Foreign Country.
- 5080. Proof to be sent to Assignee; his Duty; other Evidence.
  - NOTE 111.—Withdrawal of Proof.
  - 112.—Quantum of Proof.
- 5081. Examination by Court into Proof of Claims.
  - NOTE 113.—Examination of Proof.
- 5082. Withdrawal of Evidences of Debt.
- 5083. Postponement of Proofs.
  - NOTE 114.—The same subject.
- 5084. Surrender of Preferences; Penalty for Failure.
  - NOTE 115.—The same subject.
  - 116.—When Surrender may be made.
- 5085. Allowance and debts.
- 5086. Examination of Bankrupt.
  - NOTE 117.—The same subject.
- 5087. Witnesses Compelled to Attend.
  - NOTE 118.—Mode of Procuring Testimony; Privilege of Witness.
- 5087a. Bankrupt or Party Competent Witness.
- 5088. Examination of Bankrupt's Wife.
- 5089. Examination of Imprisoned or Disabled Debtor.
- 5090. No Abatement upon Death of Debtor.
- 5091. Distribution of Bankrupt's Estate; Bail, Surety, Guarantor.
  - NOTE 119.—Preferred Creditors.
- 5092. Second Meeting of Creditors; Assignee to Report; Creditors to decide as to Dividend; Assignee to decide, when.
  - NOTE 120.—When Meeting should not be called.
- 5093. Third meeting of Creditors; Fi-

SECTION
  nal Dividend; Further Dividends.
  - NOTE 121.—Who may participate.
- 5094. Notice of Meetings and Dividends.
- 5095. Creditor may act by Attorney.
  - NOTE 122. Acknowledgment of Power of Attorney.
- 5096. Settlement of Assignee's Account; his Examination and Discharge.
- 5097. Dividends not to be Disturbed.
- 5098. Omission of Assignee to call Meetings.
- 5099. Disbursements and Compensation of Assignee.
  - NOTE 123. Fees and Allowances of Assignee.
  - 124. Allowances for Rent.
  - 125. Discretionary Allowances.
  - 126. State Taxation.
- 5100. Commissions Allowed Assignee; need not Proceed without Funds.
- 5101. Dividends; Priorities; Fees, Public Debts, Wages, etc.
  - NOTE 127. Priorities; Attorney's Fees; Services of Expert; Taxes; Costs of Attachment; Sheriff's Fees.
  - 128. Debts due the United States; Subrogation.
- 5102. Notice of Dividend to each Creditor.
- 5103. Superseding Proceedings by Arrangement; Trustees; Court to Approve; Consent of Creditors to be Filed; Conveyances to Trustees — their Title; Effect of these Proceedings; Duties of Trustees, their Rights and Powers; Examination of Bankrupt, Witnesses, etc.; Books and Papers; Discharge of Bankrupt; if Resolution is not Approved, what.
  - NOTE 129. Superseding Provisions by Arrangement.
- 5103a. Composition with Creditors; Number and Value of Creditors Consenting; What Creditors Reckoned; who may not vote; Debtor to be present or present Statement; Resolution to be Ap-

§§ 5032–5034.] Notice to Creditors—Assignee. [Note 64.

SECTION
proved and Recorded; Terms of Composition may be afterwards Varied; Binding upon what Creditors; Provision in Case of Outstanding Commercial Paper; Correction of Mistakes; Payments to be made pro *rata*, etc.; Enforcement of Provisions of Compositions; Court may set aside Composition, etc.

NOTE 130.—Constitutionality.
131.—Resolution must pass.
132.—Must be confirmed.
133.—Oath not required of Creditors.
134.—What Creditors Reckoned and what not. (1) Creditors whose Debts do not exceed $50. (2) Creditors who purchase claims against Bankrupt. (3) Secured Creditors.
135.—Unliquidated Claims.
136.—Terms of the Resolution.
137.—Debtor should be Present; Objection; Mistake or Omission in Statement of Assets.
NOTE 138.—Recording the Resolution.
139.—Proceedings binding on whom.
140.—Attachments not Dissolved.
141.—Practice under Compositions.
142.—Compositions Conclusive upon State Courts.
143.—Adjudication and Discharge not Necessary.
144.—Composition does not release Surety or Co-obligor.
145.—Effect on Secured Creditors.
146.—Composition procured by Fraud, invalid.
147.—Provision applies to Corporations.
148.—In Case of Partnerships.

ORIGINAL ACT OF 1867, § 11; R. S. § 5032.—The notice to creditors under warrant shall state: 1, that a warrant in bankruptcy has been issued against the estate of the debtor; 2, that the payment of any debts and the delivery of any property belonging to such debtor to him or for his use, and the transfer of any property by him, are forbidden by law; 3, that a meeting of the creditors of the debtor, giving the names, residences, and amounts, so far as known, to prove their debts and choose one or more assignees of his estate, will be held at a court of bankruptcy, to be holden at a time and place designated in the warrant, not less than ten nor more than ninety days after the issuing of the same.

NOTICE TO CREDITORS: Shall state what.

IBID. § 12; R. S. § 5033.—At the meeting held in pursuance of the notice, one of the registers of the court shall preside, and the messenger shall make return of the warrant and of his doings thereon; and if it appears that the notice to the creditors has not been given as required in the warrant, the meeting shall forthwith be adjourned, and a new notice given as required.

First meeting of creditors: Marshal's return.

64. *Construed.*—*Re* Hill, 1 Ben. 321; *Re* Pulver, 1 Ben. 381.

IBID. § 13; R. S. § 5034.—The creditors shall, at the first meeting held after due notice from the messenger in presence of a register designated by the court, choose one or more assignees of the estate of the debtor; the choice to be made

ASSIGNEE: How chosen.

§§ 5034–5037.] Election of Assignee—Bond—Contempt. [Note 65.

by the greater part in value and in number of creditors who have proved their debts. If no choice is made by the creditors at the meeting, the judge, or if there be no opposing interest, the register, shall appoint one or more assignees. If an assignee, so chosen or appointed, fails within five days to express in writing his acceptance of the trust, the judge or register may fill the vacancy. All elections or appointments of assignees shall be subject to the approval of the judge; and when in his judgment it is for any cause needful or expedient, he may appoint additional assignees, or order a new election.

65. *Election of Assignee — Eligibility — Qualification* — The "greater part," etc., means the majority in number and value of the creditors who have proved their debts. *Re* Scheiffer, 2 N. B. R. 591. Where co-partners are adjudged bankrupt, only partnership creditors can participate in the election of assignee. *Re* Scheiffer, 2 N. B. R. 591; *Re* Phelps, 1 N. B. R. 525. Preferred creditor may surrender preference and vote. *Re* Saunders, 13 N. B. R. 164. A near relative of the bankrupt is not eligible. *Re* Zinn, 4 N. B. R. 376; s. C., 4 N. B. R. 436; *Re* Powell, 2 N. B. R. 45. An attorney for the bankrupt may be assignee. *Re* Clairmont, 1 N. B. R. 276. An attorney for a creditor may also. *Re* Barrett, 2 N. B. R. 533. A register can only appoint in case there is no choice and no opposing interest. *Re* Scheiffer, *supra*. Where proceedings are pending in different districts against the same debtor, an assignee should be elected in each district, it seems. *Re* Boston, Hartford & Erie R. R., 5 N. B. R. 233. Assignee must accept trust in writing. *Re* Major, 14 N. B. R. 71.

IBID. § 18; R. S. § 5035.—No person who has received any preference contrary to the provisions of this title shall vote for or be eligible as assignee; but no title to property, real or personal, sold, transferred, or conveyed by an assignee, shall be affected or impaired by reason of his ineligibility.[1] *Who can not vote for or be chosen assignee.*

IBID. § 13; R. S. § 5036.—The district judge at any time may, and upon the request in writing of any creditor who has proved his claim shall, require the assignee to give good and sufficient bond to the United States, with a condition for the faithful performance and discharge of his duties; the bond shall be approved by the judge or register by his indorsement thereon, shall be filed with the record of the case, and enure to the benefit of all creditors proving their claims, and may be prosecuted in the name and for the benefit of any injured party. If the assignee fails to give the bond within such time as the judge or register orders, not exceeding ten days after notice to him of such order, the judge shall remove him and appoint another in his place.[2] *Bond of assignee: Failing to give, removed.*

IBID. § 18; R. S. § 5037.—Any assignee who refuses or unreasonably neglects to execute an instrument when lawfully required by the court, or disobeys a lawful order or decree of the court in the premises, may be punished as for a contempt of court. *Assignee liable for contempt.*

(1) See note to preceding section.
(2) Re Fernberg, 2 N. B. R. 353.

§§ 5038-5044.] Resignation—Vacancies—Conveyance—Assignment. [Note 66.

Resignation of the assignee.
IBID. § 18; R. S. § 5038.—An assignee may, with the consent of the judge, resign his trust and be discharged therefrom.

Removal of assignee.
IBID.; R. S. § 5039.—The court, after due notice and hearing, may remove an assignee for any cause which, in its judgment, renders such removal necessary or expedient. At a meeting called for the purpose by order of the court, in its discretion, or called upon the application of a majority of the creditors in number and value, the creditors may, with consent of the court, remove any assignee by such a vote as is provided for the choice of assignee.

66. *Removal of Assignee.*—This provision places matters of this sort in the discretion of the court. The removal must be "n.cessary or expedient." *Re* Blodgett, 5 N. B. R. 472. The court, and not the register, is the proper party to entertain motion to remove an assignee. *Re* Stokes, 1 N. B. R. 489. See *Re* Price, 4 N. B. R. 406. It seems that a register may have a rule issued on the assignee to show cause why he should not be removed. *Re* Price, *supra.*

Effect of resignation or removal.
IBID.; R. S. § 5040.—The resignation or removal of an assignee shall in no way release him from performing all things requisite on his part for the proper closing up of his trust and the transmission thereof to his successors, nor shall it affect the liability of the principal or surety on the bond given by the assignee.

Vacancies, how filled.
IBID.; R. S. § 5041.—Vacancies caused by death or otherwise in the office of assignee may be filled by appointment of the court, or at its discretion by an election by the creditors, in the same manner as in the original choice of an assignee, at a regular meeting, or at a meeting called for the purpose, with such notice thereof in writing to all known creditors, and by such person as the court shall direct.

Estate vested in remaining assignee.
IBID.; R. S. § 5042.—When, by death or otherwise, the number of assignees is reduced, the estate of the debtor not lawfully disposed of shall vest in the remaining assignee or assignees, and in the persons selected to fill vacancies, if any, with the same powers and duties relative thereto as if they were originally chosen.

Conveyance to new assignee: Court to make orders.
IBID.; R. S. § 5043.—Any former assignee, his executors or administrators, upon request, and at the expense of the estate, shall make and execute to the new assignee all deeds, conveyances and assurances, and do all other lawful acts requisite to enable him to recover and receive all the estate. And the court may make all orders which it may deem expedient to secure the proper fulfillment of the duties of any former assignee, and the rights and interests of all persons interested in the estate.

Assignment: Relates back: Vests estate: Dissolves attachments.
IBID. § 14; R. S. § 5044.—As soon as an assignee is appointed and qualified, the judge, or, where there is no opposing interest, the register shall, by an instrument under his hand, assign and convey to the assignee all the estate, real and personal, of the bankrupt, with all his deeds,

§ 5044.]   Assignment—Relates back—Effect on Attachments.   [Notes 67-69.

books and papers relating thereto, and such assignment shall relate back to the commencement of the proceedings in bankruptcy, and by operation of law shall vest the title to all such property and estate, both real and personal, in the assignee, although the same is then attached on mesne process as the property of the debtor, and shall dissolve any such attachment made within four months next preceding the commencement of the bankruptcy proceedings.

67. *Assignment not Acknowledged—Relates Back.*—An assignment by a register in bankruptcy to the assignee, although not acknowledged and recorded, is good as against all persons having notice of bankruptcy. Brady v. Otis, 14 N. B. R. 345. The title of the assignee relates back to the commencement of proceedings in bankruptcy. Re Vogel, 7 Blatch. 18; Re Hufnagel, 12 N. B. R. 554. Assignee must pay rent from that day. Re Hufnagel, *supra*.

68. *What Assignee Takes—Effect of Equities, Judgments, etc.*—The general doctrine is thus stated by Mr. Justice Clifford: Assignees in bankruptcy, except in cases of fraud, take only such rights and interests in the property of the bankrupt as he himself had and could have himself claimed and asserted at the time of his bankruptcy, and they are affected with all the equities which would affect the bankrupt himself, if he were asserting those rights and interests. Barnard v. Norwich & Worcester R. R., 14 N. B. R. 469; Hayes v. Dickinson, 15 N. B. R. 350. An assignee in possession of mortgaged property is entitled to the accruing rents for the benefit of the general estate, up to the time the mortgagee makes claim for them. Re Bennett, 12 N. B. R. 257. A devise of property to a trustee to pay the income thereof to a third person free from liability for his debts, is not such an interest as will pass to the latter's assignee. Nichols v. Eaton, 13 N. B. R. 421; s. c., 91 U. S. 716. The policy of the bankrupt law is to preserve judgments existing against bankrupts, according to the right of the creditors when the bankruptcy intervened, unless the judgment is offensive to some express provision of the law, or successfully impeached for fraud. Trimble v. Williamson, 14 N. B. R. 53; s. c., 49 Ala. 525; Re Gold Mining Co. 15 N. B. R. 545. Creditors holding an order for part of a general or particular fund obtained from a bankrupt before bankruptcy, hold an equitable assignment of that fund *pro tanto* though the drawee has refused payment. The creditors' rights must, however, be passed upon by the court in bankruptcy; they will be enjoined from pursuing the drawee for the fund in the state court. Walker v. Siegel, 12 N. B. R. 394; s. c., 2 Cent L. J. 508. Where a firm parts with its property through fraud of a party, the property does not lose its identity, and, if recovered back, or its proceeds, from the party who obtained the property after the party's known insolvency, they would not be liable to his assignee. Montgomery v. Bucyrus Machine Works, 14 N. B. R. 193; 92 U. S. 257. The assignee represents the creditors as well as the bankrupt, and is bound to protect their interests. Re Collins, 12 N. B. R. 379. A bankrupt is not entitled to retain money to pay the probable costs of obtaining a discharge. Re Thompson, 13 N. B. R. 300. The assignee acquires no title to *exempted property*, and when he sets apart to the bankrupt the exemptions, the liens upon it which existed before bankruptcy still adhere to it. Bush v. Lester, 15 N. B. R. 36; s. c., 55 Ga. 579. And a bankrupt is entitled to retain such sum as the assignee may consider necessary for the temporary support of himself and family, not exceeding, with his furniture and other articles, the sum of five hundred dollars. Re Thompson, 13 N. B. R. 300.

69. *Effect of Assignment upon Attachments.*—All attachments sued out within four months prior to the commencement of proceedings in bankruptcy are dissolved, *ipso facto*, by the bankruptcy. King v. Loudon, 14 N. B. R. 383: s. c., 53 Ga. 64; Bracken v. Johnston, 15 N. B. R. 106; Re Badenheim, 15 N. B. R. 370; Hatch v. Seely, 13 N. B. R. 380, and cases cited; Re Jack, 13 N. B. R. 296; Henkelman v. Smith, 12 N. B. R. 121; Re Ellis, 1 N. B. R. 555. *Contra*, Sims v. Jacobson, 51 Ala. 186. The bank-

§ 5045.]   Effect of Assignment upon Attachments—Exemptions.   [Note 69.

ruptcy proceedings and assignment might be made known to the state court. Ibid. But if judgment is obtained in the attachment proceedings, and the creditor realizes his money prior to the filing of the bankruptcy petition, he may retain it, even though the attachment was sued out within four months prior thereto. Hiukelman v. Smith, 12 N. B. R. 121. Otherwise, if after petition is filed. Dickerson v. Spaulding, 15 N. B. R. 312. But if judgment is entered therein after proceedings in bankruptcy are commenced, it is void. King v. Loudon, 14 N. B. R. 383; s. c., 53 Ga. 64; Re Ellis, 1 N. B. R. 555. An attachment issued more than four months prior to the commencement of proceedings in bankruptcy is not dissolved, and may be enforced by any proceedings not involving a judgment *in personam* against the bankrupt. Hatch v. Seely, 13 N. B. R. 380; Batchelder v. Putnam, 13 N. B. R. 404; s. c., 54 N. H. 84; Bowman v. Harding, 4 N. B. R. 20; s. c., 56 Me. 559; Valliant v. Childress, 11 N. B. R. 317; s. c., 21 Wall. 642; Ray v. Wight, 14 N. B. R. 563; s. c., 119 Mass. 426; Mason v. Warthen, 14 N. B. R. 346. In case of a corporation defendant, a judgment for the amount claimed may be had. Munson v. Boston, Hartford & Erie R. R., 14 N. B. R. 173; s. c., 120 Mass. 80. Bankruptcy proceedings against one partner will not dissolve an attachment sued out against the firm, although issued within four months prior. Mason v. Warthen, 14 N. B. R. 346. An attachment upon exempt property is not dissolved, though sued out less than three months before bankruptcy, and may be enforced in the state court. Robinson v. Wilson, 14 N. B. R. 565. Contra, 8. C., 15 Kas. 595; Re Ellis, 1 N. B. R. 555; Re Hambright, 2 N. B. R. 498; Re Stevens, 5 N. B. R. 298. The provisions of the bankrupt law for the dissolution of attachments apply to attachments sued out in the state courts. Bank of Columbia v. Overstreet, 13 N. B. R. 154; s. c., 10 Bush, 148. The obligation of a bond for the production of the property, seized in an attachment proceeding, toward satisfaction of any execution to be issued or any judgment to be recovered in the action, is superseded by proceedings in bankruptcy, begun within four months after the institution of the attachment proceedings, and the surety on the bond is released. Kaiser v. Richardson, 14 N. B. R. 391. If a bankrupt, after the commencement of proceedings in bankruptcy, gives a bond to dissolve an attachment issued more than four months before that time, and subsequently pleads a discharge, no special judgment can be entered to be enforced by action upon the bond. Hamilton v. Bryant, 14 N. B. R. 479; Carpenter v. Turrell, 100 Mass. 450. See Holyoke v. Adams, 13 N. B. R. 413. The state laws govern the rights of an assignee in bankruptcy in the estate of the bankrupt held by attachment under its laws, and where the bankrupt's property is attached more than four months prior to proceedings in bankruptcy being begun, the assignee is vested with title, and may dissolve the attachment by giving bond. Braley v. Boomer, 12 N. B. R. 303; s. c., 116 Mass. 527.

EXEMPTIONS: What property exempt in hands of bankrupt: Exemption, how to operate.

IBID. § 14. AS AMENDED;[1] R. S. § 5045.—There shall be excepted from the operation of the conveyance the necessary household and kitchen furniture, and such other articles and necessaries of the bankrupt as the assignee shall designate and set apart, having reference in the amount to the family, condition and circumstances of the bankrupt, but altogether not to exceed in value, in any case, the sum of five hundred dollars; also the wearing apparel of a bankrupt, and that of his wife and children, and the uniform, arms and equipments of any person who is or has been a soldier in the militia, or in the service of the United States; and such other property as now is, or hereafter shall be, exempted from attachment, or seizure, or levy on execution by the laws of

(1) The original section was so amended by the act of June 8, 1872, and Act of March 3, 1873.

the United States, and such other property not included in the foregoing exceptions as is exempted from levy and sale upon execution or other process or order of any court by the laws of the state in which the bankrupt has his domicile at the time of the commencement of the proceedings in bankruptcy, to an amount allowed by the constitution and laws of each state, as existing in the year eighteen hundred and seventy-one; and such exemptions shall be valid against debts contracted before the adoption and passage of such state constitution and laws, as well as those contracted after the same, and against liens by judgment or decree of any state court, any decision of any such court rendered since the adoption and passage of such constitution and laws to the contrary notwithstanding. These exceptions shall operate as a limitation upon the conveyance of the property of the bankrupt to his assignee; and in no case shall the property hereby excepted pass to the assignee, or the title of the bankrupt thereto be impaired or affected by any of the provisions of this title; and the determination of the assignee in the matter shall, on exception taken, be subject to the final decision of the said court.

70. *What is Exempt.*—Real estate can not be set apart as exempt under the head of "articles or necessaries." Re Hunt, 5 N. B. R. 493; Re Thornton, 2 N. B. R. 189; Nor money. Re Welch, 5 N. B. R. 348. But a life insurance interest may. Re Bennett, 2 N. B. R. 181.

71. *No Title passes to Assignee.*—The title to exemptions is unaffected by the bankrupt act. Re Hunt, 5 N. B. R. 493; Re Hester, 5 N. B. R. 285; Bush v. Lester, 15 N. B. R. 36. It is the duty of the bankruptcy court to see that the exempted property is secured to the bankrupt. Re Stevens, 5 N. B. R. 298; Re Griffin, 2 N. B. R. 254. But see Re Hunt, 5 N. B. R. 493.

72. *Setting apart Exempt Property—Remedy of Debtor.*—The assignee must select the property to be exempt under the bankrupt law, and the bankrupt should select the property exempt under the state law. Re Cobb, 1 N. B. R. 414. Where creditor's claim that the exemptions are unauthorized, they must except under general order 19, when reference is had to exemptions of personalty; but as to real estate an unauthorized exemption is void, no title passes from the assignee; the creditors need not except, but can hold the assignee accountable. Re Gainey, 2 N. B. R. 525.

73. *Exemption extends to what Property—How affected by Judgment Liens, Mortgages, etc.*—The exemption privilege applies even though the property is held by the lien of execution before proceedings in bankruptcy were commenced. Re Owens, 12 N. B. R. 518; Re Martin, 13 N. B. R. 397. The right of exemption must exist at the date of the commencement of the bankruptcy proceedings. Re Duerson, 13 N. B. R. 183. An allotment of exemption does not impair the lien of a judgment. Haworth v. Travis, 13 N. B. R. 145; s. c., 67 Ills. 301. Where the homestead claimed is worth more than the sum allowed, a judgment is a lien on the excess. Haworth v. Travis, 13 N. B. R. 45; s. c., 67 Ill. 301. A bankrupt is entitled to his homestead, though his wife owns a house. Re Tonne, 13 N. B. R. 170. A mortgagee may enforce his mortgage in a state court if he does not prove his debt, although the assignee set the property apart to the mortgagor. Hatcher v. Jones, 14 N. B. R. 387; Cumming v. Clegg, 14 N. B. R. 49; s. c. 52 Geo. 605.

74. *Homestead purchased in Fraud of Creditors.*—A purchase of a homestead by an insolvent trader upon the eve of bankruptcy with knowledge of his insolvent condition and for the purpose of placing the property beyond the reach of process, is a legal fraud and the court would declare it void as to creditors. Re Boothroyd, 14 N. B. R. 230.

§§ 5046–5047.]   Exemptions—Assignment—Powers of Assignee.   [Notes 75–79.

75. *Physical Character of Homestead.*—Where a bankrupt built a block for business purposes upon ground where his dwelling stood, and moved his family into it, upon becoming insolvent he can not claim it as exempt under the laws of Wisconsin. Re Lammer, 14 N. B. R. 460. See also Re Wright, 8 N. B. R. 430; s. c., 3 Biss. 359. A debtor can not retain portions of property not auxiliary to his homestead. Greeley v. Scott, 12 N. B. R. 248.

76. *Partners* not entitled to exemption out of partnership estate. Re Tonne, 13 N. B. R. 170; Re Boothroyd, 14 N. B. R. 230; Re Stewart, 13 N. B. R. 295; Re Handlin, 12 N. B. R. 49; s. c. 2 Cent. L. J. 264.

77. *Statute Laws Existing in 1871 Govern.*—The statutes of the states regarding exemptions in force at the close of the year 1871 govern the exemptions allowed a bankrupt. Re Anthony Baer, 14 N. B. R. 97.

78. *Constitutionality.*—There is nothing in the constitution which forbids Congress to pass laws impairing the obligation of contracts. Congress may by the enactment of a uniform bankrupt law, discharge debtors entirely from their obligations. Re Owens, 12 N. B. R. 518. Congress, in adopting the exemption laws of a state, can not dispense with any of the limitations imposed by that law. Re Duerson, 13 N. B. R. 183. The amendatory act of March 3, 1873, has been held constitutional in some circuits, and unconstitutional in others. The latest authority on its constitutionality is the decision in Re Smith, 14 N. B. R. 295, in the fifth circuit. Held *unconstitutional* in Re Deckert, 10 N. B. R. 2; Re Dillard, 9 N. B. R. 8; Re Duers on, 13 N. B. R. 183. Held *constitutional* in Re Jordan, 8 N. B. R. 180; Re Kean, 8 N. B. R. 367; Re Smith, 8 N. B. R. 401; Re Jordan, 10 N. B. R. 427. But the act did not make unconstitutional provisions in state laws a part of the system of bankruptcy. Bush v. Lester, 15 N. B. R. 36; s. c. 55 Geo. 579. The original act of 1867, § 14, was held constitutional. Re Beckerford, 1 Dill. 45.

IBID. § 14; R. S. § 5046.—All property conveyed by the bankrupt in fraud of his creditors; all rights in equity, choses in action, patent-rights, and copy-rights; all debts due him, or any person for his use, and all liens and securities therefor; and all his rights of action for property or estate, real or personal, and for any cause of action which he had against any person arising from contract or from the unlawful taking or detention, or injury to the property of the bankrupt; and all his rights of redeeming such property or estate; together with the like right, title, power, and authority to sell, manage, dispose of, sue for, and recover or defend the same, as the bankrupt might have had if no assignment had been made, shall, in virtue of the adjudication of bankruptcy and the appointment of his assignee, but subject to the exceptions stated in the preceding section, be at once vested is such assignee.

What property vests in the assignee.

79. *Property Conveyed in Fraud of Creditors, etc.*—This section vests in the assignee "all the property conveyed by the bankrupt in fraud of his creditors," not only property conveyed in fraud of the bankrupt act, but such also as has been conveyed in fraud of creditors generally. Pratt v. Curtis, 6 N. B. R. 139. An assignee in bankruptcy can not recover in an action of trover the value of property seized under an execution and levy of judgment-creditor and sold before proceedings in bankruptcy were begun. Gates v. American, 14 N. B. R. 141.

IBID. §§ 14, 16; R. S. § 5047.—The assignee shall have the like remedy to recover all the estate, debts and effects in his own name, as the debtor might have had if the decree in bankruptcy had not been rendered and no assignment had been made. If at the time of the commencement of

Assignee may recover debts: Be admitted to pending suit: Defend actions.

§§ 5047–5049.]   Powers of Assignee—Death or Removal—Evidence.   [Note 8ᵒ.

the proceedings in bankruptcy an action is pending in the name of the debtor for the recovery of a debt or other thing which might or ought to pass to the assignee by the assignment, the assignee shall, if he requires it, be admitted to prosecute the action in his own name, in like manner and with like effect as if it had been originally commenced by him. And if any suit at law or in equity, in which the bankrupt is a party in his own name, is pending at the time of the adjudication of bankruptcy, the assignee may defend the same in the same manner and with the like effect as it might have been defended by the bankrupt.

80. *Decisions under this Section—Rights of Assignee, Bankrupt, etc.*—A suit to recover damages for the alleged malicious abuse of legal process is an action for personal injury, and does not pass to the bankrupt's assignee. Noonan v. Orton, 12 N. B. R. 405; s. c., 34 Wis. 259. If the assigee does not intervene in such actions as do not pass to him, they may proceed in the name of the bankrupt. Noonan v. Orton, 12 N. B. R. 405; s. c., 34 Wis. 259. Upon the filing of a petition in bankruptcy suits pending in the state courts, in which the bankrupt is a party, do not abate, but such courts must determine the questions as they arise, subject to the final judgment of the proper appellate tribunal. Hewett v. Norton, 13 N. B. R. 276; Re Clark, 3 N. B. R. 491; Samson v. Burton, 4 N. B. R. 1. As soon as the petition in bankruptcy is filed, the property of the insolvent is *eo instanti* brought into the custody of the bankrupt court, and no person acting under a process from any other court can, without the permission of the bankrupt court, interfere with it. Hewett v. Norton, 13 N. B. R. 276. An assignee can appear in a suit in which the bankrupt was a party, and which was settled and dismissed since bankruptcy proceedings were begun, all parties having notice of that fact, and have the entry stricken out. Home Ins. Co. v. Hollis, 14 N. B. R. 337. An assignee in bankruptcy can have no relief in a suit founded upon the idea that proceedings to foreclose a mortgage and a sale thereunder in a state court are invalid, because the decree of foreclosure and sale was made after bankruptcy proceedings were begun, or because he was not made a party to the proceedings. The decree is also a bar to the assignee's right to raise the question of usury in the mortgage. Outter v. Dingee, 14 N. B. R. 294. Where the laws of a state do not permit an assignee of a *chose in action* to sue in his own name, the purchaser of a bankrupt's *choses in action* from the assignee in bankruptcy can not bring suit in his own name. Leach v. Green, 12 N. B. R. 376; s. c., 116 Mass. 534. A debtor assigned a chose in action and afterwards was adjudged a bankrupt. No assignee was appointed, and the proceedings were discontinued. In an action by the assignee of the chose in action, it was held that he could maintain it; that the bankruptcy alone had not divested the debtor of his property. Kline v. Bauendahl, 12 N. B. R. 575; s. c., 6 N. Y. Sup. 546. A bankrupt may appeal from a judgment obtained against him while in bankruptcy. Sanford v. Sanford, 12 N. B. R. 565; s. c., 58 N. Y. 67. See Herndon v. Howard, 4 N. B. R. 212; s. c., 9 Wall. 664.

IBID. § 16; R. S. § 5048.—No suit pending in the name of the assignee shall be abated by his death or removal; but upon the motion of the surviving or remaining or new assignee, as the case may be, he shall be admitted to prosecute the suit in like manner and with like effect as if it had been originally commenced by him.

Suits not to abate by death or removal.

IBID. § 14; R. S. § 5049.—A copy duly certified by the clerk of the court, under the seal thereof, of the assignment, shall be conclusive evidence of the title of the assignee to take, hold, sue for, and recover the property of the bankrupt.

Copy of assignment conclusive evidence of title.

§§ 5050-5054.] Assignee—What passes to—Notice of Appointment. [Notes 81-84.

81. *Construed—Exemplification of Part of Record.*—Herndon v. Howard, 4 N. B. R. 212; s. c. 9 Wall. 664. A certified copy of that part of the record containing the assignment is conclusive evidence of the assignee's right to sue. Michener v. Payson, 13 N. B. R. 49. The proceedings in bankruptcy are not deemed to constitute an integral record, but a copy of each proceeding may be authenticated as a separate record, and is presumptive evidence of the facts stated in it. Ibid.

Bankrupt's books of account.

IBID.; R. S. § 5050.—No person shall be entitled, as against the assignee, to withhold from him possession of any books of account of the bankrupt, or claim any lien thereon.

Debtor must execute instruments.

IBID.; R. S. § 5051.—The debtor shall, at the request of the assignee and at the expense of the estate, make and execute any instruments, deeds, and writings which may be proper to enable the assignee to possess himself fully of all the assets of the bankrupt.

Certain mortgages not invalidated.

IBID.; R. S. § 5052.—No mortgage of any vessel or of any other goods or chattels, made as security for any debt, in good faith and for a present consideration and otherwise valid, and duly recorded pursuant to any statute of the United States or of any state, shall be invalidated or affected by an assignment in bankruptcy.

82. *Construed.*—Re Eldridge, 4 N. B. R. 498; Potter v. Coggeshall, 4 N. B. R. 73; Re Griffith, 3 N. B. R. 731; Re Soldier's Business Co., 3 Ben. 204. If not recorded, valid, if valid by the laws of the state where made. Re Dow, 6 N. B. R. 10.

Trust property.

IBID.; R. S. § 5053.—No property held by the bankrupt in trust shall pass by the assignment.

83. *Identity of Trust Property, etc.*—The trust property must be *in specie*, otherwise the *cestuis que trust* come in as general creditors only. Coan Carriage Co., 12 N. B. R. 203; Re Janeway, 4 N. B. R. 100; White v. Jones, 6 N. B. R. 175. Where bankrupts held a fund in a fiduciary capacity, and the identity of the fund can be traced, the court will order it to be paid to the claimant. Voight v. Lewis, 14 N. B. R. 543; Re Hapgood, 14 N. B. R. 495. Although the funds of the trust and the trustee had been mingled, the court will ascertain by equitable principles how much belongs to the trust estate. Ibid. A consignor may reserve a special property in goods consigned for bills of exchange drawn against them; but not in the choses in action into which the goods have been converted. These are part of the general assets. Re Chamberlaines, 12 N. B. R. 230.

Notice of appointment of assignee and recording of assignment.

IBID.; R. S. § 5054.—The assignee shall immediately give notice of his appointment by publication at least once a week for three successive weeks in such newspapers as shall for that purpose be designated by the court, due regard being had to their general circulation in the district or in that portion of the district in which the bankrupt and his creditors shall reside, and shall, within six months, cause the assignment to him to be recorded in every registry of deeds or other office within the United States, where a conveyance of any lands owned by the bankrupt ought by law to be recorded.

84. *Construed.*—The assignment passes the title to the assignee; the recording is not essential to the validity of the transfer. Davis v. Anderson, 6 N. B. R. 145. "Once a week" means once every seven days. Re Bellamy, 1 Ben. 390.

§§ 5055-5060.] Assignee—Suits by—Limitation—Keep Moneys, how. [Notes 85-86.

IBID. § 15; R. S. § 5055.—The assignee shall demand and receive, from all persons holding the same, all the estate assigned or intended to be assigned.   *Assignee to demand all assigned estate.*

IBID. § 14; R. S. § 5056.—No person shall be entitled to maintain an action against an assignee in bankruptcy for anything done by him as such assignee, without previously giving him twenty days' notice of such action, specifying the cause thereof, to the end that such assignee may have an opportunity of tendering amends, should he see fit to do so.   *Notice prior to suit against assignee.*

85. *Property of Stranger.*—This does not apply to cases where the assignee has seized property as belonging to the bankrupt, but which in fact belongs to a stranger. Such person may sue in replevin in the state court without giving such notice. Leighton v. Harwood, 12 N. B. R. 360; s. c., 111 Mass. 67.

IBID. § 2; R. S. § 5057.—No suit, either at law or in equity, shall be maintainable in any court between an assignee in bankruptcy and a person claiming an adverse interest, touching any property or rights of property transferable to or vested in such assignee, unless brought within two years from the time when the cause of action accrued for or against such assignee. And this provision shall not in any case revive a right of action barred at the time when an assignee is appointed.   *Suits to be brought within two years; Rights barred not revived hereby.*

86. *Construction of this Section.*—A suit by an assignee in bankruptcy to collect debts or claims due the estate must be brought within two years from the time when the cause of action accrued to the assignee. Walker v. Towner, 5 Cent. L. J. 206; Payson v. Coffin, Ib. 220. This limitation applies as well to those causes of action which existed before bankruptcy as to those which arise after. Norton v. De La Villebeuve, 13 N. B. R. 304. This limitation does not bar ordinary money demands. Sedgwick v. Casey, 4 N. B. R. 496; Re Krogman, 5 N. B. R. 116. It applies only to actions respecting property held adversely to the bankrupt and his assignee. Davis v. Anderson, 6 N. B. R. 145; Bailey v. Wier, 12 N. B. R. 24; s. c., 21 Wall. 342. And only to controversies of which the circuit court of the district has concurrent jurisdiction under § 4979. Sedgwick v. Casey, 4 N. B. R. 496. It does not apply to a bill of review to set aside a decree in equity. Wilt v. Stickney, 15 N. B. R. 23. "In any court whatsoever,"—those words were in the original act and have been omitted by the revisors. The limitation was then held to apply in a suit in the state court. Peiper v. Harmer, 5 N. B. R. 252. A right of action is barred after two years, although the assignee did not discover the right within that time. Norton v. De La Villebeuve, 13 N. B. R. 304.

R. S. § 5058.—[Superseded by Act of June 22, 1874; § 4, *post*, § 5065a.]

IBID. § 17; R. S. § 5059.—The assignee shall, as soon as may be after receiving any money belonging to the estate, deposit the same in some bank in his name as assignee, or otherwise keep it distinct from all other money in his possession; and shall, as far as practicable, keep all goods and effects belonging to the estate separate from all other goods in his possession, or designated by appropriate marks, so that they may be easily and clearly distinguished, and may not be liable to be taken as his property or for the payment of his debts.   *Assignee to deposit money and keep effects separate.*

IBID.; R. S. § 5060.—When it appears that the distribution of the es-

§§ 5060–5062.]   May Submit to Arbitration—Make Sales.   [Notes 87–88.

Temporary investment of money. tate may be delayed by litigation or other cause, the court may direct the temporary investment of the money belonging to such estate in securities to be approved by the judge or register, or may authorize it to be deposited in any convenient bank, upon such interest, not exceeding the legal rate, as the bank may contract with the assignee to pay thereon.[1]

IBID.; R. S. § 5061.—The assignee, under the direction of the court, may submit any controversy arising in the settlement of demands against the estate, or of debts due to it, to the determination of arbitrators to be chosen by him and the other party to the controversy, and, under such direction, may compound and settle any such controversy, by agreement with the other party, as he thinks proper and most for the interest of the creditors.

May submit to arbitration.

May settle controversies.

87. *Construed.*— Application must be to court. *Re* Graves, 2 Ben. 100. Court can not empower assignee "to compound all doubtful claims with the consent and approbation of a committee of creditors." *Re* Dibble, 3 Ben. 354.

§ 5061a; AMENDATORY ACT OF 1874, § 1.—That the court may, in its discretion, on sufficient cause shown, and upon notice and hearing, direct the receiver or assignee to take possession of the property, and carry on the business of the debtor, or any part thereof, under the direction of the court, when, in its judgment, the interest of the estate as well as of the creditors will be promoted thereby, but not for a period exceeding nine months from the time the debtor shall have been declared a bankrupt: *Provided,* that such order shall not be made until the court shall be satisfied that it is approved by a majority in value of the creditors.

May carry on business, when.

ORIGINAL ACT OF 1867, § 15; R. S. § 5062.—The assignee shall sell all such unincumbered estate, real and personal, which comes to his hands, on such terms as he thinks most for the interest of the creditors; but upon petition of any person interested, and for cause shown, the court may make such order concerning the time, place, and manner of sale as will, in its opinion, prove to the interest of the creditors.

SALES: Assignee may make, but court may make order.

88. *Assignee's Sales.*—Creditors who apply to set aside a sale and offer to bid at such resale a specified sum, are bound to fulfil their offer. *Re* Troy Woolen Co., 8 Blatch. 465. A claim against the bankrupt before his bankruptcy can not be set off against an indebtedness for goods purchased from the assignee. Moran v. Bogert, 14 N. B. R. 393. The solicitor of an assignee can not bid at an assignee's sale, but an agreement between the solicitor and a party who intends to bid at a sale; that if the property is bought by the latter he will sell it to the former for a fixed price, without any reference to the sum at which it may be bought, does not vitiate the sale. Citizens Bank v. Ober, 13 N. B. R. 328. The assignee must obey the order of court strictly. *Re* Ryan, 6 N. B. R. 235. The court alone is entrusted with the discretion whether to sell or not, also as to how long notice shall be given; the power can not be delegated; such sale should be public, after public notice. *Re* Major, 14 N. B. R. 71.

---

(1) Sedgwick v. Place, 3 Ben. 360.

§§ 5063-5065a.]   Assignee's Sales—Notice of—Supervisory Power over.   [Note 80.

A register can not order a sale; a sale under his order would be void. Ibid. Notice of sale must be given to parties holding adversely. Ibid.

IBID. § 25; R. S. § 5063.—Whenever it appears to the satisfaction of the court that the title to any portion of an estate, real or personal, which has come into possession of the assignee, or which is claimed by him, is in dispute, the court may, upon the petition of the assignee, and after such notice to the claimant, his agent or attorney, as the court shall deem reasonable, order it to be sold, under the direction of the assignee, who shall hold the funds received in place of the estate disposed of; and the proceeds of the sale shall be considered the measure of the value of the property in any suit or controversy, between the parties in any court. But this provision shall not prevent the recovery of the property from the possession of the assignee by any proper action commenced at any time before the court orders the sale. *Sale of disputed property.*

89. *Sale of Disputed Property.*—This section is well considered in Knight v. Cheney, 5 N. B. R. 305. The court has no power to order the sale of property claimed by the assignee which is in dispute and in the possession of the claimant. Knight v. Cheney, 5 N. B. R. 305. *Contra,* Bill v. Beckwith, 2 N. B. R. 241. See also Foster v. Ames, 2 N. B. R. 455; Markson v. Heaney, 1 Dill. 497.

IBID. §.28; R. S. § 5064.—The assignee may sell and assign, under the direction of the court and in such manner as the court shall order, any outstanding claims or other property in his hands, due or belonging to the estate, which can not be collected and received by him without unreasonable or inconvenient delay or expense. *Sale of uncollectible assets.*

IBID. § 25; R. S. § 5065.—When it appears to the satisfaction of the court that the estate of the debtor, or any part thereof, is of a perishable nature, or liable to deteriorate in value, the court may order the same to be sold, in such manner as may be deemed most expedient, under the direction of the messenger or assignee, as the case may be, who shall hold the funds received in place of the estate disposed of. *Sale of perishable property.*

§ 5065a; AMENDATORY ACT OF 1874, § 4.—That unless otherwise ordered by the court, the assignee shall sell the property of the bankrupt, whether real or personal, at public auction, in such parts or parcels and at such times and places as shall be best calculated to produce the greatest amount with the least expense. All notices of public sales under this act by any assignee or officer of the court shall be published once a week for three consecutive weeks, in the newspaper or newspapers, to be designated by the judge, which, in his opinion, shall be best calculated to give general notice of the sale. And the court, on the application of any party in interest, shall have complete supervisory power over such sales, including the power to set aside the same and to order a *Sales to be at auction. Notice of, how published. Supervisory power of court.*

§§ 5065a–5065b.] Accounting and Reports of Assignee—Penalties.

re-sale, so that the property sold shall realize the largest sum. And the court may, in its discretion, order any real estate of the bankrupt, or any part thereof, to be sold for one-fourth cash at the time of sale, and the residue within eighteen months in such instalments as the court may direct, bearing interest at the rate of seven per centum per annum, and secured by proper mortgage or lien upon the property so sold.

Sales on Credit.

§ 5065b; IBID.—And it shall be the duty of every assignee to keep a regular account of all moneys received or expended by him as such assignee, to which account every creditor shall, at reasonable times, have free access. If any assignee shall fail or neglect to well and faithfully discharge his duties in the sale or disposition of property as above contemplated, it shall be the duty of the court to remove such assignee, and he shall forfeit all fees and emoluments to which he might be entitled in connection with such sale. And if any assignee shall, in any manner, in violation of his duty aforesaid, unfairly or wrongfully sell or dispose of, or in any manner fraudulently or corruptly combine, conspire, or agree with any person or persons, with intent to unfairly or wrongfully sell or dispose of the property committed to his charge, he shall, upon proof thereof, be removed, and forfeit all fees or other compensation for any and all services in connection with such bankrupt's estate, and, upon conviction thereof before any court of competent jurisdiction, shall be liable to a fine of not more than ten thousand dollars, or imprisonment in the penitentiary for a term of not exceeding two years, or both fine and imprisonment, at the discretion of the court. And any person so combining, conspiring, or agreeing with such assignee for the purpose aforesaid shall, upon conviction, be liable to a like punishment. That the assignee shall report, under oath, to the court, at least as often as once in three months, the condition of the estate in his charge, and the state of his accounts in detail, and at all other times when the court, on motion or otherwise, shall so order. And on any settlement of the accounts of any assignee, he shall be required to account for all interest, benefit or advantage received, or in any manner agreed to be received, directly or indirectly, from the use, disposal, or proceeds of the bankrupt's estate. And he shall be required, upon such settlement, to make and file in court an affidavit declaring, according to the truth, whether he has or has not, as the case may be, received, or is or is not, as the case may be, to receive, directly or indirectly, any interest, benefit or advantage from the use or deposit of such funds; and such assignee may be examined orally upon the same subject, and if he shall wilfully swear falsely, either in such affidavit or examination, or to his report provided for in this section,

Assignee: To keep account.

Penalties against.

Punishment of co-conspirator.

Reports of.

To account for all interest, benefits, etc.

Affidavit and examination of.

Penalty for false swearing.

§§ 5065b–5067.] Discharge of Liens—Debts and Proof of Claims. [Notes 90–92.

he shall be deemed to be guilty of perjury, and, on conviction thereof, be punished by imprisonment in the penitentiary not less than one and not more than five years.

ORIGINAL ACT OF 1867, § 14; R. S. § 5066.—The assignee shall have authority, under the order and direction of the court, to redeem and discharge any mortgage or conditional contract, or pledge or deposit, or lien upon any property, real or personal, whenever payable, and to tender due performance of the condition thereof, or to sell the same subject to such mortgage, lien, or other incumbrance.[1]

Discharge of liens: Perform conditional contracts.

IBID. § 19; R. S. § 5067.—All debts due and payable from the bankrupt at the time of the commencement of proceedings in bankruptcy, and all debts then existing but not payable until a future day, a rebate of interest being made when no interest is payable by the terms of the contract, may be proved against the estate of the bankrupt. All demands against the bankrupt for or on account of any goods or chattels wrongfully taken, converted, or withheld by him may be proved and allowed as debts to the amount of the value of the property so taken or withheld, with interest. When the bankrupt is liable for unliquidated damages arising out of any contract or promise, or on account of any goods or chattels wrongfully taken, converted, or withheld, the court may cause such damages to be assessed in such mode as it may deem best, and the sum so assessed may be proved against the estate.

DEBTS AND PROOF OF CLAIMS: What debts provable: Demands for conversion of chattels: Unliquidated damages.

90. *Debts due the United States.*—A claim of the United States for the value of goods forfeited for violation of the revenue laws, is a provable debt against a bankrupt's estate. Barnes v. United States, 12 N. B. R. 526.

91. *Statutes of Limitation.*—Courts of bankruptcy, like courts of equity, recognize statutes of limitation, and the Federal courts are bound to pay the same regard to the state statutes of limitation as is paid them by the states. Re Eldridge, 12 N. B. R. 540. The statutes of limitations did not run during the war. Ibid. The petition in bankruptcy is an act which stops the running of the statutes of limitation; it is a new promise, and is the creation of a trust; the bankrupt's goods are in the custody of the law. Ibid. See also Re Eldridge. 12 N. B. R. 540. A debt barred by limitation of the state where the bankrupt resides, can not be proved against his estate in bankruptcy. Re Kingsley, 1 N. B. R. 329; Re Harden, 1 N. B. R. 395; Re Noesen, 12 N. B. R. 422. See Re Sheppard, 1 N. B. R. 439; Re Ray, 1 N. R. R. 203. Contra, Re Cornwall, 6 N. B. R. 305. It is, however, such a provable debt as will be discharged by the certificate, if the bankrupt obtains one. Re Kingsley, *supra.* See also Re Noesen, *supra.*

92. *What are Provable Debts.*—Accrued interest is part of a debt provable. Sloan v. Lewis, 12 N. B. R. 173; s. c., 22 Wall. 150; Re Orne, 1 Ben. 361. A verdict without judgment is not a provable debt in bankruptcy; it does not come within the category of a claim whose payment is postponed to a future day. Black v. McClelland, 12 N. B. R. 481. A judgment after commencement of proceedings in bankruptcy for a personal tort is not a provable debt. Ibid. A proof of debt is not a "suit." Re Eldridge, 12 N. B. R. 540. Where a payment of a claim was oppressively obtained from a debtor, and his assignee in bankruptcy recovered it back, the creditor was

(1) See note 89, *supra.*

§§ 5068–5070.]   Proof of Claims—Contingent Liabilities—Sureties.   [Notes 92–94.

permitted to prove the original demand against the estate. Brookmire v. Bean, 12 N. B. R. 217; s. c., 3 Dill. 136. A judgment obtained after proceedings in bankruptcy are begun is not provable, and a discharge does not affect it. Re Williams, 2 N. B. R. 229; Re Gallison, 5 N. B. R. 353. A secured debt is provable. Re Bloss, 4 N. B. R. 147. Debt contracted for liquors, the sale of which is prohibited, is not provable. Re Paddock, 6 N. B. R. 132. The word "debt," as used in the act, is synonymous with the word claim. Stokes v. Mason, 12 N. B. R. 498; s. c., 10 R. I. 261. Damages for tort are not provable until assessed. Re Bailey, 2 Woods, 222. An attaching creditor can not prove the costs of the attachment as a demand against the debtor's estate, unless it be shown that the attachment proceedings were auxiliary to contemplated bankruptcy, or otherwise beneficial to the estate. Re Hatje, 12 N. B. R. 548. A cause of action for breech of a warranty of title contained in a deed which exists prior to the time of the warrantor's bankruptcy, is a debt provable in bankruptcy, and is barred by the bankrupt's discharge. Williams v. Harkins, 15 N. B. R. 34; s. c., 55 Ga. 172. Where a banking corporation is prohibited by its charter from discounting notes or making loans upon personal security, such notes and such loans are void, and are not provable under the bankrupt act. Re Jaycox, 13 N. B. R. 122. Wager contracts void, and loss can not be proven. Re Green, 15 N. B. R. 198.

Contingent debts and liabilities.

IBID.; R. S. § 5068.—In all cases of contingent debts and contingent liabilities contracted by the bankrupt, and not herein otherwise provided for, the creditor may make claim therefor, and have his claim allowed, with the right to share in the dividends, if the contingency happens before the order for the final dividend; or he may, at any time, apply to the court to have the present value of the debt or liability ascertained and liquidated, which shall then be done in such manner as the court shall order, and he shall be allowed to prove for the amount so ascertained.

93. *Contingent Liabilities.*—A loss on a fire insurance policy is provable in bankruptcy against the bankrupt company, though the loss occurred after adjudication, if proved before the final dividend. Re Am. Plate Glass & Ins. Co., 12 N. B. R. 56. It may be an equitable demand. Sigsby v. Willis, 3 Ben. 371. Liability of surety on guardian's bond before breach is a contingent liability, and surety's discharge discharges such. Reitz v. People, 72 Ills. 435.

Liability of bankrupt as drawer, indorser, etc.

IBID.; R. S. § 5069.—When the bankrupt is bound as drawer, indorser, surety, bail, or guarantor upon any bill, bond, note or any other specialty or contract, or for any debt of another person, but his liability does not become absolute until after the adjudication of bankruptcy, the creditor may prove the same after such liability becomes fixed, and before the final dividend is declared.

94. *Liability as Drawer, Indorser, etc.*—He must be *bound* under the laws relating to commercial paper. Re Crawford, 5 N. B. R. 301; *Ex parte* Balch, 13 N. B. R. 160. The holder of a note can only prove against the estate of an indorser the amount due upon the note at the date of the proof. Re Weeks, 13 N. B. R. 263. If, after such proof, the maker make payments upon the note, the holder is still entitled to his dividends upon the whole amount due upon the note at date of proof; provided, that such dividends added to such payments, do not amount to a sum greater than that due upon the note. Ibid.

Sureties for bankrupt.

IBID.; R. S. § 5070.—Any person liable as bail, surety, guarantor, or otherwise for the bankrupt, who shall have paid the debt, or any part thereof, in discharge of the whole, shall be entitled to prove such debt or to stand in the place of the

§§ 5070–5073.]   Rent—Landlord's Lien—Set-offs.   [Notes 95–97.

creditor if the creditor has proved the same, although such payments shall have been made after the proceedings in bankruptcy were commenced. And any person so liable for the bankrupt, and who has not paid the whole of such debt, but is still liable for the same or any part thereof, may, if the creditor fails or omits to prove such debt, prove the same either in the name of the creditor or otherwise, as may be provided by the general orders, and subject to such regulations and limitations as may be established by such general orders.

95. *A bond to return Property*, if the court requires it, is not a provable debt, unless the decision of the court is rendered before the final dividend. United States v. Rob Roy, 13 N. B. R. 235.

IBID.; R. S. § 5071.—Where the bankrupt is liable to pay rent or other debt falling due at fixed and stated periods, the creditor may prove for a proportionate part thereof up to the time of the bankruptcy, as if the same grew due from day to day, and not at such fixed and stated periods.   *Debts falling due at stated periods.*

96. *Rent—Landlord's Lien.*—The assignee's title to movable property found on demised premises is subject to the rights of all other persons; and where, under the laws of the state, a landlord has a lien for rent, it is subject to it. Longstreth v. Pennock, 12 N. B. R. 95; s. o., 20 Wall. 575. As to lien, see also *Re* Trim, 5 N. B. R. 23; *Re* Wynne, 4 N. B. R. 23. The landlord's lien is not lost by his acquiescence in the sale of the goods subject to the lien. *Re* Browne, 12 N. B. R. 529. Nor does the taking of a note for the rent release the lien. Ibid.

97. *Assignee's Occupation of Leased Premises.*—The landlord of premises occupied by a bankrupt, is entitled to reasonable compensation for the premises, during the occupancy of the same by the officers of the court. *Re* Hamburger, 12 N. B. R. 277; *Re* McGrath, 5 N. B. R. 254; *Re* Breck, 12 N. B. R. 215; *Re* Commercial Bulletin Co., 2 Woods, 220. Rent accruing after adjudication is not a provable debt. Bailey v. Loeb, 2 Woods, 578; Wylie v. Breck, 2 Woods, 673. A lease which can not be assigned without the landlord's consent is terminated by the tenant's bankruptcy. *Re* Breck, 12 N. B. R. 215. *Semble*, that an adjudication cancels a lease. *Re* Hamburger, 12 N. B. R. 277; *Re* Metz, 6 Ben. 571. But this is still an open question. The landlord has no provable claim for rent falling due under the lease, after the surrender of possession by the assignee. *Re* Hufnagel, 12 N. B. R. 554. The subsequent rent is unaffected by a discharge. Ibid.

IBID.; R. S. § 5072.—No debts other than those specified in the five preceding sections shall be proved or allowed against the estate.   *No other debts provable.*

IBID. § 20; R. S. § 5073 AS AMENDED.—In all cases of mutual debts or mutual credits between the parties, the account between them shall be stated, and one debt set off against the other, and the balance only shall be allowed or paid; but no set-off shall be allowed in favor of any debtor to the bankrupt of a claim in its nature not provable against the estate, or of a claim purchased by or transferred to him after the filing of the petition, [or in cases of compulsory bankruptcy, after the act of bankruptcy upon or in respect of which the adjudication shall be made, and with a view of making such set-off.][1]   *Set-offs.*

(1) So amended by Act of June 22, 1874, § 6.

§§ 5074–5075.]   Set-off—Mixed Liabilities—Secured Debts.   [Notes 98–100.

98. *Set-off—Claim of Stockholder—Of Bailee.*—The claim of a stockholder in a bankrupt insurance company for losses sustained by him on policies issued by such company, can not be set off against his indebtedness to the company for unpaid subscriptions to its stock. Such unpaid subscriptions constitute a fund to be applied to the payment of *all* the creditors of the company. Scammon v. Kimball, 13 N. B. R. 445; Sawyer v. Hoag, 9 N. B. R. 145; s. c., 17 Wall. 610; Jenkins v. Armour, 14 N. B. R. 276. A creditor who holds goods or chattels at the time of bankruptcy belonging to the bankrupt with power of sale, or choses in action with power of collection, may sell the goods or collect the claims, and set them off against the debt the bankrupt owes him. *Re* Dow, 14 N. B. R. 307. So also a banker who has for collection drafts of the bankrupt, the proceeds of which come into his hands after bankruptcy, may retain them by virtue of his lien. *Re* Farnsworth, 14 N. B. R. 148.

99. *Claim Purchased or Transferred.*—Choses in action purchased by a debtor of a bankrupt can not be set off against the claim of the assignee in bankruptcy where the assignee of the choses in action has no rights which he could enforce in his own name. Rollins v. Twitchell, 14 N. B. R. 201. The consent of the bankrupt to the assignment of a chose in action against him to his debtor after an act of bankruptcy has been committed, gives the assignee no better right than he had when he purchased. Ibid.; Hitchcock v. Rollo, 4 N. B. R. 690; s. c., 3 Biss. 278; *Contra*, *Re* City Bank, 6 N. B. R. 71. This case was decided, however, before the amendment of 1874.

IBID. § 21; R. S. § 5074.—When the bankrupt, at the time of adjudication, is liable upon any bill of exchange, promissory note, or other obligation in respect to distinct contracts as a member of two or more firms carrying on separate and distinct trades, and having distinct estates to be wound up in bankruptcy, or as a sole trader and also as a member of a firm, the circumstance that such firms are in whole or in part composed of the same individuals, or that the sole contractor is also one of the joint contractors, shall not prevent proof and receipt of dividend in respect of such distinct contracts against the estates respectively liable upon such contracts.

Mixed liabilities.

IBID. § 20; R. S. § 5075.—When a creditor has a mortgage or pledge of real or personal property of the bankrupt, or a lien thereon for securing the payment of a debt owing to him from the bankrupt, he shall be admitted as a creditor only for the balance of the debt after deducting the value of such property, to be ascertained by agreement between him and the assignee, or by a sale thereof, to be made in such manner as the court shall direct; or the creditor may release or convey his claim to the assignee upon such property, and be admitted to prove his whole debt. If the value of the property exceeds the sum for which it is so held as security, the assignee may release to the creditor the bankrupt's right of redemption therein on receiving such excess; or he may sell the property, subject to the claim of the creditor thereon; and in either case the assignee and creditor, respectively, shall execute all deeds and writings necessary or proper to consummate the transaction. If the property is not so sold or released and delivered up, the creditor shall not be allowed to prove any part of his debt.

Secured debts; Where value of security exceeds debt.

100. *Practice where Debt is Secured.*—A secured creditor can resort to one of three rem-

§ 5075.] Practice in Case of Secured Debts. [Notes 100–104.

edies: 1. He can rely upon his security; 2. He may abandon it and prove the whole debt as unsecured; 3. He may be admitted only as a creditor for the balance remaining after the deduction of the value of the security. If he takes either of the last two, he must prove his debt; if he choses the first, he need not prove it, unless he seeks the aid of the bankrupt court to enforce his lien. Wicks v. Perkins, 13 N. B. R. 280. All the necessary requirements of a statute giving a lien must be complied with before the petition in bankruptcy against a debtor is filed, before it can effect the estate in the assignee's hands. Re Sabin, 12 N. B. R. 142. But see Re Brunquest, 14 N. B. R. 529; Thornton v. Hogan, 63 Mo. 143. Where one of the statutory requirements is to commence suit for the lien claim, a lien claimant may, as an equivalent, assert his lien in the bankruptcy court within the time limited by the statute creating the lien. Re Brunquest, supra. See also Phelps v. Sellick, 8. N. B. R 390; Re Eldridge, 12 N. B. R. 540; Re Firemen's Ins. Co., 8 N. B. R. 123; s. c., 3 Biss 462.

101. *Who are Lien Creditors.*—Bankers have a general lien on the securities of their customers for balance. Sparhawk v. Drexel, 12 N. B. R. 450. Where one partner has pledged his individual property for a firm debt, proof may be made in full against the assets of the firm without a valuation of the securities. Re Dow, 14 N. B. R. 307. Proving a secured as a general claim does not waive the security, unless there was concealment of the fact that it was secured. Hatch v. Seeley, 13 N. B. R. 380. A judgment creditor's lien obtained after an assignment for creditor's benefit is made, and which assignment is subsequently set aside in bankruptcy, is a valid lien as against the assignee in bankruptcy. MacDonald v. Moore, 15 N. B. R. 26. But see Johnson v. Rogers, 15 N. B. R. 2. Where money is loaned on commercial paper by a bank, indorsed by a bankrupt, such paper is not collateral security. Re Weeks, 13 N. B. R. 263. See Re Peebles, 13 N. B. R. 149. Judgment docketed on Sunday does not create a valid lien. Re Worthington, 14 N. B. R. 390. A landlord, with right of distress for rent, is entitled to priority of payment for rent which has accrued; this right is in the nature of a lien, and the courts have classed it as a lien within the meaning of the bankrupt act. Austin v. O'Reilly, 12 N. B. R. 329. See note 96, supra.

102. *Sale of Incumbered Property.*—The district court in bankruptcy may direct the sale of the bankrupt's property free from all incumbrances. Secured creditors must have due opportunity to defend their interests, and must be notified to appear. Ray v. Brigham, 12 N. B. R. 145; s. c., 23 Wall. 128. A sale without order of court conveys only such interest as the bankrupt had. Ibid.; Wicks v. Perkins, 13 N. B. R. 280. Sale under an illegal order is void. Davis v. R. R. Co., 13 N. B. R. 258. If the proceeds are not in excess of the lien, the court has no control over them; they go to the claimant. Re Blue Ridge Co., 13 N. B. R. 315.

102a. *Failure to Prove Debt.*—A mortgagee does not lose his lien by omitting to prove his debt. He may enforce his lien after the termination of the bankruptcy proceedings. Wicks v. Perkins, 13 N. B. R. 280. See also Brown v. Gibbons, 13 N. B. R. 407; McKay v. Funk, 13 N. B. R. 334; s. c., 87 Iowa, 661. So may a judgment lien creditor. Bush v. Lester, 15 N. B. R. 36; s. c., 55 Ga. 579.

103. *Sale at Request of Creditor.*—Secured creditors may petition court for order to sell the security, upon notice to the assignee. Re Davis, 2 N. B. R. 391. But their debt must first be proven as secured. Re Frizelle, 5 N. B. R. 122; Re Bigelow, 2 Ben. 480. A claimant who has a judgment lien should prove his judgment as a secured debt and obtain permission to sell the property by virtue of his execution. Re Hufnagel, 12 N. B. R. 554. See Heard v. Jones, 15 N. B. R. 402. Bankrupt court is the proper tribunal to administer remedies to enforce liens. Blum v. Ellis, 76 N. C. 293. The same decision holds that all claimants must prove their debts, however evidenced.

104. *Marshalling Securities.*—Where a creditor of a bankrupt holds two classes of security for his debt, he will be compelled to exhaust that class which he holds, and from which the other creditors would be excluded. Re Sauthoff, 14 N. B. R. 364. See also Re Peebles, 13 N. B. R. 149.

§§ 5076-5077.]   Secured Debts—Proof of Claims, how made.   [Notes 105-108.

105. *What not Secured.*—Creditors who hold security for their claim against a bankrupt, on property not the bankrupt's, may prove for their entire debt as unsecured. Re Dunkerson, 12 N. B. R. 413. A guaranty of a third party does not constitute security within the meaning of this section. Re Anderson, 12 N. B. R. 502; Re Cram, 1 N. B. R. 504. An indorsee of a note, of which the bankrupt is maker, is not a secured creditor. Re Breich, 15 N. B. R. 11.

106. *Action in State Court to enforce Lien stayed.*—An action to foreclose a mortgage given by a bankrupt, instituted in a state court after proceedings in bankruptcy were commenced, will be stayed at the instance of the assignee, until the close of proceedings in bankruptcy. Markson v. Haney, 12 N. B. R. 484; s. C., 47 Ind. 31. If not stayed, it is valid as against all persons who are parties thereto. Brown v. Gibbon, 13 N. B. R. 407; s. C., 37 Ia. 665.

IBID. § 22; R. S. § 5076.—Creditors residing within the judicial district where the proceedings in bankruptcy are pending shall prove their debts before one of the registers of the court, or before a commissioner of the circuit court, within the said district. Creditors residing without the district, but within the United States, may prove their debts before a register in bankruptcy, or a commissioner of a circuit court, in the judicial district where such creditor, or either one of joint creditors, reside; but proof taken before a commissioner, shall be subject to revision by the register of the court.

Debts provable before what officers.

107. Re Sheppard, 1 N. B. R. 439; Re Haley, 2 N. B. R. 36; Re Strauss, 2 N. B. R. 48.

§ 5076a; AMENDMENT OF 1874, § 20.—That in addition to officers now authorized to take proof of debts against the estate of a bankrupt, notaries public are hereby authorized to take such proof, in the manner and under the regulations provided by law; such proof to be certified by the notary and attested by his signature and official seal.

Notary may take proof of debts.

108. *Power of Notaries—Use of Seal.*—A notary may also take acknowledgments of letters of attorney. Re McDuffee, 14 N. B. R. 336. The seal of a notary who takes a proof of debt need not contain his name and be impressed upon the paper. Re Phillips, 14 N. B. R. 219. Contra, Re Nebe, 11 N. B. R. 289.

ORIGINAL ACT OF 1867, § 22; R. S. § 5077.—To entitle a claimant against the estate of a bankrupt to have his demand allowed, it must be verified by a deposition in writing, under oath, and signed by the deponent, setting forth the demand, the consideration thereof, whether any and what securities are held therefor, and whether any and what payments have been made thereon; that the sum claimed is justly due from the bankrupt to the claimant; that the claimant has not, nor has any other person, for his use, received any security or satisfaction whatever other than that by him set forth; that the claim was not procured for the purpose of influencing the proceedings in bankruptcy; and that no bargain or agreement, express or implied, has been made or entered into, by or on behalf of such creditor, to sell, transfer, or dispose of the claim, or any part thereof, or to take or receive, directly or indirectly, any money, property, or consideration whatever, whereby the vote of such creditor

Claims, how verified.

§§ 5077–5080.]   Proof of Claims—Requisites of—How made.   [Notes 109–110.

for assignee, or any action on the part of such creditor, or any other person in the proceedings, is or shall be in any way affected, influenced, or controlled. No claim shall be allowed unless all the statements set forth in such deposition shall appear to be true.

109. *Proof must show what.*—The proof of debt must show the items of the indebtedness as well as the consideration. Re Port Huron Dock Co., 14 N. B. R. 253. Also christian names of claimant and debtor. Re Reed, 12 N. B. R. 390. Where the debt is a note held by a third party, he must state the consideration which passed from him. Re Port Huron Dock Co., *supra*; Re L. J. Ship Canal R. R. & Iron Co., 10 N. B. R. 76.

IBID. § 22; R. S. § 5078.—Such oath shall be made by the claimant, testifying of his own knowledge, unless he is absent from the United States or prevented by some other good cause from testifying, in which case the demand may be verified by the attorney or authorized agent of the claimant, testifying to the best of his knowledge, information, and belief, and setting forth his means of knowledge. Corporations may verify their claims by the oath of their president, cashier, or treasurer. The court may require or receive further pertinent evidence either for or against the admission of any claim.   *Oath, by whom made: Corporations: Other evidence received.*

110. *Who may make Proof.*—Where an officer of a corporation makes proof, he must, on oath, disclose that fact. When proof is made by an agent, he must state why not made by the claimant in person. Re Port Huron Dock Co., 14 N. B. R. 253. An agent who has had exclusive management and can testify to the subject-matter of his own knowledge, can make proof. Re Watrous, 14 N. B. R. 258. Not otherwise. Re Saunders, 13 N. B. R. 164. A bankrupt is a competent witness to prove a claim of his wife, against the estate, if a competent witness under the state laws. Re Bean, 14 N. B. R. 182. "Some other good cause" construed. Re Jackson, 14 N. B. R. 449.

IBID.; R. S. § 5079.—Such oath may be taken in any district before any register or any commissioner of the circuit court authorized to administer oaths; or, if the creditor is in a foreign country, before any minister, consul, or vice-consul of the United States. When the proof is so made it shall be delivered or sent by mail to the register having charge of the case.   *Oath, before whom taken and how transmitted: Creditors in foreign country.*

IBID.; R. S. § 5080.—If the proof is satisfactory to the register it shall be delivered or sent by mail to the assignee, who shall examine the same and compare it with the books and accounts of the bankrupt, and shall register, in a book to be kept by him for that purpose, the names of creditors who have proved their claims, in the order in which such proof is received, stating the time of receipt of such proof, and the amount and nature of the debts. Such books shall be open to the inspection of all the creditors. The court may require or receive further pertinent evidence either for or against the admission of any claim.   *Proof to be sent to assignees: His duty: Other evidence.*

111. *Withdrawal of Proof.*—Giving the right to withdraw a proof of debt inadvertently filed is a discretionary power of the court, and will be exercised only where

§§ 5081–5084.] Examination of Proof—Postponement of Proof. [Notes 111–114.

the general estate is to be benefitted. *Re* Wiener, 14 N. B. R. 218. See Hubbard's Case, 1 N. B. R. 679; s. c., 1 Lowell, 190.

112. *Quantum of Proof.*—A creditor is not obliged, by the mere interposition of an objection to a proof of claim, to produce such evidence as would be necessary at an ordinary trial. *Re* Saunders, 13 N. B. R. 164. A proof of debt in due form makes out a *prima facie* case, subject to the discretion of the register and court to order further proof, and to the right of a creditor to offer counter proof. *Re* Saunders, 13 N. B. R. 164.

IBID.; R. S. § 5081.—The court may, on the application of the assignee,
Examination by court into proof of claims.
or of any creditor, or of the bankrupt, or without any application examine upon oath the bankrupt, or any person tendering or who has made proof of a claim, and may summon any person capable of giving evidence concerning such proof, or concerning the debt sought to be proved, and shall reject all claims not duly proved, or where the proof shows the claim to be founded in fraud, illegality, or mistake.

113. *Examination of Proof.*—McKinsey v. Harding, 4 N. B. R. 38; *Re* Ray, 2 Ben. 53. Creditor proving his debt is subject to examination and to the jurisdiction of the court, without regard to his place of residence. *Re* Kyler, 2 Ben. 414.

113*a*. *Competency of Bankrupt.*—A bankrupt is a competent party to move that a claim proven against the estate be expunged. *Re* McDonald, 14 N. B. R. 477.

IBID. § 24; R. S. § 5082.—A bill of exchange, promissory note, or
Withdrawal of evidences of debt.
other instrument, used in evidence upon the proof of a claim, and left in court or deposited in the clerk's office, may be delivered, by the register or clerk having the custody thereof, to the person who used it, upon his filing a copy thereof, attested by the clerk of the court, who shall indorse upon it the name of the party against whose estate it has been proved, and the date and amount of any dividend declared thereon.

IBID. § 23; R. S. § 5083.—When a claim is presented for proof before
Postponement of proof.
the election of the assignee, and the judge or register entertains doubts of its validity or of the right of the creditor to prove it, and is of opinion that such validity or right ought to be investigated by the assignee, he may postpone the proof of the claim until the assignee is chosen.

114. *Postponement of Proof.*—It is not required, in order to justify postponement of proof of claim, that the register shall have positive evidence that the claim is invalid. If there are any facts or circumstances which create in his mind substantial doubt upon the question of validity, or of the creditor's right, it is his duty to postpone it. *Re* Jackson, 14 N. B. R. 449; Lake Sup. Ship Canal R. R. Co., 7 N. B. R. 376, 389; *Re* Northern Iron Co., 14 N. B. R. 359; *Re* Stevens, 4 N. B. R. 367. If creditor's name does not appear in the bankrupt's schedule, it is sufficient. *Re* Milwain, 12 N. B. R. 358. Proofs that are postponed must be presented anew. *Re* Herrman, 4 Ben. 126.

IBID.; R. S. § 5084.—Any person who, since the second day of March,
Surrender of preference: Penalty for failure.
eighteen hundred and sixty-seven, has accepted any preference, having reasonable cause to believe that the same was made or given by the debtor, contrary to any provisions of the act of March two, eighteen hundred and

sixty-seven, chapter one hundred and seventy-six, to establish a uniform system of bankruptcy, or to any provisions of this title, shall not prove the debt or claim on account of which the preference is made or given, nor shall he receive any dividend therefrom until he shall first surrender to the assignee all property, money, benefit, or advantage received by him under such preference.

115. *Surrender of Preferences—Penalty for Failure.*—*Re* Davidson, 4 Ben. 10. A preferred creditor can not prove his debt until he has surrendered, voluntarily or by compulsion, his preference. *Re* Currier, 13 N. B. R. 68. A mere repayment to the debtor can not take the place of a surrender to the assignee. Ibid.

116. *When Surrender may be Made.*—The authorities on this point are conflicting, some maintaining that the surrender may be made at any time before the actual entry of judgment in the suit to set aside the preference (Burr v. Hopkins, 12 N. B. R. 211), and others, that it is too late to make the surrender after the creditor has elected to contest the assignee's title to the property preferentially received. *Re* Lee, 14 N. B. R. 89. The amendments of 1874 to the foregoing may be found in § 5021, which see. It has been held that the amendments are not retroactive. *Re* Lee, 14 N. B. R. 89. Section 5021 provides that in cases of actual fraud on the part of the creditor, he shall not be allowed to prove for more than a moiety of his debt. This must be understood to mean that in such a case, a creditor can do so only when he has fulfilled the requirements of § 5084, by making a surrender of the advantage obtained by the preference. Where there is no actual fraud and the requirements of this section are fulfilled, the whole debt may be proven. *Re* Riorden, 14 N. B. R. 332; *Re* Cramer, 13 N. B. R. 225; Burr v. Hopkins, 12 N. B. R. 211; *Re* Lee, 14 N. B. R. 89. Payment of the decree in a suit to set aside a preference is not a surrender. *Re* Tonkin, 4 N. B. R. 52; *Re* Richter, 1 Dill. 544.

IBID.; R. S. § 5085.—The court shall allow all debts duly proved, and shall cause a list thereof to be made and certified by one of the registers. Allowance and list of debts.

IBID. § 26; R. S. § 5086.—The court may, on the application of the assignee, or of any creditor, or without any application, at all times require the bankrupt, upon reasonable notice, to attend and submit to an examination, on oath, upon all matters relating to the disposal or condition of his property, to his trade and dealings with others, to his accounts concerning the same, to all debts due to or claimed from him, and to all other matters concerning his property and estate and the due settlement thereof according to law. Such examination shall be in writing, and shall be signed by the bankrupt and filed with the other proceedings. Examination of bankrupt.

117. *Examination of Bankrupt.*—A bankrupt who has fully submitted to an examination has a right to be protected against unreasonable demands for further examination; and where the examination already had is apparently full, unless it be made to appear that such examination was collusive, or in some material and specified particulars deficient, an application for further examination may properly be refused. *Re* Frisbie, 13 N. B. R. 349. Time to examine does not expire with the bankrupt's application for discharge. *Re* Solis, 4 Ben. 143. Upon hearing of a motion to expunge a claim, an examination of the bankrupt will not be granted; he may be summoned as a witness. Canby v. McLear, 13 N. B. R. 22.

IBID.; R. S. § 5087.—The court may, in like manner, require the at-

§§ 5087-5091.]　　Testimony—Distribution of Bankrupt's Estate.　　[Note 118.

Witness compelled to attend. tendance of any other person as a witness, and if such person fails to attend, on being summoned thereto, the court may compel his attendance by warrant directed to the marshal, commanding him to arrest such person and bring him forthwith before the court, or before a register in bankruptcy, for examination as a witness.

118. *Mode of Procuring Testimony—Privilege of Witnesses.*—An assignee may be subpœnaed. *Re* Smith, 14 N. B. R. 432. Registers in bankruptcy have "all the powers of the district court for the summoning of witnesses;" consequently may subpœna witnesses who reside out of the district, in conformity to § 876 of the Revised Statutes of the United States. *Re* Woodward, 12 N. B. R. 297. A commission may issue from the bankrupt court and be sent to another state for the taking of testimony. *Re* Johnston, 14 N. B. R. 569. The examination of a witness by the assignee, under § 26 of the act, is an *ex parte* proceeding. The assignee is the only party. Consequently the witness is not entitled to counsel, nor can a creditor interfere with or be represented by counsel in such a proceeding. *Re* Comstock, 13 N. B. R. 193, and cases cited. Witness need not answer questions tending to degrade him, if not relevant to a matter of fact in issue. *Re* Lewis, 4 Ben. 67.

§ 5087*a*. AMENDMENT OF 1874.—In all causes and trials arising *Bankrupt or party competent witness.* or ordered under this act, the alleged bankrupt, and any party thereto, shall be a competent witness.[1]

IBID.; R. S. § 5088.—For good cause shown, the wife of any bankrupt may be required to attend before the court to the end *Examination of bankrupt's wife.* that she may be examined as a witness; and if she does not attend at the time and place specified in the order, the bankrupt shall not be entitled to a discharge unless he proves to the satisfaction of the court that he was unable to procure her attendance.[2]

IBID.; R. S. § 5089.—If the bankrupt is imprisoned, absent, or disabled from attendance, the court may order him to be *Examination of imprisoned or disabled bankrupt.* produced by the jailer, or any officer in whose custody he may be, or may direct the examination to be had, taken, and certified at such time and place and in such manner as the court may deem proper, and with like effect as if such examination had been had in court.

No abatement upon death of debtor. IBID. § 12; R. S. § 5090.—If the debtor dies after the issuing of the warrant, the proceedings may be continued and concluded in like manner as if he had lived.

IBID. § 27; R. S. § 5091.—All creditors whose debts are duly proved *DISTRIBUTION OF BANKRUPT'S ESTATE; Bail, surety, guarantor.* and allowed shall be entitled to share in the bankrupt's property and estate, pro rata, without any priority or preference whatever, except as allowed by section fifty-one hundred and one. No debt proved by any person liable, as bail, surety, guarantor, or otherwise, for the bankrupt, shall be paid to the person so proving the same until satisfactory evidence shall be produced of the payment of such debt by such person so liable.

(1) Act of June 22, 1874, § 8.
(2) Re Woolford, 4 Ben. 9.

§§ 5092-5093.]   Second and Third Meeting of Creditors.   [Notes 119-120.

and the share to which such debt would be entitled may be paid into court, or otherwise held for the benefit of the party entitled thereto, as the court may direct.

119. *Preferred Creditors.*—A bank having suspended payment advertised that it would receive deposits to be kept separate from the old deposits. Subsequently the bank was adjudged bankrupt. The depositors under the advertisement petitioned to have their deposits first paid out of the fund. The petition was refused, and it was held that they were general creditors only. *Re* Mut. Building Society, 15 N. B. R. 44. Where a debtor had given an irrevocable power of attorney to sell stock to an attorney as security for a debt, and after the attorney's death and before the power was executed the debtor became bankrupt, it was held that the power was not revoked, and the creditor for whose security the power was made could hold it against the assignee. Lightner v. First Nat. Bank, 15 N. B. R. 69; s. o., 82 Penn. 301.

IBID.; R. S. § 5092.—At the expiration of three months from the date of the adjudication of bankruptcy in any case, or as much earlier as the court may direct, the court, upon request of the assignee, shall call a general meeting of the creditors, of which due notice shall be given, and the assignee shall then report, and exhibit to the court and to the creditors just and true accounts of all his receipts and payments, verified by his oath, and he shall also produce and file vouchers for all payments for which vouchers are required by any rule of the court; he shall also submit the schedule of the bankrupt's creditors and property as amended, duly verified by the bankrupt, and a statement of the whole estate of the bankrupt as then ascertained, of the property recovered and of the property outstanding, specifying the cause of its being outstanding, and showing what debts or claims are yet undetermined, and what sum remains in his hands. The majority in value of the creditors present shall determine whether any and what part of the net proceeds of the estate, after deducting and retaining a sum sufficient to provide for all undetermined claims which, by reason of the distant residence of the creditor, or for other sufficient reason, have not been proved, and for other expenses and contingencies, shall be divided among the creditors; but unless at least one-half in value of the creditors attend the meeting, either in person or by attorney, it shall be the duty of the assignee so to determine.
SECOND MEETING OF CREDITORS: Assignee to report; Creditors to decide as to dividend: Assignee to decide, when.

120. *No meeting should be called* unless there are funds in the hands of the assignee for distribution. *Re* Son, 1 N. B. R. 310.

IBID. § 28; R. S. § 5093. — Like proceedings shall be had at the expiration of the next three months, or earlier, if practicable, and a third meeting of creditors shall then be called by the court, and a final dividend then declared, unless any suit at law or in equity is pending, or unless some other estate or effects of the debtor afterward come to the hands of the assignee, in which case the assignee shall, as soon as may be, convert such estate and effects into money, and within two months after the same are so converted they shall be divided in manner aforesaid.
THIRD MEETING OF CREDITORS: Final dividend: Further dividends.

§§ 5094–5099.] Meetings and Dividends—Accounting of Assignee. [Notes 121–122.

Further dividends shall be made in like manner as often as occasion requires, and after the third meeting of creditors no further meeting shall be called, unless ordered by the court.

121. *Who may Participate.*—So long as there is a fund to distribute, all who have claims will, upon making proof, be permitted to participate in it. *Re* Maybin, 15 N. B. R. 468.

Notice of meetings and dividends.
IBID. § 17; R. S. § 5094.—The assignee shall give such notice to all known creditors, by mail or otherwise, of all meetings, after the first, as may be ordered by the court.

Creditor may act by attorney.
IBID. § 23; R. S. § 5095.—Any creditor may act at all meetings by his duly constituted attorney the same as though personally present.

122. *Powers of Attorney* need not be acknowledged. *Re* Powell, 2 N. B. R. 45; *Re* Barnes, 1 Lowell, 580. It would seem that under the general orders in bankruptcy they must be. They may be acknowledged before a notary public. *Re* Butterfield, 14 N. B. R. 195. *Contra, Re* Christley, 10 N. B. R. 268. See Gen. Ord. 34, *post*. A Good power of attorney must be shown. *Re* Hill, 1 Ben. 321; *Re* Knœpfel, 1 Ben. 330.

IBID. § 28; R. S. § 5096.—Preparatory to the final dividend, the as-
Settlement of assignee's account. His examination and discharge.
signee shall submit his account to the court and file the same, and give notice to the creditors of such filing, and shall also give notice that he will apply for a settlement of his account, and for a discharge from all liability as assignee, at a time to be specified in such notice, and at such time the court shall audit and pass the accounts of the assignee, and the assignee shall, if required by the court, be examined as to the truth of his account, and if it is found correct he shall thereby be discharged from all liability as assignee to any creditor of the bankrupt. The court shall thereupon order a dividend of the estate and effects, or of such part thereof as it sees fit, among such of the creditors as have proved their claims, in proportion to the respective amount of their debts.

IBID.; R. S. § 5097.—No dividend already declared shall be disturbed by
Dividends not to be disturbed.
reason of debts being subsequently proved, but the creditors proving such debts shall be entitled to a dividend equal to those already received by the other creditors before any further payment is made to the latter.

IBID.; R. S. § 5098.—If by accident, mistake, or other cause, without
Omission of assignee to call meetings.
fault of the assignee, either or both of the second and third meetings should not be held within the times limited, the court may, upon motion of an interested party, order such meetings, with like effect as to the validity of the proceedings as if the meeting had been duly held.

IBID.; R. S. § 5099.—The assignee shall be allowed, and may retain out
Disbursements and compensation of assignee.
of money in his hands, all the necessary disbursements made by him in the discharge of his duty, and a reasonable compensation for his services, in the discretion of the court.

§§ 5100-5101.]   Allowances of Assignee—Dividends—Priorities.   [Notes 123-127.

123. *Fees—Allowances of Assignee.*—As to fees generally, see *Re* Dean, 1 N. B. R. 249 *Attorneys* for an assignee in bankruptcy will not be allowed compensation, unless the services rendered were absolutely necessary. *Re* Drake, 14 N. B. R. 150.

124. *Allowance for Rent.*— Where an assignee continues to occupy the premises leased by the bankrupt, he is liable personally for the rent, and the landlord has a lien upon the goods upon the premises, the same as against other tenants. This rent has priority over all the expenses of administration of the estate. A suit triable by a jury may be brought for such liability. Buckner v. Jewell, 14 N. B. R. 287. See note to § 5071, *ante.*

125. *Discretionary Allowances.*—No. 30 of the General Orders, which permits no other allowance to be made than therein specified, does not prevent the court from exercising its discretion in allowing an assignee further compensation. *Re* Colwell, 15 N. B. R. 92.

126. *State Taxation.*—The bankrupt's estate in the hands of an assignee is not subject to state taxation. *Re* Booth, 14 N. B. R. 232.

IBID.; R. S. § 5100.—In addition to all expenses necessarily incurred by him in the execution of his trust, in any case, the assignee shall be entitled to an allowance for his services in such case on all moneys received and paid out by him therein, for any sum not exceeding one thousand dollars, five per centum thereon; for any larger sum, not exceeding five thousand dollars, two and a half per centum on the excess over one thousand dollars; and for any larger sum, one per centum on the excess over five thousand dollars. If, at any time, there is not in his hands a sufficient amount of money to defray the necessary expenses required for the further execution of his trust, he shall not be obliged to proceed therein until the necessary funds are advanced or satisfactorily secured to him. Commissions allowed: Need not proceed without funds.

IBID.; R. S. § 5101.—In the order for a dividend, the following claims shall be entitled to priority, and to be first paid in full in the following order: 1, the fees, costs, and expenses of suits, and of the several proceedings in bankruptcy under this title, and for the custody of property as herein provided; 2, all debts due to the United States, and all taxes and assessments under the laws thereof; 3, all debts due to the state in which the proceedings in bankruptcy are pending, and all taxes and assessments made under the laws thereof; 4, wages due to any operative, clerk, or house-servant, to an amount not exceeding fifty dollars, for labor performed within six months next preceding the first publication of the notice of proceedings in bankruptcy; 5, all debts due to any persons who, by the laws of the United States are, or may be entitled to a priority, in like manner as if the provisions of this title had not been adopted. But nothing contained in this title shall interfere with the assessment and collection of taxes by the authority of the United States or any state.   DIVIDENDS: PRIORITIES: Fees: Public Debts: Wages, etc.

127. *Priorities— Attorney's Fees—Services of Expert—Taxes—Costs of Attachment— Sheriff's Fee.*—Attorneys for a bankrupt who aid him in the preparation of his schedules, are general creditors of the estate, either in a voluntary or an involuntary proceeding. An attorney may obtain compensation before rendering services, or take

security therefor from the bankrupt. *Re* Gies, 12 N. B. R. 179, and cases cited; *Re* Handell, 15 N. B. R. 71. Even though the debtor is insolvent and known to be so by him. Triplett v. Hanley, 1 Dill. 217. An expert who was employed by a bankrupt just prior to bankruptcy to examine and straighten out his books, is a "clerk," and entitled to priority of payment to the amount of fifty dollars. *Ex parte* Rocket, 15 N. B. R. 95. State taxes duly assessed have a priority. Foster v. Inglee, 13 N. B. R. 239. Costs of attachment which has been dissolved may be paid out of the fund in full, unless it can be affirmatively proved that the attachment did not and could not preserve the property for the general creditors. *Re* Holmes, 14 N. B. R. 493. The sheriff has a lien. *Re* Houseberger, 2 Ben. 504.

128. *Debts due the United States—Subrogation.*—The United States is entitled to priority of payment; it need not prove its debt. U. S. v. Lewis, 13 N. B. R. 33. This priority will be enforced against the separate estate of the members of the firm, as well as the partnership assets. The equity rule, recognized by the bankrupt law, that individual creditors are to be paid out of the individual assets, and partnership creditors out of partnership assets, does not apply. The United States is in no wise bound by the bankrupt act. Lewis v. U. S., 14 N. B. R. 64. If a party pays a duty on an imported article, in order to get it out of the bonded warehouse, he is subrogated to the rights of the United States against the failing sureties. *Re* Chase, 14 N. B. R. 139; s. c. 14 N. B. R. 157.

IBID. § 27; R. S. § 5102.—Whenever a dividend is ordered, the register shall, within ten days after the meeting, prepare a list of creditors entitled to dividend, and shall calculate and set opposite to the name of each creditor who has proved his claim the dividend to which he is entitled out of the net proceeds of the estate set apart for dividend, and shall forward, by mail, to every creditor a statement of the dividend to which he is entitled, and such creditors shall be paid by the assignee in such manner as the court may direct.

Notice of dividend to each creditor.

IBID. § 43; R. S. § 5103.—If at the first meeting of creditors, or at any meeting of creditors specially called for that purpose, and of which previous notice shall have been given for such length of time and in such manner as the court may direct, three-fourths in value of the creditors whose claims have been proved shall resolve that it is for the interest of the general body of the creditors that the estate of the bankrupt shall be settled by trustees, under the inspection and direction of a committee of the creditors, the creditors may certify and report such resolution to the court, and may nominate one or more trustees to take and hold and distribute the estate, under the direction of such committee. If it appears, after hearing the bankrupt and such creditors as desire to be heard, that the resolution was duly passed, and that the interests of the creditors will be promoted thereby, the court shall confirm it; and upon the execution and filing, by or on behalf of three-fourths in value of all the creditors whose claims have been proved, of a consent that the estate of the bankrupt shall be wound up and settled by trustees, according to the terms of such resolution, the bankrupt, or, if an assignee has been appointed, the assignee, shall,

Superseding proceedings by arrangement: Trustees.

Court to approve.

Consent of creditors to be filed.

§ 5103.] Proceedings in Case of Appointment of Trustees. [Note 129.

under the direction of the court, and under oath, convey, transfer, and deliver all the property and estate of the bankrupt to the trustees, who shall, upon such conveyance and transfer, have and hold the same in the same manner, and with the same powers and rights, in all respects, as the bankrupt would have had or held the same if no proceedings in bankruptcy had been taken, or as the assignee in bankruptcy would have done, had such resolution not been passed. Such consent and the proceedings under it shall be as binding in all respects on any creditor whose debt is provable, who has not signed the same, as if he had signed it, and on any creditor whose debt, if provable, is not proved, as if he had proved it. The court, by order, shall direct all acts and things needful to be done to carry into effect such resolution of the creditors, and the trustees shall proceed to wind up and settle the estate under the direction and inspection of such committee of the creditors, for the equal benefit of all such creditors; and the winding up and settlement of any estate under the provisions of this section shall be deemed to be proceedings in bankruptcy; and the trustees shall have all the rights and powers of assignees in bankruptcy. The court, on the application of such trustees, shall have power to summon and examine, on oath or otherwise, the bankrupt, or any creditor, or any person indebted to the estate, or known or suspected of having any of the estate in his possession, or any other person whose examination may be material or necessary to aid the trustees in the execution of their trust, and to compel the attendance of such persons and the production of books and papers in the same manner as in other proceedings in bankruptcy; and the bankrupt shall have the like right to apply for and obtain a discharge after the passage of such resolution and the appointment of such trustees as if such resolution had not been passed, and as if all the proceedings had continued in the manner provided in the preceding sections of this title. If the resolution is not duly reported, or the consent of the creditors is not duly filed, or if, upon its filing, the court does not think fit to approve thereof, the bankruptcy shall proceed as if no resolution had been passed, and the court may make all necessary orders for resuming the proceedings. And the period of time which shall have elapsed between the date of the resolution and the date of the order for resuming proceedings shall not be reckoned in calculating periods of time prescribed by this title.

Conveyances to trustees: Their Title.

Effect of these proceedings.

Trustees: Their duties.

Their rights and powers: Examination of bankrupt, witnesses, etc.: Books and papers.

Discharge of bankrupt.

If resolution be not approved, etc.

129. *Superseding Proceeding by Arrangement.*—This provision has been invoked in but few cases. The bankruptcy proceedings are superseded by arrangement under this section. Creditors need not prove their claims as in ordinary bankruptcy proceedings. *Re* Darby, 4 N. B. R. 211, 309. *Contra, Re* Bakewell, 4 N. B. R. 619. An assignee

[§ 5103a.] Composition with Creditors—Proceedings.

may be removed, and proceedings had under this section. *Re* Jones, 2 N. B. R. 59. No meetings are had as provided for by §§ 5092, 5093. *Re* Hinsdale, 12 N. B. R. 480.

§ 5103a; ACT JUNE 22, 1874, § 17.—In all cases of bankruptcy now pending, or to be hereafter pending, by or against any person, whether an adjudication in bankruptcy shall have been had or not, the creditors of such alleged bankrupt may, at a meeting called under the direction of the court, and upon not less than ten days' notice to each known creditor of the time, place, and purpose of such meeting, such notice to be personal or otherwise, as the court may direct, resolve that a composition, proposed by the debtor shall be accepted in satisfaction of the debts due to them from the debtor. And such resolution shall, to be operative, have been passed by a majority in number and three-fourths in value of the creditors of the debtor assembled at such meeting either in person or by proxy, and shall be confirmed by the signatures thereto of the debtor and two-thirds in number and one-half in value of all the creditors of the debtor. And in calculating a majority for the purposes of a composition under this section, creditors whose debts amount to sums not exceeding fifty dollars shall be reckoned in the majority in value, but not in the majority in number; and the value of the debts of secured creditors above the amount of such security, to be determined by the court, shall, as nearly as circumstances admit, be estimated in the same way. And creditors whose debts are fully secured shall not be entitled to vote upon or to sign such resolution without first relinquishing such security for the benefit of the estate. The debtor, unless prevented by sickness or other cause satisfactory to such meeting, shall be present at the same, and shall answer any enquiries made of him; and he, or, if he is so prevented from being at such meeting, some one in his behalf, shall produce to the meeting a statement showing the whole of his assets and debts, and the names and addresses of the creditors to whom such debts respectively are due. Such resolution, together with the statement of the debtor as to his assets and debts, shall be presented to the court; and the court shall, upon notice to all the creditors of the debtor of not less than five days, and upon hearing, enquire whether such resolution has been passed in the manner directed by this section; and if satisfied that it has been so passed, it shall, subject to the provisions hereinafter contained, and upon being satisfied that the same is for the best interest of all concerned, cause such resolution to be recorded and statement of assets and debts to be filed; and until such record and filing shall have taken place, such resolution shall be of no validity. And any creditor of the debtor may inspect such record and statement at all reasonable times. The creditors may, by resolution passed in the manner and under the circum-

§ 5103a.] Composition with Creditors—Proceedings.

stances aforesaid, add to, or vary the provisions of, any composition previously accepted by them, without prejudice to any persons taking interests under such provisions who do not assent to such addition or variation. Terms of composition may be afterwards varied.
And any such additional resolution shall be presented to the court in the same manner and proceeded with in the same way and with the same consequences as the resolution by which the composition was accepted in the first instance. The provisions of a composition accepted by such resolution in pursuance of this section shall be binding on all the creditors whose names and addresses and the amounts of the debts due to whom are shown in the statement of the debtor produced at the meeting at which the resolution shall have been passed, but shall not affect or prejudice the rights of any other creditors. Binding upon what creditors. Where a debt arises on a bill of exchange or promissory note, if the debtor shall be ignorant of the holder of any such bill of exchange or promissory note, he shall be required to state the amount of such bill or note, the date on which it falls due, the name of the acceptor and of the person to whom it is payable, and any other particulars within his knowledge respecting the same; and the insertion of such particulars shall be deemed a sufficient description by the debtor in respect to such debt. Provision in case of outstanding commercial paper. Any mistake made inadvertently by a debtor in the statement of his debts may be corrected upon reasonable notice, and with the consent of a general meeting of his creditors. Correction of mistakes.
Every such composition shall, subject to priorities declared in said act, provide for a *pro rata* payment or satisfaction, in money, to the creditors of such debtor in proportion to the amount of their unsecured debts, or their debts in respect to which any such security shall have been duly surrendered and given up. Payments to be pro rata, etc. The provisions of any composition made in pursuance of this section may be enforced by the court, on motion made in a summary manner by any person interested, and on reasonable notice; and any disobedience of the order of the court made on such motion shall be deemed to be a contempt of court. Enforcement of provisions of compositions. Rules and regulations of court may be made in relation to proceedings of composition herein provided for, in the same manner and to the same extent as now provided by law in relation to proceedings in bankruptcy. If it shall at any time appear to the court, on notice, satisfactory evidence, and hearing, that a composition under this section can not, in consequence of legal difficulties, or for any sufficient cause, proceed without injustice or undue delay to the creditors or to the debtor, the court may refuse to accept and confirm such composition, or may set the same aside; and, in either case, the debtor shall be proceeded with as a bankrupt in conformity with the provisions of law, and proceedings may Court may set aside composition, etc.

[§ 5103a.] Composition with Creditors—Decisions. [Notes 130-138.

be had accordingly; and the time during which such composition shall have been in force shall not, in such case, be computed in calculating periods of time prescribed by said act.

130. *Constitutionality.*—This act is constitutional. *Re* Reiman, 13 N. B. R. 128.

131. *Resolution must Pass*—by the requisite vote. *Re* Spades, 13 N. B. R. 72. When so passed or rejected, the business of the meeting is over. *Re* Spillman, 13 N. B. R. 214.

132. *Must be Confirmed.*—It must then be *confirmed* by the requisite vote, signed by the debtor. *Re* Spades, *supra.* And the confirmation need not be made at a meeting of creditors, nor be presented to the register. *Re* Spillman, *supra.* But see *Re* Scott, 15 N. B. R. 73; s. C., 4 Cent. L. J. 29.

133. *The Oath* required by § 5077 is not required of creditors voting upon a resolution of compromise. *Re* Morris, 12 N. B. R. 170.

134. *What Creditors Reckoned.*—(1.) Creditors whose debts do not exceed fifty dollars are only to be reckoned in determining the *value*, and not the number requisite to both *pass* and *confirm* a resolution. *Re* Spades, *supra.* See *Re* Wald, 12 N. B. R. 491. (2.) *Creditors who purchase claims* against a bankrupt may vote them at a meeting, held for composition purposes to defeat the resolution of compromise, when the object of the purchase is not for the purpose of oppression or to commit a fraud. *Re* Morris, 12 N. B. R. 170. (3.) *Secured creditors* are not counted. *Re* Van Auken, 14 N. B. R. 425. They may vote where their debt is in excess of their security. *Re* Spades, 13 N. B. R. 72. A creditor having personal security is not a secured creditor within the meaning of the act. *Re* Spades, *supra.*

135. *Unliquidated Claims.*—If a claim is unliquidated or disputed, the court should provide as if the proceedings were in bankruptcy; that is, by permitting a pending action or suit to be prosecuted to judgment, in order to ascertain the amount, or by ordering an inquiry at the bar of the bankruptcy court into the matter. *Re* Trafton, 14 N. B. R. 507.

136.—*Terms of Resolution.*—A resolution which provides for payment in indorsed notes is valid. *Re* Hurst, 13 N. B. R. 455; *Re* Reiman, 11 N. B. R. 21. *Contra*, *Re* Langdon, 18 N. B. R. 60. In this case stress is laid upon the phraseology of the resolution, which was that the notes were to be *payment*, and not merely evidences of indebtedness, to be payment when paid. The debtor is not entitled to his discharge unless the amount agreed upon is actually paid. *Re* Hurst, *supra;* *Re* Reiman, *supra.* The resolution must name the indorser of the notes, or provide for a committee to decide upon his sufficiency. *Re* Reiman, *supra.* A resolution for a composition which provides that payment shall be guaranteed by the giving of a satisfactory bond to a committee of creditors, may be recorded. *Re* Lewis, 14 N. B. R. 144. A stipulation that the debtor retain the assets is surplusage. *Re* Van Auken, 14 N. B. R. 425.

137. *Debtor should be Present—Objection—Mistake or Omission in Statement of Assets.*— The debtor should be present at the meeting to enable any creditor who may be dissatisfied with the statement which the debtor produces at the meeting, to inquire into its accuracy and to obtain a true exhibit of his affairs. *Re* Holmes, 12 N. B. R. 86. If objection is made, no vote should be taken on the proposition until the examination is completed. *Re* Holmes, *supra; Re* Asten, 14 N. B. R. 7; *Re* Morris, 11 N. B. R. 443. Amount due each creditor should be stated; if incorrectly stated by mistake, the composition would not be vitiated. *Re* Trafton, 14 N. B. R. 507. As to omission to state assets correctly, see *Re* Reiman, 13 N. B. R. 128. Statement if incorrect can only be corrected at a meeting of creditors. *Re* Asten, *supra.*

138. *Recording the Resolution.*—It is in the discretion of the court to refuse to record a composition if opposed by even a small minority of creditors, when it is made to appear that a settlement in bankruptcy would be more for their interest. *Re* Weber Furniture Co., 13 N. B. R. 529; *Re* Whipple, 11 N. B. R. 524. An illegal vote does not nullify the proceedings, if its absence would not have changed the result. *Re* Walshee, 2 Woods, 225. It is error to refuse to record without notice and hearing of the

§ 5103a.]   Composition with Creditors—Decisions.   [Notes 138-148.

parties concerned. *Re* Weber Furniture Co., 13 N. B. R. 559. It should be recorded, unless there is some feature in it so gross as to excite suspicion of fraud when viewed in conjunction with the statement of the debtor. Ibid. The decision of the majority of the creditors is conclusive as to the *amount* of the compromise being for the best interests of all concerned. Ibid. See *Re* Morris, 11 N. B. R. 443.

139. *Binding.*—A composition is binding upon all creditors who have *provable* debts and who have notice. *Re* Trafton, 14 N. B. R. 507; *Re* Bechet, 12 N. B. R. 201, s. c., 2 Woods, 173.

140. *Attachments not Dissolved.*—A resolution of compromise does not affect attaching creditors whose attachments are less than four months old, unless an assignee has been elected and an assignment is made of the bankrupt's effects. *Re* Clapp, 14 N. B. R. 191; *Re* Shields, 15 N. B. R. 532; s. c., 4 Cent. L. J. 557. *Contra,* Miller v. Mackenzie, 13 N. B. R. 496; Smith v. Eagle, 14 N. B. R. 481. An exhaustive discussion of this whole subject may be found in *Re* Scott, 15 N. B. R. 73; s. c., 4 Cent. L. J.

141. *Practice under Composition.*—See *Re* scott, *supra.* A second meeting for composition purposes may be held. *Re* McDowell, 6 Biss. 193.

142. *Conclusive on State Courts.*—If the jurisdiction of the bankrupt court is shown to have attached, the subsequent proceedings are presumed to be regular, and its decision, whether correct or otherwise, upon every question properly arising in the case, is binding and conclusive until reversed. Smith v. Eagle, 14 N. B. R. 481. The decision of the district court on any question arising in the course of composition proceedings is conclusive in a collateral action. Ibid.

143. *Adjudication and Discharge not Necessary.*—The omission of the court in a voluntary case to adjudicate the debtor a bankrupt does not defeat a composition made before an adjudication is ordered. *Re* Van Auken, 14 N. B. R. 435. Nor a discharge; the composition in itself is a discharge. *Re* Bechet, 12 N. B. R. 201.

144. *Surety—Co-obligor.*—A composition does not release a co-obligor or surety. Mason Organ Co. v. Bancroft, 4 Cent. L. J. 295.

145. *Effect on Secured Creditors.*—If a resolution of composition has been duly approved and recorded, it confines the secured creditor to his security and discharges the debtor from personal liability for the secured debt. *Re* Lytle, 14 N. B. R. 457. The jurisdiction of the federal court will not be exercised to restrain a creditor from following his liens or security in the state courts, even though such courts have the power. *Re* Lytle, *supra; Re* Tooker, 14 N. B. B. 35.

146. *Composition procured by Fraud invalid.*—If a creditor is induced to vote or to sign a composition by any unfair means, whether known to the debtor or not, his vote operates as a fraud on the other creditors and makes the composition voidable by any of them. And if a creditor withdraws his intended opposition, but does not vote for or sign a proposed composition for a consideration, whether known to the debtor or not, the presumption is that it is for the debtors benefit, and an order to record a resolution of compromise under such circumstances will be set aside. *Re* Sawyer, 14 N. B. R. 241.

147. *Corporations.*—This act applies to corporations. *Re* Weber Furniture Co., 13 N. B. R. 529.

148. *In Case of Partnerships.*—Where a partnership desires a composition, the creditors may make the composition by a general vote and general confirmation, but if any one class of creditors perceives that the other class is about to force upon it an unjust composition, it may demand a separate vote. *Re* Spades, *supra.* One member of a firm which has been adjudged bankrupt may submit a proposition of compromise to creditors of firm and separate creditors. Pool v. McDonald, 15 N. B. R. 560.

Protection and Discharge of Bankrupts.

CHAPTER FIVE.

PROTECTION AND DISCHARGE OF BANKRUPTS.

SECTION
5104. Bankrupt subject to Orders of Court.
5105. *As Amended.*—Waiver of Suit by Proof of Debt.
  NOTE 149.—The same Subject.
5106. Creditors not to Prosecute Suit; Stay of Proceedings.
  NOTE 150.—Stay of Suits.
5107. Exemption from Arrest.
  NOTE 151.—Exemption from Arrest; Habeas Corpus.
5108. *As Amended.*—Discharge of Bankrupt.
  NOTE 152.—The same Subject.
5109. Notice of Application for Discharge.
5110. What will Prevent or Avoid Discharge.
  (1. False Oath.
  NOTE 153.—False Oath.
  (2.) Concealment; Fraud; Negligence; Waste.
  NOTE 154.—Concealment; Omission.
  (3.) Fraudulent Attachment, etc.
  (4.) Falsification of Books.
  (5.) Removal of Property; Fraudulent Payments, Conveyances, etc.
  NOTE 155.—What necessary to Show.
  (6.) Gaming Debts; Fictitious Debts.
  (7.) Failure to keep Books.
  NOTE 156.—The same Subject.
    157.—"Tradesman" defined.
  (8.) Purchasing Assent of Creditors.

SECTION
  NOTE 158.—Purchase of Claim to secure Assent of Creditors.
  (9.) Fraudulent Assignment; Preferences.
  (10.) Misdemeanor.
  NOTE 159.—In General.
5111. Specification of Grounds of Opposition.
  NOTE 160. — Burden of Proof; What Creditors may may file Specification; Requisites of.
5112. Assets must equal 50 per centum of Debts.
5112*a*. The Foregoing applicable to Compulsory Bankrupts; Voluntary Bankrupts to pay 30 per centum, etc.; Repeal.
  NOTE 161.—Construction; Statute Retroactive; Consent to be in Writing; In Partnership Cases.
5113. Final Oath of Bankrupt.
  NOTE 162—The same Subject.
5114. Discharge and Certificate thereof.
5115. Form of the Certificate.
5116. Second Bankruptcy; Discharge.
  NOTE 163.—Second Bankruptcy.
5117. Certain Debts not released.
  NOTE 164.—Fiduciary Debts; Conversion; Fraud.
5118. Liability of other Persons not Released.
5119. Effect of Discharge; How Pleaded; Certificate of same is Evidence.

BANKRUPT LAW. 65

§§5104–5106.]   Protection and Discharge of Bankrupts.   [Note 149.

NOTE 165.—Application for Discharge.
166.—What Debts Discharged. (1) Debts omitted from Schedule. (2) Security Debts.
167.—What Debts not Discharged. (1) Debts due United States.

SECTION
(2) Security Debts.
(3) Lien Debts.
168.—Plea of Discharge.
169.—In Maine.
5120. Application to annul Discharge; Proceedings thereunder.
NOTE 170.—This Remedy Exclusive.
171.—"Within two years."

ORIGINAL ACT OF 1867, § 27; R. S. § 5104.—The bankrupt shall at all times, until his discharge, be subject to the order of the court, and shall, at the expense of the estate, execute all proper writings and instruments, and do all acts required by the court touching the assigned property or estate; and to enable the assignee to demand, recover, and receive all the property and estate assigned, wherever situated. For neglect or refusal to obey any order of the court, the bankrupt may be committed and punished as for a contempt of court. If the bankrupt is without the district, and unable to return and personally attend at any of the times or do any of the acts which may be required pursuant to this section, and if it appears that such absence was not caused by willful default, and if, as soon as may be after the removal of such impediment, he offers to attend and submit to the order of the court in all respects, he shall be permitted so to do, with like effect as if he had not been in default. *Bankrupt subject to orders of court.*

IBID. § 21; R. S. § 5105, AS AMENDED.—No creditor proving his debt or claim shall be allowed to maintain any suit at law or in equity therefor against the bankrupt, but shall be deemed to have waived all right of action against him; and all proceedings already commenced or unsatisfied judgments already obtained thereon against the bankrupt shall be deemed to be discharged and surrendered thereby. [But a creditor proving his debt or claim shall not be held to have waived his right of action or suit against the bankrupt where a discharge has been refused or the proceedings have been determined without a discharge.][1] *Waiver of suit by proof of debt.*

149. *Waiver of Right to Sue by Proving Debt.*—This does not apply to debts not dischargable by the act. *Re* Migel, 2 N. B. R. 481; *Re* Robinson, 6 Blatch. 253. The mere proof of debt in bankruptcy does not discharge the debt so as to prevent the creditor from suing upon it, but it is the bankrupt's discharge which bars the action. Miller v. O'kain, 14 N. B. R. 145; Dingee v. Becker, 9 N. B. R. 508. A judgment for a debt created by fraud is not within the purview of this provision. *Re* Robinson, 6 Blatch. 253; *Re* Wright, 2 Ben. 509.

IBID.; R. S. § 5106.—No creditor whose debt is provable shall be allowed to prosecute to final judgment any suit at law or in equity therefor against the bankrupt, until the question of the debtor's discharge shall have been determined; and any such suit or proceedings shall, upon the appli- *Creditor not to prosecute suit: Stay of proceedings.*

(1) So amended by Act of June 22, 1874, § 7.

§§ 5106–5108.]   Stay of Suits—Exempt from Arrest—Habeas Corpus.   [Notes 150–151.

cation of the bankrupt be stayed to await the determination of the court in bankruptcy on the question of the discharge, provided there is no unreasonable delay on the part of the bankrupt in endeavoring to obtain his discharge, and provided, also, that if the amount due the creditor is in dispute, the suit, by leave of the court in bankruptcy, may proceed to judgment for the purpose of ascertaining the amount due, which amount may be proved in bankruptcy, but execution shall be stayed.

150. *Stay of Suits.*—Bankrupt court may stay suits, but cannot try the issues of a suit pending in the state courts. Sampson v. Burton, 4 N. B. R. 1. An adjudication must be had on the bankruptcy petition. Maxwell v. Faxton, 4 N. B. R. 210. A proceeding on the application of a bankrupt to revive a judgment so that it may operate as a lien, (which was not a lien) recovered before bankruptcy, may be stayed. Bratton v. Anderson, 14 N. B. R. 99. For a full discussion of this whole subject see Bratton v. Anderson, *supra.* No decision indicates how a discharge is properly brought to the attention of the appellate court. On this subject see Flanagan v. Pearson, 14 N. B. R. 37; Haggerton v. Morrison, 59 Mo. 324; Todd v. Barton, 13 N. B. R. 197. The debt need only be *provable;* whether discharged by a discharge or not, it will be stayed. *Re* Migel, 2 N. B. R. 481; *Re* Rosenberg, 3 Ben. 14. See *Re* Seymour, 1 Ben. 348. In the absence of any suggestion of bankruptcy, a judgment against a bankrupt is not a nullity. Flanagan v. Pearson, 14 N. B. R. 37. It would seem that such is the case in attachment suits sued out even within four months prior to the commencement of bankruptcy proceedings. Haber v. Clayburg, 4 Cent. L. J. In attachment suits sued out more than four months prior to bankruptcy proceedings being begun, plaintiff may have special judgment against property attached. See § 5044, note, *ante.* In case of bankrupt corporations, creditors are not restrained from prosecuting suits to charge stockholders. Munson v. Boston R. R., 14 N. B. R. 173; Chamberlain v. Manuf. Co., 118 Mass. 532; Lamp Co. v. Brass Co., 13 N. B. R. 385. The right to grant writs of injunction to stay proceedings in state courts is only given to federal courts in proceedings in bankruptcy. See act of March 2, 1793, c. 22, § 5; Rev. Stat. U. S. § 720. The court in which the bankruptcy proceedings are pending is the court to grant the injunction. *Re* Richardson, 2 Ben. 517. State courts will stay suits, on affidavit of defendant setting up that proceedings in bankruptcy are pending against him, and that the time for applying for a discharge has not arrived. Frostman v. Hicks, 15 N. B. R. 41. Judgments of state courts appealed from are not final judgments, and their prosecution will be stayed. *Re* Metcalf, 2 Ben. 78; *Re* Leszynsky, 3 Ben. 487.

IBID. § 26; R. S. § 5107.—No bankrupt shall be liable during the pendency of the proceedings in bankruptcy to arrest in any civil action, unless the same is founded on some debt or claim from which his discharge in bankruptcy would not release him.

Exemption from arrest.

151. *Exemption from Arrest—Habeas Corpus.*—*Re* Devoe, 2 N. B. R. 27. During pendency of bankruptcy proceedings an arrest made prior thereto will not be disturbed. Minon v. Van Nostrand, 4 N. B. R. 108. As to power of court on writ of *habeas corpus* to inquire whether the debt for which the arrest is made is dischargeable, see *Re* Valk, 3 Ben. 431.

IBID. § 29; R. S. § 5108, AS AMENDED.—At any time after the expiration of six months from the adjudication of bankruptcy, or if no debts have been proved against the bankrupt, or if no assets have come to the hands of the assignee, at

DISCHARGE OF BANKRUPT.

§§ 5408-5110.]   Notice of Application of Discharge—False Oath.   [Notes 152-154.

any time after the expiration of sixty days, and [before the final disposition of the cause,]¹ the bankrupt may apply to the court for a discharge from his debts.

152. *Discharge of Bankrupt.*—Under the law as it stood prior to the amendment of July 26, 1876, bankrupts had to apply for their discharge within one year from date of adjudication, where no assets had come to the hands of the assignee or no debts had been proved against the estate. *Re* Sloan, 12 N. B. R. 69; *Re* Holmes, 14 N. B. R. 209. Inability to obtain the assent of the requisite number under § 5112 is no excuse for failure to apply for a discharge within the time required by the act. *Re* Lowenstein, 13 N. B. R. 479. The amendment of 1876 construed in *Re* Brightman, 15 N. B. R. 213.

IBID. § 29; R. S. § 5109.—Upon application for a discharge being made the court shall order notice to be given by mail to all creditors who have proved their debts, and by publication at least once a week in such newspapers as the court shall designate, due regard being had to the general circulation of the same in the district, or in that portion of the district in which the bankrupt and his creditors shall reside to appear on a day appointed for that purpose, and show cause why a discharge should not be granted to the bankrupt.
<small>Notice of application for discharge.</small>

IBID.; R. S. § 5110.—No discharge shall be granted, or, if granted, shall be valid, in any of the following cases:

1. If the bankrupt has willfully sworn falsely in his affidavit, annexed to his petition, schedule, or inventory, or upon any examination in the course of the proceedings in bankruptcy, in relation to any material fact.
<small>What will prevent or avoid discharge. False oath.</small>

153. *False Oath.*—The specifications must allege that the bankrupt *wilfully* swore falsely. *Re* Beardsley, 1 N. B. R. 304; *Re* Keefer, 4 N. B. R. 389; *Re* Smith, 5 N. B. R. 20. Omitting to name creditor in schedule is not fraudulent, if done with such creditor's assent. *Re* Needham, 2 N. B. R. 387.

2. If the bankrupt has concealed any part of his estate or effects, or any books or writings relating thereto, or has been guilty of any fraud or negligence in the care, custody, or delivery to the assignee of the property belonging to him at the time of the presentation of his petition and inventory, excepting such property as he is permitted to retain under the provisions of this title, or if he has caused, permitted, or suffered any loss, waste, or destruction thereof.
<small>Concealment: Fraud: Negligence: Waste.</small>

154. *Concealment—Omission.*—Specifications must allege what property was omitted or concealed. *Re* Beardsley, *supra*; *Re* Hill, 1 N. B. R. 16, 275, 431; *Re* Rathborne, 1 N. B. R. 294, 324, 536. Concealment includes *title* to property as well as *property* itself. *Re* Hussman, 2 N. B. R. 437; *Re* O'Bannon, 2 N. B. R. 15; *Re* Beal, 2 N. B. R. 587; *Re* Rainsford, 5 N. B. R. 381. It must be a *fraudulent* omission. *Re* Smith, 13 N. B. R. 256.

3. If, within four months before the commencement of such proceedings, the bankrupt has procured his lands, goods, money, or chattels to be attached, sequestered, or seized on execution.²
<small>Fraudulent attachment, etc.</small>

(1) So amended by Act of July 26, 1876.
(2) Re Belden, 2 N. B. R. 42.

§ 5110.]   What will Prevent or Avoid Discharge.   [Notes 155–158.

4. If, at any time after the second day of March, eighteen hundred and sixty-seven, the bankrupt has destroyed, mutilated, altered, or falsified any of his books, documents, papers, writings, or securities, or has made or been privy to the making of any false or fraudulent entry in any book of account or other document, with intent to defraud his creditors; or has removed or caused to be removed any part of his property from the district, with intent to defraud his creditors.

Falsification of books.

5. If the bankrupt has given any fraudulent preference contrary to the provisions of the act of March two, eighteen hundred and sixty-seven, to establish a uniform system of bankruptcy, or to the provisions of this title, or has made any fraudulent payment, gift, transfer, conveyance, or assignment of any part of his property, or has lost any part thereof in gaming, or has admitted a false or fictitious debt against his estate.

Removal of property; Fraudulent payments. conveyances. etc.; Gaming: Fictitious Debt.

155. *What necessary to Show.*—This provision is general in its terms, and under it is sufficient to show a preference under any of the provisions of the act. The provision in the ninth subdivision of this section is specific, and the proofs must bring the case clearly within its terms, and the preference must be shown to have been made "in contemplation of becoming bankrupt." *Re* Warner, 5 N. B. R. 414, and cases there cited; *Re* Cretiew, 5 N. B. R. 423; *Re* Jones, 13 N. B. R. 286.

6. If the bankrupt, having knowledge that any person has proved such false or fictitious debt, has not disclosed the same to his assignee within one month after such knowledge.

Fictitious Debts.

7. If the bankrupt, being a merchant or tradesman, has not, at all times after the second day of March, eighteen hundred and sixty-seven, kept proper books of account.

Failure to keep books.

156. *Omission to Keep Proper Books of Account.*—"Proper books of account," what are, is a question of fact, depending upon the nature of and amount of the bankrupt's business. *Re* Reed, 12 N. B. R. 390. Omission to keep a stock or invoice book is fatal. *Re* White, 2 N. B. R. 590. Or cash book. *Re* Gay, 2 N. B. R. 358; *Re* Mackay, 4 N. B. R. 66. The omission need not be fraudulent. *Re* Solomon, 2 N. B. R. 285; *Re* Newman, 2 N. B. R. 302.

157.—"*Tradesman*" means shopkeeper. *Re* Cote, 14 N. B. R. 503. Who is such, see *Re* Cocks, 3 Ben. 260; *Re* O'Bannon, 2 N. B. R. 15; *Re* Tyler, 4 N. B. R. 104.

8. If the bankrupt, or any person in his behalf, has procured the assent of any creditor to the discharge, or influenced the action of any creditor at any stage of the proceedings, by any pecuniary consideration or obligation.

Purchasing assent of creditors.

158. *Purchase of Claim to Secure Requisite Number of Creditors.*—Where the assent of creditors is required, a discharge will be refused, if a claim has been purchased on behalf of the bankrupt, for the purpose of getting the requisite number of creditors to assent; and a rebuttable presumption will arise that such is the purpose where a claim is purchased. *Re* Whitney, 14 N. B. R. 1. And it is immaterial whether the assent purchased was necessary or not to make the requisite proportion. *Re* Palmer, 14 N. B. R. 437.

9. If the bankrupt has, in contemplation of becoming bankrupt, made

§§ 5110-5112a.] Discharge—Specifications—Per centum of Assets. [Notes 159-160.

any pledge, payment, transfer, assignment, or conveyance of any part of his property, directly or indirectly, absolutely or conditionally, for the purpose of preferring any creditor or person having a claim against him, or who is or may be under liability for him, or for the purpose of preventing the property from coming into the hands of the assignee, or of being distributed in satisfaction of his debts.[1] *Fraudulent assignment: Preferences.*

10. If the bankrupt has been convicted of any misdemeanor under this title. *Misdemeanor.*

159. *In General.*—A bankrupt must have complied with all the requirements of the act before he can demand a discharge, and if it appear in the regular course of proceedings that an applicant for a discharge has failed in any particular to perform his duty as a bankrupt, the discharge must be refused. *Re* Palmer, 14 N. B. R. 437.

IBID. § 31; R. S. § 5111.—Any creditor opposing the discharge of any bankrupt may file a specification in writing of the grounds of his opposition, and the court may, in its discretion, order any question of fact so presented to be tried at a stated session of the district court. *Specification of grounds of opposition.*

160. *Burden of Proof—Specifications—What Creditors may file—Generally.*—The burden of proof is on the opposing creditor in support of his specifications. Creditors who wish to oppose discharge must appear at the return day. *Re* Smith, 5 N. B. R. 20. But see *Re* Levin, 14 N. B. R. 385. Specifications in opposition to a bankrupt's discharge must be as precise as those of an indictment. *Re* Butterfield, 14 N. B. R. 147. And if not filed in accordance with the law they will be disregarded. *Re* Buxbaum, 13 N. B. R. 478. Creditors who have not proved their debts can oppose discharge of bankrupt, but they must show that they are *bona fide* creditors. *Re* Bontelle, 2 N. B. R. 129.

ACT OF JULY 27, 1868, § 1; R. S. § 5112.—In all proceedings in bankruptcy commenced after the first day of January, 1869, no discharge shall be granted to a debtor whose assets shall not be equal to fifty per centum of the claims proved against his estate upon which he shall be liable as the principal debtor, unless the assent in writing of a majority in number and value of his creditors to whom he shall have become liable as principal debtor, and who shall have proved their claims, is filed in the case at or before the time of the hearing of the application for discharge; but this provision shall not apply to those debts from which the bankrupt seeks a discharge which were contracted prior to the first day of January, 1869.[2] *Assets equal to fifty per cent. required.*

§ 5112 *a*; AMENDMENT OF 1874.—That in cases of compulsory or involuntary bankruptcy, the provisions of said act, and any amendment thereof, or of any supplement thereto, requiring the payment of any proportion of the debts of the bankrupt, or the assent of any portion of his creditors, as a condition of his discharge from his debts, shall not apply; but he may, if otherwise entitled thereto, be discharged by the court in the *The foregoing not applicable to compulsory bankrupts.*

---

(1) See note 156, supra.
(2) This last clause was taken from the Act of July 14, 1870, § 1.

§§ 5112–5115.] Discharge—Assent of Creditors—Final Oath, etc. [Notes 161–162.

Voluntary bankrupts to pay thirty per cent., etc.

same manner and with the same effect as if he had paid such per centum of his debts, or as if the required proportion of his creditors had assented thereto. And in cases of voluntary bankruptcy, no discharge shall be granted to a debtor whose assets shall not be equal to thirty per centum of the claims proved against his estate, upon which he shall be liable as principal debtor, without the assent of at least one-fourth of his creditors in number, and one-third in value; and the provision in section thirty-three of said act of March second, eighteen hundred and sixty-seven, requiring fifty per centum of such assets, is hereby repealed.[1]

Repeal.

161. *Construction—Statute Retroactive—Assent in Writing—Partnership.*—This provision relates to all cases whether commenced before its passage or after. *Re* Lowenstein, 13 N. B. R. 480; S. C., 3 Dill. 145; *Re* King, 10 N. B. R. 556; *Re* Griffiths, 10 N. B. R. 456; *Re* Perkins, 10 N. B. R. 529; *Re* Jones, 12 N. B. R. 48. *Contra*, *Re* Francke, 10 N. B. R. 438; *Re* Sheldon, 12 N. B. R. 63. The act of June 22, 1874, does not repeal the first section of the act of 1870 or the last clause of section 5112. *Re* Sheldon, 12 N. B. R. 63. Where a judgment is obtained after January 1, 1869, upon a debt contracted prior to that time, it is not proper to hold that the debt was contracted after January 1, 1869. The assent required by this act must be in writing. *Re* Derby, 12 N. B. R. 241. Where a firm is declared bankrupt, upon the petition of one of the partners, the denial of his co-partner that he is such co-partner, and his resistance to the proceedings upon that ground, does not make the case an involuntary one as to him, and to obtain his discharge he must comply with the provisions of the act in regard to voluntary bankrupts. *Re* Wilson, 13 N. B. R. 253.

ORIGINAL ACT OF 1867, § 29; R. S. § 5113.—Before any discharge is granted, the bankrupt must take and subscribe an oath to the effect that he has not done, suffered, or been privy to any act, matter or thing specified as a ground for withholding such discharge, or as invalidating such discharge if granted.

Final oath of bankrupt.

162. *Final Oath.*—Oath must be taken; if bankrupt dies before taking oath no discharge can be granted. *Re* Gunike, 4 N. B. R. 92; *Re* O'Farrell, 3 Ben. 191. Where specifications in opposition to discharge are filed and then withdrawn, the bankrupt must take the oath after the withdrawal. *Re* Macbad, 2 N. B. R. 352.

IBID. § 32; R. S. § 5114.—If it shall appear to the court that the bankrupt has in all things conformed to his duty under this title, and that he is entitled, under the provisions thereof, to receive a discharge, the court shall grant him a discharge from all his debts except as hereinafter provided, and shall give him a certificate thereof under the seal of the court.[2]

Discharge and certificate thereof.

IBID. R. S. § 5115.—The certificate of a discharge in bankruptcy shall be in substance in the following form:

Form of the certificate.

District court of the United States, district of

Whereas   has been duly adjudged a bankrupt under the Revised Statutes of the United States, title "BANKRUPTCY," and appears to have conformed to all the requirements of law in that behalf, it is therefore ordered by the court that said   be forever

(1) So amended by Act of June 22, 1874, § 9.
(2) Re Palmer, 14 N. B. R. 437; Re Bunster, 5 N. B. R. 82.

§§ 5115-5118.]   Discharge—Second Bankruptcy—Debts not Released.   [Notes 163-164.

discharged from all debts and claims which by said title are made provable against his estate, and which existed on the   day of   , on which day the petition for adjudication was filed by (or against) him; excepting such debts, if any, as are by law excepted from the operation of a discharge in bankruptcy. Given under my hand and the seal of the court at   . in the said district, this   day of   ,   .
(Seal.)   , Judge.

IBID. § 30; R. S. § 5116.—No person who has been discharged, and afterward becomes bankrupt on his own application, shall be again entitled to a discharge whose estate is insufficient to pay seventy per centum of the debts proved against it, unless the assent in writing of three-fourths in value of his creditors who have proved their claims is filed at or before the time of application for discharge; but a bankrupt who proves to the satisfaction of the court that he has paid all the debts owing by him at the time of any previous bankruptcy, or who has been voluntarily released therefrom by his creditors, shall be entitled to a discharge in the same manner and with the same effect as if he had not previously been bankrupt. *Second bankruptcy ; Discharge.*

163. *Second Bankruptcy.*— A party who has contracted new debts since his first bankruptcy may file a second petition, although not yet discharged under the first. *Semble*, that the creditors under the first petition are not affected by the second. *Re Drisco*, 14 N. B. R. 551; s. C., 13 N. B. R. 112.

IBID. § 33; R. S. § 5117.—No debt created by the fraud or embezzlement of the bankrupt, or by his defalcation as a public officer, or while acting in any fiduciary character, shall be discharged by proceedings in bankruptcy; but the debt may be proved, and the dividend thereon shall be a payment on account of such debt. *Certain debts not released.*

164. *Fiduciary Debts—Conversion—Fraud.*—If goods were consigned to the bankrupt to sell on commission and he failed to account for the proceeds, this is a fiduciary debt and will not be released by a discharge. Meador v. Sharpe, 14 N. B. R. 492; s. C., 54 Geo. 125; Jones v. Russell, 44 Geo. 460; Treadwell v. Holloway, 12 N. B. R. 61; s. C., 46 Cal. 547. *Contra*, Woolsey v. Cade, 15 N. B. R. 238; s. C., 4 Cent. L. J. 202; Owsley v. Cobin, 15 N. B. R. 489. A conversion by an attorney of money belonging to his client is a debt created while acting in a fiduciary capacity. Flanagan v. Pearson, 14 N. B. R. 37. The claim is *provable* but not *discharged*, and the claimant may sue on it after the question of discharge is determined. Stokes v. Mason, 12 N. B. R. 498; s. C., 10 R. I. 261. A conditional vendor does not lose his claim for a conversion of the property by proving his debt, nor is such claim barred by a discharge. Johnson v. Worden, 13 N. B. R. 335; s. C., 47 Vt. 457. A judgment obtained in an action the gravamen of which was fraud, is not released by a discharge. Warner v. Cronkhite, 13 N. B. R. 52; s. C., 6 Biss. 453, and cases cited. The word "*debt*" used in the bankrupt act is synonymous with *claim*. Stokes v. Mason, 12 N. B. R. 498; s. C., 10 R. I. 261.

IBID.; R. S. § 5118.—No discharge shall release, discharge, or affect any person liable for the same debt for or with the bankrupt, either as partner, joint-contractor, indorser, surety, or otherwise. *Liability of other persons not released.*

§ 5119.]   Effect of Discharge and how Pleaded, etc.   [Notes 165-169.

IBID. § 34; R. S. § 5119.—A discharge in bankruptcy duly granted shall, subject to the limitations imposed by the two preceding sections, release the bankrupt from all debts, claims, liabilities, and demands which were or might have been proved against his estate in bankruptcy. It may be pleaded by a simple averment that on the day of its date such discharge was granted to the bankrupt, setting a full copy of the same forth in its terms as a full and complete bar to all suits brought on any such debts, claims, liabilities, or demands. The certificate shall be conclusive evidence in favor of such bankrupt of the fact and the regularity of such discharge.

Effect of discharge: How pleaded; Certificate evidence.

165. *Application for Discharge.*—Section 5109 governs notices of application for discharge, and not this section. Pattison v. Wilbur, 12 N. B. R. 193.

166. *What Debts Discharged*—(1.) *Debts Omitted from Schedule.*—A debt is barred though omitted from the schedule, if with no fraudulent intention on the part of the bankrupt, and although the creditor has received no notice of the pendency of the proceedings. Lamb v. Brown, 12 N. B. R. 522; Platt v. Parker, 13 N. B. R. 14; Payne v. Able, 4 N. B. R. 220; Stevens v. Bank, 101 Mass. 109; Thurman v. Andrews, 13 N. B. R. 157. Or of the application for a discharge. Lamb v. Brown, *supra*; Williams v. Butcher, 12 N. B. R. 143; Pattison v. Wilbur, 12 N. B. R. 193; s. c., 10 R. I. 448; Thurman v. Andrews, *supra*. If the omission was fraudulent, the proper course is to have the discharge set aside. Thurman v. Andrews, *supra;* Lamb v. Brown, *supra;* Humble v. Carson, 6 N. B. R. 84.

(2.) *Security Debts.*—The security on an appeal bond is discharged where the principal has been discharged in bankruptcy subsequent to the appeal. Odell v. Wootten, 4 N. B. R. 183; s. c. 38 Ga. 224. *Contra*, Merritt v. Glidden, 39 Cal. 559; Knapp v. Anderson, 15 N. B. R. 316. A promise to pay a debt made after adjudication need not be in writing, and the amount of the debt may be recovered. Henley v. Lanier, 15 N. B. R. 260, Fraley v. Kelly, 67 N. C. 78. Where a holder of an indorsed note consents to the discharge in bankruptcy of the maker, he discharges the indorser, although the claim against the indorser is merged in a judgment. *Re* McDonald, 14 N. B. R. 477.

167. *What Debts not Discharged.*—(1.) *Debts due the United States*—United States v. Rob Roy, 13 N. B. R. 35; United States v. Herron, 20 Wall. 251.

(2.) *Security Debts.*—A discharge does not release a bankrupt from his liability as a surety on an injunction bond, when the injunction proceedings are not determined until after the granting thereof. Eastman v. Hibbard, 13 N. B. R. 3 0.

(3.) *Lien Debts.*—A judgment creditor may pursue realty upon which he has lien, and which was sold by the debtor before proceedings in bankruptcy were commenced. Winship v. Phillips, 14 N. B. R. 50; s. c., 52 Ga. 593; Phillips v. Bowdoin, 14 N. B. R. 43; s. c., 52 Ga. 545. But see Blum v. Ellis, 13 N. B. R. 345; s. c., 73 N. C. 293.

168. *Plea of Discharge.*—A discharge should be pleaded; it can not be set up after judgment as a reason why the judgment should not be enforced. Goodrich v. Hunton, 2 Woods, 137. A plea of discharge which does not set out a copy of the discharge and aver what court adjudged the defendant to be a bankrupt, is bad. Stoll v. Wilson, 14 N. B. R. 571; s. c., 38 N. J. (Law) 198. A plea of discharge may be amended. Ibid. It is not sufficient for a plea in bar to aver that since the commencement of suit the defendant has been adjudged bankrupt and plaintiff has proven his claim. Brandon Mfg. Co. v. Frazer, 13 N. B. R. 362; s. c., 47 Vt. 88. *Contra*, Bennet v. Goldthaite, 109 Mass. 494.

169. *Maine.*—A petition for review will be granted a bankrupt against whom a judgment has been obtained by default, on account of the mistake of his counsel, in order that he may plead his discharge. Shurtleff v. Thompson, 12 N. B. R. 524; s. c., 63 Me. 118.

§ 5120.] Proceedings to Annul Discharge. [Notes 170-171a.

IBID.; R. S. § 5120.—Any creditor of a bankrupt, whose debt was proved or provable against the estate in bankruptcy, who desires to contest the validity of the discharge on the ground that it was fraudulently obtained, may, at any time within two years after the date thereof, apply to the court which granted it to annul the same. The application shall be in writing, and shall specify which, in particular, of the several acts mentioned in section 5110, it is intended to prove against the bankrupt, and set forth the grounds of avoidance; and no evidence shall be admitted as to any other of such acts; but the application shall be subject to amendment at the discretion of the court. The court shall cause reasonable notice of the application to be given to the bankrupt, and order him to appear and answer the same, within such time as to the court shall seem proper. If, upon the hearing of the parties, the court finds that the fraudulent acts, or any of them, set forth by the creditor against the bankrupt, are proved, and that the creditor had no knowledge of the same until after the granting of the discharge, judgment shall be given in favor of the creditor, and the discharge of the bankrupt shall be annulled. But if the court finds that the fraudulent acts and all of them so set forth are not proved, or that they were known to the creditor before the granting of the discharge, judgment shall be rendered in favor of the bankrupt, and the validity of his discharge shall not be affected by the proceedings. *Application to annul discharge. Proceedings thereunder.*

170. *This Remedy Exclusive.*—This remedy is exclusive of any other mode of impeaching the validity of a discharge, either in the federal or state courts. Black v. Blazo, 13 N. B. R. 195; s. c., 117 Mass. 17; May v. Howe, 4 N. B. R. 677; s. c., 108 Mass. 502; Burper v. Sparhawk, 4 N. B. R. 685; s. c., 108 Mass. 111; Smith v. Ramsey, 27 Ohio St. Com. 339; Bay v. Lapham, 27 Ohio St. Com. 452; Seymour v. Street, 5 Neb. 85.

171. *"Within Two Years."*—Suit must be brought within two years, even though the ground for setting aside the discharge did not become known for a long period after that time. Pickett v. McGavick, 14 N. B. R. 236; Alton v. Robinett, 9 N. B. R. 74; Way v. Howe, *supra. Contra,* Perkins v. Gay, 3 N. B. R. 772.

171a. *Newly discovered evidence.*—To set aside a discharge, a creditor can not rely upon testimony known to him at the time the discharge was granted. *Re* Marionneaux, 13 N. B. R. 222.

[§ 5121.] Proceedings Peculiar to Partnerships and Corporations.

CHAPTER SIX.

PROCEEDINGS PECULIAR TO PARTNERSHIPS AND CORPORATIONS.

SECTION
5121. Bankruptcy of Partnerships; Joint and Separate Estate to be Taken: Assignee to keep Accounts separate: Estate, how Distributed: Discharge: Jurisdiction where Partners reside in Different Districts.
   NOTE 172.—In General.
   173.—In Voluntary Cases.
   174.—In Involuntary Cases.
   175.—Distribution.
   176.—Exemption from Partnership Debts.
   177.—Discharge.
   178.—In Case of Several Petitions.

SECTION
5122. Bankruptcy of Corporations and Joint Stock Companies.
   NOTE 179.—Adjudication.
   180.—Not discharged.
   181.—Railroad Companies.
   182.—Vote of Stockholders necessary.
   183.—Number and Value of Creditors.
5123. Authority of State Courts in Proceedings against Corporations, etc.
5123a. Union Pacific Railroad Company.

ORIGINAL ACT OF 1867, § 36; R. S. § 5121.—Where two or more persons who are partners in trade are adjudged bankrupt, either on the petition of such partners or of any one of them, or on the petition of any creditor of the partners, a warrant shall issue, in the manner provided by this title, upon which all the joint stock and property of the copartnership, and also all the separate estate of each of the partners, shall be taken, excepting such parts thereof as are hereinbefore excepted. All the creditors of the company, and the separate creditors of each partner, may prove their respective debts. The assignee shall be chosen by the creditors of the company. He shall keep separate accounts of the joint stock or property of the copartnership and of the separate estate of each member thereof; and after deducting out of the whole amount received by the assignee the whole of the expenses and disbursements, the net proceeds of the joint stock shall be appropriated to pay the creditors of the copartnership,

BANKRUPTCY OF PARTNERSHIP: Joint and separate estate to be taken.

Assignee to keep account separate.

§ 5121.]   Bankruptcy of Partnerships—Proceedings—Distribution. [Notes 172-175.

and the net proceeds of the separate estate of each partner shall be appropriated to pay his separate creditors. If there is any balance of the separate estate of any partner, after the payment of his separate debts, such balance shall be added to the joint stock for the payment of the joint creditors; and if there is any balance of the joint stock after payment of the joint debts, such balance shall be appropriated to and divided among the separate estates of the several partners according to their respective right and interest therein, and as it would have been if the partnership had been dissolved without any bankruptcy; and the sum so appropriated to the separate estate of each partner shall be applied to the payment of his separate debts. The certificate of discharge shall be granted or refused to each partner as the same would or ought to be if the proceedings had been against him alone. In all other respects the proceedings against partners shall be conducted in the like manner as if they had been commenced and prosecuted against one person alone. If such copartners reside in different districts, that court in which the petition is first filed shall retain exclusive jurisdiction over the case.

Estate: How Distributed.

Discharge.

Jurisdiction where partners reside in different districts.

172. *In General.*—This section contemplates that persons who are copartners may be adjudicated bankrupts on three kinds of petitions: 1. The petition of all the copartners; 2. The petition of one of the co-partners; 3. The petition of creditors of the copartners. *Re* Penn, 5 N. B. R. 30. See general order XVIII.

173. *In Voluntary Cases.*—An adjudication in bankruptcy can not be made on one petition filed on behalf of two distinct firms, unless each partner is partner of both firms. *Re* Wallace, 12 N. B. R. 191.

174. *In Involuntary Cases.*—In such a petition all the members of the firm must be proceeded against. *Re* Pitt, 14 N. B. R. 59. A defect of parties can not be amended. Ibid. See *Re* Stevens, 5 N. B. R. 112. After the dissolution of a co-partnership, one partner can not petition for adjudication of the firm, unless the insolvency of the retiring partner is clearly shown. *Re* Bennett, 12 N. B. R. 181. Bankruptcy of one partner *ipso facto* dissolves the co-partnership. Wilkins v. Davis, 15 N. B. R. 60. As to bankruptcy of a firm composed of general and special partners, see Wilkins v. Davis, *supra*. An order to show cause, upon a petition in bankruptcy against a partnership, may be refused, where it appears on the face of the petition that the estate of the co-partnership is then in actual course of administration, by the probate court, under provisions of the state statute in respect to winding up partnership estates where one of the partners is deceased. *Re* Sectional Dock Co., 3 Dill. 83.

175. *Distribution.*—Firm creditors can not share in the individual estate until the individual creditors are paid in full, *where there are firm assets*. *Re* Smith, 13 N. B. R. 500; *Re* Morse, 13 N. B. R. 376; *Re* McEwen, 12 N. B. R. 11; s. c., 6 Biss. 294; *Re* McLean, 15 N. B. R. 333. If the firm assets are expended in the payment of costs, then the firm and individual creditors are to be paid *pari passu* out of the separate estate of each partner. *Re* McEwen, *supra;* *Re* Knight, 8 N. B. R. 436. Where there are firm and individual assets, each estate must pay its proportion of the expense of administration of the estate. *Re* Smith, *supra.* If partners file separate petitions, firm creditors are postponed to separate creditors, whether there are joint assets or not. *Re* Morse, *supra.* If a debtor is a member of two firms, one of which becomes bankrupt, the creditors of the firm which are not bankrupt are only entitled to

§ 5122.] Bankruptcy of Corporations, etc. [Notes 175-178.

dividends out of the surplus of the debtor's individual assets with the creditor of the other firm. *Re* Dunkerson, 12 N. B. R. 391. The rule as to distribution of the assets of a firm, where one partner only is bankrupt, does not apply. *Re* Pease, 13 N. B. R. 168. Where partners dissolve and transfer all their separate estate to one of the firm who assumes all the debts, and the firm is adjudged bankrupt, firm creditors and individual creditors share *pari passu* in the estate. *Re* Collier, 12 N. B. R. 266. The rule which obtains in England requiring creditors, both of the joint and separate estate in bankruptcy, to elect which fund they will pursue, does not obtain here. *Re* Foot, 12 N. B. R. 337. Where firm creditors have received payment, of their claims after bankruptcy out of the individual estate of one of the firm which they held as security, the individual creditors of such partner are entitled to share in the dividends of the partnership assets on a sum equal to that received by the joint creditors from the individual estate. Ibid.

176. *Exemption from Partnership Debts.*—The rights of the wives of a bankrupt firm in the real estate vested in the assignee are simply those of inchoate dower interests. Hiscock v. Jaycox, 12 N. B. R. 507. As to real estate which is partnership assets, no dower interest attaches until all the partnership accounts and debts have been settled. Ibid. Individual exemptions are not allowed co-partners out of the partnership effects. See § 5045, *ante*.

177. *Discharge.*—Where there are firm debts and assets, the firm must be declared bankrupt before any member of it can be discharged. This applies only to actually existing co-partnerships, or where there are assets belonging to the firm, and not to co-partnerships terminated heretofore by bankruptcy, insolvency, assignment, or otherwise. *Re* Winkens, 2 N. B. R. 349. See *Re* Abbe, 2 N. B. R. 75; *Re* Stevens, 5 N. B. R. 112; *Re* Leland, 5 N. B. R. 232; Hudgius v. Lane, 11 N. B. R. 462. *Contra*, Wilkins v. Davis, 15 N. B. R. 60, where it is held that if one member of a firm becomes bankrupt and obtains his discharge, he is released from liability on his joint as well as separate debts. See also Compton v. Conklin, 15 N. B. R. 417.

178. *In case of several petitions*, the petition first filed takes precedence. *Re* Leland, 5 N. B. R. 222; *Re* Penn, 5 N. B. R. 30.

IBID. § 37; R. S. § 5122.—The provisions of this title shall apply to all moneyed business or commercial corporations and joint stock companies, and upon the petition of any officer of any such corporation or company, duly authorized by a vote of a majority of the corporators at any legal meeting called for the purpose, or upon the petition of any creditor of such corporation or company, made and presented in the manner provided in respect to debtors, the like proceedings shall be had and taken as are provided in the case of debtors. All the provisions of this title which apply to the debtor, or set forth his duties in regard to furnishing schedules and inventories, executing papers, submitting to examinations, disclosing, making over, secreting, concealing, conveying, assigning, or paying away his money or property, shall in like manner, and with like force, effect, and penalties, apply to each and every officer of such corporation or company in relation to the same matters concerning the corporations or company, and the money and property thereof. All payments, conveyances, and assignments declared fraudulent and void by this title when made by a debtor, shall in like manner, and to the like extent, and with like remedies, be fraud-

Of Corporations and Joint-Stock Companies: Proceedings.

Provisions of this title apply to officers of.

Fraudulent preferences by.

ulent and void when made by a corporation or company. Whenever any corporation by proceedings under this title is declared bankrupt, all its property and assets shall be distributed to the creditors of such corporations in the manner provided in this title in respect to natural persons. But no allowance or discharge shall be granted to any corporation or joint-stock company, or to any person or officer or member thereof.

Distribution of assets: No allowance or discharge.

179. *The adjudication* of a corporation is in the nature of a decree *in rem.* New Lamp Co. v. Ausonia Co., 13 N. B. R. 385; s. c., 91 U. S. 656.

180. *Not Discharged.*—A corporation is not given a discharge. Re Leavenworth Sav. Bank, 14 N. B. R. 82. A creditor who has proved his claim against a bankrupt corporation and received a dividend thereon, is not precluded from instituting suit and recovering a judgment for the balance. New Lamp Co. v. Ausonia Co., *supra.* It would seem that a fraudulent representation made to a purchaser of stock by the officers of a corporation, is no defense to an action brought by the assignee for balance due on stock. Farrar v. Walker, 13 N. B R. 82; Michener v. Payson, 13 N. B. R. 49.

181. *Railroad Companies* amenable to the act. Rankin v. Florida R. R. Co., 1 N. B. R. 647; Adams v. Boston R. R. Co., 4 N. B. R. 314; Ala. R. R. Co. v. Jones, 5 N. B. R. 97; Sweatt v. Boston R. R., 5 N. B. R. 234; Re California R. R. 3 Sawy. 240. But not the Union Pacific Railroad. *Infra*, 5123a.

182. *Vote of Stockholders.*—Vote of trustees or directors not sufficient. Re Bryan Mining Co., 4 N. B. R. 144; s. c., 4 N. B. R. 394. Petition must show that corporation is a "moneyed," etc., one. Re Oregon Pub. Co., 14 N. B. R. 405.

183. *Number and Value of Creditors.*—The amendments of 1874, requiring a certain proportion of creditors to join in the petition to have a person adjudged bankrupt, applies to corporations. Re Detroit Car Works, 14 N. B. R. 243; Re Leavenworth Savings Bank, 14 N. B. R. 82; s. c., 14 N. B. R. 92; s. c., 3 Cent. L. J. 207; Re Oregon Publishing Co., 14 N. B. R. 405; overruling s. c., 13 N. B. R. 200.

AMENDATORY ACT OF FEB. 13, 1873; R. S. § 5123.—Whenever a corporation created by the laws of any State, whose business is carried on wholly within the State creating the same, and also any insurance company so created, whether all its business shall be carried on in such State or not, has had proceedings duly commenced against such corporation or company before the courts of such State for the purpose of winding up the affairs of such corporation or company and dividing its assets ratably among its creditors and lawfully among those entitled thereto prior to proceedings having been commenced against such corporation or company under the bankrupt laws of the United States, any order made, or that shall be made, by such court agreeably to the State law for the ratable distribution or payment of any dividend of assets to the creditors of such corporation or company while such State court shall remain actually or constructively in possession or control of the assets of such corporation or company shall be deemed valid notwithstanding proceedings in bankruptcy may have been commenced and be pending against such corporation or company.[1]

Authority of State courts in proceedings against corporations, etc.

(1) Construed in Re National Life Ins. Co., 6 Biss. 35.

§ 5123a.] Additional Amendment—Union Pacific Railroad.

§ 5123a. ADDITIONAL AMENDMENT. — The laws of the United States providing for proceedings in bankruptcy shall not be held to apply to said corporation.[1] [The Union Pacific Railroad Company.].

Union Pacific Railroad Company.

(1) This clause is found in § 4 of the Legislative, Executive and Judicial Appropriation Act of 1873, ch. 226, 17 Stat. 509.

§ 5124.] Fees and Costs. [Note 184.

CHAPTER SEVEN.

FEES AND COSTS.

SECTION
5124. Fees of Register; Entitled to a Priority.
    NOTE 184.—This section construed.
5125. Traveling and Incidental Expenses.
5126. Marshal's Fees.
5127. Justices of Supreme Court may change Tariff of Fees.
5127a. Fees and Allowances to be reduced one-half, and to be revised by Justices of Supreme Court; Register, Clerk, etc., not to be of Counsel nor Interested.
5127b. Reports of Officers; of Marshal.
5127c. Reports of Register.
5127d. Reports of Assignee.
5127e. Reports of Clerk.
5127f. Penalties under these Sections.

ORIGINAL ACT OF 1867, § 47; R. S. § 5124.—In each case there shall be allowed and paid, in addition to the fees of the clerk of the court as now established by law, or as may be established by general order for fees in bankruptcy, the following fees, which shall be applied to paying for the services of the registers: 1 For issuing every warant, two dollars; 2. For each day in which a meeting is held, three dollars; 3. For each order for a dividend, three dollars; 4. For every order substituting an arrangement by trust deed for bankruptcy, two dollars; 5. For every bond with sureties, two dollars; 6. For every application for any meeting in any matter under this act, one dollar; 7. For every day's service while actually employed under a special order of the court, a sum not exceeding five dollars, to be allowed by the court; 8. For taking depositions, the fees now allowed by law; 9. For every discharge when there is no opposition, two dollars. Such fees shall have priority of payment over all other claims out of the estate, and, before a warrant issues, the petitioner shall deposit with the clerk of the court fifty dollars as security for the payment thereof; and if there are not sufficient assets for the payment of the fees, the person upon whose petition the warrant is issued shall pay the same, and the court may issue an execution against him to compel payment to the register. *Fees of Registers. To have priority.*

184. *Construed.*—For a discussion of this, see *Re* Dean, 1 N. B. R. 249; *Re* Sherwood, 1 N. B. R. 344; *Re* Burnell, 14 N. B. R. 498.

IBID. § 5; R. S. § 5125.—The traveling and incidental expenses of the register, and of any clerk or other officer attending him, shall be settled by the court in accordance with the rules prescribed by the justices of the supreme court, and paid out of the assets of the estate in respect of which such register has acted; or if there are no such assets, or if the assets are insufficient, such expenses shall form a part of the costs in the case in which the register acts, to be apportioned by the judge.[1]

Traveling and incidental expenses.

IBID. § 47; R. S. § 5126.—Before any dividend is ordered, the assignee shall pay out of the estate to the messenger the following fees, and no more: 1. For service of warrant, two dollars; 2. For all necessary travel, at the rate of five cents a mile each way; 3. For each written note to creditor named in the schedule, ten cents; 4. For custody of property, publication of notices, and other services, his actual and necessary expenses upon returning the same in specific items, and making oath that they have been actually incurred and paid by him, and are just and reasonable, the same to be taxed or adjusted by the court, and the oath of the messenger shall not be conclusive as to the necessity of such expenses. For cause shown, and upon hearing thereon, such further allowance may be made as the court, in its discretion, may determine.[2]

Marshal's Fees.

IBID. R. S. § 5127.—The enumeration of the foregoing fees shall not prevent the justices of the supreme court from prescribing a tariff of fees for all other services of the officers of courts of bankruptcy, or from reducing the fees prescribed in the three preceding sections, in classes of cases to be named in their general orders.

Justices of Supreme Court may change tariff of fees.

§ 5127a. AMENDMENT OF 1874 TO PRECEDING.—That from and after the passage of this act the fees, commissions, charges and allowances, excepting actual and necessary disbursements of, and to be made by the officers, agents, marshals, messengers, assignees, and registers in cases of bankruptcy, shall be reduced to one-half of the fees, commissions, charges, and allowances heretofore provided for or made in like cases: *Provided,* That the preceding provision shall be and remain in force until the justices of the Supreme Court of the United States shall make and promulgate new rules and regulations in respect to the matters aforesaid, under the powers conferred upon them by sections ten and forty-seven of said act, and no longer, which duties they shall perform as soon as may be. And said justices shall have power under said sections, by general regulations, to simplify and, so far as in their judgment will conduce to the benefit of creditors, to consolidate the duties of the register, assignee,

Fees, etc., to be reduced one-half.

And revised by Judges of Supreme Court.

---

(1) Re Dean, 1 N. B. R. 249.
(2) Re Talbot, 2 N. B. R. 280.

§§ 5127a–5127c.]   Reports of Officers.

marshal, and clerk, and to reduce fees, costs, and charges, to the end that prolixity, delay, and unnecessary expense may be avoided. And no register or clerk of court, or any partner or clerk of such register or clerk of court, or any person having any interest with either in any fees or emoluments in bankruptcy, or with whom such register or clerk of court shall have any interest in respect to any matter in bankruptcy, shall be of counsel, solicitor, or attorney, either in or out of court, in any suit or matter pending in bankruptcy in either the circuit or district court of his district, or in an appeal therefrom. Nor shall they, or either of them, be executor, administrator, guardian, commissioner, appraiser, divider, or assignee of or upon any estate within the jurisdiction of either of said courts of bankruptcy; nor be interested, directly or indirectly, in the fees or emoluments arising from either of said trusts. And the words "except such as are established by this act or by law," in section ten of said act, are hereby repealed.[1]

Register, clerk, etc., not to be of counsel or trustee or interested.

§ 5127b. SUPPLEMENTAL PROVISION OF 1874.—That it shall be the duty of the marshal of each district, in the month of July of each year, to report to the clerk of the district court of such district, in a tabular form, to be prescribed by the justices of the Supreme Court of the United States, as well as such other or further information as may be required by said justices: 1, the number of cases in bankruptcy in which the warrant prescribed in section eleven of said act has come to his hands during the year ending June 30th, preceding; 2, how many such warrants were returned, with the fees, costs, expenses, and emoluments thereof, respectively and separately; 3, the total amount of all other fees, costs, expenses and emoluments, respectively and separately, earned or received by him during such year from or in respect of any matter in bankruptcy; 4, a summarized statement of such fees, costs, and emoluments, exclusive of actual disbursements in bankruptcy, received or earned for such year; 5. a summarized statement of all actual disbursements in such cases for such year.[2]

Reports of officers: Of marshal.

IBID. § 5127c.—And in like manner, every register shall, in the same month and for the same year, make a report to such clerk of: 1, the number of voluntary cases in bankruptcy coming before him during said year; 2, the amount of assets and liabilities, as nearly as may be, of the bankrupts; 3, the amount and rate per centum of all dividends declared; 4, the disposition of all such cases; 5, the number of compulsory cases in bankruptcy coming before him in the same way; 6, the amount of assets and liabilities, as nearly as may be, of such bankrupt; 7, the disposition of all such cases; 8, the amounts and rate per centum of all dividends declared in such cases; 9, the total

Of register.

---

(1) Act of June 22, 1874, § 18.
(2) Act of June 22, 1874, § 19

§§ 5127c–5127f.] Reports of Officers—Penalties under these Sections.

amount of fees, charges, costs, and emoluments of every sort, received or earned by such register during said year in each class of cases above stated.[1]

§ 5127d. IBID.—And in like manner, every assignee shall, during said
<small>Of assignee.</small> month, make like return to such clerk of: 1, the number of voluntary and compulsory cases, respectively and separately, in his charge during said year; 2, the amount of assets and liabilities therein, respectively and separately; 3, the total receipts and disbursements therein, respectively and separately; 4, the amount of dividends paid or declared, and the rate per centum thereof, in each class, respectively and separately; 5, the total amount of all his fees, charges, and emoluments, of every kind therein, earned or received; 6, the total amount of expenses incurred by him for legal proceedings and counsel fees; 7, the disposition of the cases respectively; 8, a summarized statement of both classes as aforesaid.[2]

§ 5127e. IBID.—And in like manner, the clerk of said court, in the
<small>Of Clerk.</small> month of August in each year, shall make up a statement for such year, ending June 30th, of: 1, all cases in bankruptcy pending at the beginning of the said year; 2, all of such cases disposed of; 3, all dividends declared therein; 4, the number of reports made from each assignee therein; 5, the disposition of all such cases; 6, the number of assignee's accounts filed and settled; 7, whether any marshal, register, or assignee has failed to make and file with such clerk the reports by this act required, and, if any have failed to make such reports, their respective names and residences. And such clerk shall report in respect of all cases begun during said year. And he shall make a classified statement, in tabular form, of all his fees, charges, costs, and emoluments, respectively, earned or accrued during said year, giving each head under which the same accrued, and also the sum of all moneys paid into and disbursed out of court in bankruptcy, and the balance in hand or on deposit. And all the statements and reports herein required shall be under oath, and signed by the persons respectively making the same. And said clerk shall, in said month of August, transmit every such statement and report so filed with him, together with his own statement and report aforesaid, to the attorney-general of the United States.[3]

§ 5127f. IBID.—Any person who shall violate the provisions of this
<small>Penalties under these sections.</small> section shall, on motion made, under the direction of the attorney-general, be by the district court dismissed from his office, and shall be deemed guilty of a misdemeanor, and on conviction thereof, be punished by a fine of not more than five hundred dollars, or by imprisonment not exceeding one year.[4]

(1) Act of June 22, 1874, § 19.
(2) Act of July 22, 1874, § 19.
(3) Act of June 22, 1874, § 19.
(4) Act of June 22, 1874, § 19.

§ 5128.] Prohibited and Fraudulent Transfers.

CHAPTER EIGHT.

PROHIBITED AND FRAUDULENT TRANSFERS.

SECTION
5128. *As Amended.*—Preferences by Insolvent.
NOTE 185.—Leading Cases prior to Amendments of 1874.
186.—Amendments of 1874 retroactive.
187.—What are not Fraudulent Preferences.
188.—What are Fraudulent Preferences.
189.—Intent; Burden of Proof; Evidence.
190.—General Assignments.
191.—Who liable.
192.—Jurisdiction of U. S. Circuit Court hereunder.
193.—Jurisdiction of State Courts.
194.—Allegations and Proofs.
195.—Miscellaneous Rulings.
5129. *As Amended.*—Fraudulent Transfers of Property.
5129a. Changes Periods of preceding

SECTION
Sections to two and three Months.
NOTE 196.—Not retroactive.
5129b. Verbal changes in § 35 of Original Act.
NOTE 197.—Security Taken in Good Faith.
5130. Presumptive Evidence of Fraud.
NOTE 198.—The above Section Construed.
5131. Fraudulent Agreements.
5132. Penalties against Bankrupts for secreting Property, mutilating Books, Frauds, etc.
NOTE 199.—Constitutionality of above Section.
200.—Proceeding by Information.
201.—As to Clause 6.
202.—As to Clause 9.
203.—As to Clause 10.
204.—Bankrupts not Competent Witnesses hereunder.
205.—Conspiracy.
5132a. General Repealing Clause.
NOTE 206.—Revised Statutes, how affected by Amendments of 1874.

ORIGINAL ACT OF 1867, §§ 35, 39; R. S. § 5128, AS AMENDED.—If any person, being insolvent, or in contemplation of insolvency, within *four*[1] months before the filing of the petition by or against him, with a view to give a preference to any creditor or person having a claim against him, or who is under any liability for him, procures or suffers any part of his property to be attached, sequestered, or seized on execution, or makes any payment, pledge, assignment, transfer, or conveyance of any part of his property, either directly or indirectly, absolutely or conditionally, the person re-

<small>Preferences by insolvent.</small>

(1) In compulsory cases the period is two months. Act of June 22, 1874, § 11.

84   BANKRUPT LAW.

§ 5128.]   Fraudulent Preferences.   [Notes 185-187-

ceiving such payment, pledge, assignment, transfer, or conveyance, or to be benefited thereby, or by such attachment, having reasonable cause to believe such person is insolvent, and [knowing][1] that such attachment, [sequestration, seizure,][1] payment, pledge, assignment, or conveyance is made in fraud of the provisions of this title, the same shall be void, and the assignee may recover the property, or the value of it, from the person so receiving it, or so to be benefited.

185. *The Leading Case* on the law respecting preferences before the passage of the amendments of June 22, 1874, is Wilson v. City Bank, 17 Wall. 473, which substantially overruled Buchanan v. Smith, 16 Wall. 277. See also Bartholow v. Bean. 18 Wall. 635; s. c., 1 Cent. L. J. 166; *Re* Scull, 10 N. B. R. 153; s. c., 10 Alb. L. J. 214.

186. *Amendments of* June 22, 1874, *Retroactive.*—The following authorities hold that the amendments do not apply to preferences and conveyances made prior to December 1, 1873: Tinker v. Vandyke, 11 N. B. R. 308; s. c., 14 N. B. R. 112; Brook v* McCracken, 10 N. B. R. 461; s. c., 8 P. L. R. 102; s. c., 7 Ch. L. N. 10; Hamlin v. Pettibone, 10 N. B. R. 172; s. c., 1 Cent. L. J. 404; s. c., 6 Biss. 167; *Re* Montgomery, 12 N. B. R. 321; Barnewell v. Jones, 14 N. B. R. 278; Bradbury v. Galloway, 12 N. B. R. 299; s. c., 3 Sawy. 346; Oxford Iron Co. v. Slafter, 14 N. B. R. 380; Warner v. Garber, 15 N. B. R. 409. The same authorities hold that the amendments do not affect suits brought prior to the passage of the amendatory act. See also Slafter v. Sugar Co., 13 N. B. R. 520. The following authorities hold that the amendments affect all suits brought after the passage of the amendments, though the preferences were made prior thereto. Singer v. Sloan, 12 N. B. R. 208; s. c., 3 Dill. 110; Booth v. Brooks, 12 N. B. R. 398. This last mentioned case goes still farther and decides that it affects all conveyances, where the question of validity or invalidity had not been passed upon at the time of the passage of the amendments.

187. *What are not Fraudulent Conveyances and Preferences.*—This section and the succeeding one will be treated together. As the law now stands, a failing debtor may undoubtedly suffer a friendly creditor to obtain a preference by means of legal process; he may resign himself to the purpose of the creditor with perfect tranquility and enjoy heartful pleasure in the experience. More than this, the wisdom of the law does not permit, and if, by any active participation with the creditor, he facilitates the seizure of his property, the law is transgressed and the preference is illegal. *Re* Baker, 14 N. B. R. 433. A mortgage given more than four months before the petition in bankruptcy was filed, is valid as against the assignee in bankruptcy, although the mortgagee knew the mortgagor was insolvent, and although the mortgage was made with the intent to prefer, and although the mortgage was not placed on record until a month before bankruptcy proceedings were begun. *Re* Barman, 14 N. B. R. 125; National Bank v. Conway, 14 N. B. R. 175, 513; Sawyer v. Turpin, 13 N. B. R. 271; s. c., 91 U. S. 114. If it is withheld from record, in order to conceal it from creditors, it takes effect from date of record. Exchange Bank v. Harrie, 14 N. B. R. 512; s. c., 3 Cent. L. J. 768. See also Gibson v. Warden, 14 Wall. 214; *Re* Wynne, 4 N. B. R. 23; Crajon v. Carmichael, 11 N. B. R. 511; s. c., 2 Dill. 519. For effect of the bankrupt law on chattel mortgages, see the recent work of Herman on Chattel Mortgages, p. 267. Where, by the terms of a contract, a present adequate consideration is intended to be paid for a present delivery and transfer of property, and after the consideration is paid the other fails to perform his part before his unexpected insolvency, which fact is communicated to the other party, it is no preference for the insolvent party to perform his part of the contract afterwards. Sprhawk v. Richards, 12 N. B. R. 74. A consent on the part of a judgment debtor to a revival of a judgment so as to continue the lien thereof, does not of itself charge the creditor with a reasonable

---

(1) So amended by Act of June 22, 1874, § 11. For the full section of the Act of 1874, by which the above amendments were interpolated, see post, § 5129b.

§ 5128.]   Fraudulent Preferences.   [Notes 187–189.

cause to believe the debtor insolvent. Kemmerer v. Tool, 12 N. B. R. 334; s. c., 78 Penn. St. 147. An exchange of valid securities of equal value, within four months of the filing of the petition in bankruptcy, is not a fraudulent preference, even where it is known by both debtor and creditor that the former is insolvent. Sawyer v. Turpin, 13 N. B. R. 271; s. c., 91 U. S. 114, and many cases there cited. Where a claim which has been received by an attorney through a collecting agency is collected by him in fraud of the bankrupt act, the claimant is not charged with the knowledge which the attorney had when collecting the debt, and can not be held liable. In this case, the money collected was not shown to have come into the hands of the creditor who was sued for an alleged preference, and the court intimates that that fact is material to the conclusion reached. Hoover v. Wise, 14 N. B. R. 264; s. c., 91 U. S. 308; s. c., 3 Cent. L. J. 276. An agreement made that certain and specific property shall be conveyed for advances as security, the conveyance if made within a reasonable time after the advances, will be considered as a present consideration for the conveyance, and it will be sustained. Galtman v. Honea, 12 N. B. R. 493. A payment made by an insolvent for legal services to have himself adjudicated a bankrupt is valid. Re Thompson, 13 N. B. R. 300. Where, under the provisions of the state laws, the mortgage given to a creditor is valid as against the creditors of the mortgagor, or the mortgagor himself, the bankrupt act does not give the assignee authority to set it aside, the ground of the action being that it was not filed. Re Collins, 12 N. B. R. 379. A mortgage of personal property with right of mortgagor to dispose of it is not invalid. Brett v. Carter, 14 N. B. R. 301; Barron v. Morris, 14 N. B. R. 371. And when made in good faith to secure advances, is valid to the extent of the advances made Marvin v. Chambers, 13 N. B. R. 77. Where a voluntary conveyance was made and all the debts of the grantor in existence at the time have been paid, it can not be impeached by the grantor's assignee. Smith v. Vodges, 13 N. B. R. 433; Barker v. Smith, 12 N. B. R. 474.

188. *What are Fraudulent Preferences.*—To defeat a conveyance as in fraud of the act, it must be shown, (1) that the bankrupt was insolvent or contemplated insolvency or bankruptcy; (2) that the grantee at the time of the conveyance knew, or had reasonable cause to believe, the grantor insolvent; and, (3) that the grantee knew fraud upon the law was intended. The lawmakers certainly intended something by the change, in substituting the word "knowing" for "having reasonable cause to believe;" but this knowledge of the party may be established by circumstantial evidence. Galtman v. Honea, 12 N. B. R. 493; Webb v. Sacks, 15 N. B. R. 168. A transfer of property by an insolvent to another who transfers it to a creditor of the insolvent, is the same in legal effect as if made directly from the debtor to the creditor. Gibson v. Dobie, 14 N. B. R. 156. If a mortgage is made in part to prefer the mortgagee, and in part to secure a present loan made to enable the debtor to prefer another creditor, it is entirely void. Buckman v. Goss, 13 N. B. R. 337. A bankrupt can not prefer a foreign creditor in violation of the provisions of the bankrupt act. A foreign creditor is amenable to our laws. Olcott v. MacLeans, 14 N. B. R. 379. A transfer of property to a factor that it may become subject to his lien, and with the intent thereby to give him a preference, may be set aside. Nudd v. Burrows, 13 N. B. R. 289. A creditor who had no reasonable cause to believe the debtor insolvent at the time of receiving security for his debt, is not liable to the debtor's assignee for the amount received. Rankin v. Nat. Bank, 14 N. B. R. 4. Confession of judgment, followed by an execution and seizure, is an unlawful preference, if made with a view to prefer. Webb v. Sacks, 15 N. B. R. 168. Intent will be presumed until contrary is shown. Ibid. As to the law governing preferences by means of warrants of attorney to confess judgment, see Re Herpich, 15 N. B. R. 426.

189. *Intent—Burden of Proof—Evidence.*—Burden of proof in an action to recover a preference is on the assignee, but the intent of the parties may be inferred from their acts. Parsons v. Topliff, 14 N. B. R. 547. The decision turns on the *intention* of the bankrupt. Little v. Alexander, 12 N. B. R. 134; s. c., 21 Wall. 500. The intent to prefer is essential, and is to be found by the jury. A man is presumed to intend the

§ 5128.]   Fraudulent Preferences—General Assignments.   [Note 189-193.

natural consequences of his acts; but the presumption is only one element of proof to establish actual intent. Rice v. Grafton Mills, 13 N. B. R. 209; s. c., 117 Mass. 220. Where a conspiracy to prefer is established, the declarations of the bankrupt with regard to the preference are admissible against the creditor, though not made in his presence. Nudd v. Burrow, 13 N. B. R. 289. The fact that judgment was obtained, execution issued and levied on the same day, that voluntary bankruptcy proceedings were commenced, but earlier in the day, does not prove collusion. Witt v. Hereth, 13 N. B. R. 106. The nature of transactions like these almost uniformly precludes the production of any but circumstantial evidence. *Re* Baker, 14 N. B. R. 433. Insolvency, within the meaning of the Bankrupt Act, means inability to pay debts in the ordinary course of business. Jackson v. McCulloch, 13 N. B. R. 233.

190. *General Assignments.*—An assignment of all a trader's property, which gives some creditors a preference, if made in contemplation of insolvency, is conclusive evidence of the intent of the debtor to defeat the operation of the Bankrupt Act, and is void. Ibid. An assignment without preference, though not void *ab initio*, is subject to being avoided by the assignee in bankruptcy. Cragin v. Thompson, 12 N. B. R. 81; Spahawk v. Drexel, 12 N. B. R. 450. The trustee and all persons claiming the benefit of such an assignment, are charged with knowledge of the insolvency of the debtor and his intent to evade the operation of the Bankrupt Act. Jackson v. McCulloch, 13 N. B. R. 283. A general assignment is void, though made for the equal benefit of all creditors. Globe Ins. Co. v. Cleveland Ins. Co., 14 N. B. R. 311; Rowe v. Page, 13 N. B. R. 316; s. c., 54 N. H. 190. Held not necessarily so, in *Re* Marter, 12 N. B. R. 185. See § 5021 *ante*, and note 32. Such an assignment is not invalid, if made more than six months (now four) before commencement of proceedings in bankruptcy. Mayer v. Hellman, 13 N. B. R. 440; s. c., 91 U. S. 496. An assignment by one member of a firm of his individual estate for his creditors' benefit is void. Barnewell v. Jones, 14 N. B. R. 278. A general assignee of an estate of a debtor for creditor's benefit disposed of the property assigned in accordance with his trust, although enjoined by the bankrupt court. It was held that he was not in contempt. *Re* Marter, *supra*. The assignee in bankruptcy is entitled to the possession and control of the estate. Hobson v. Markson, 1 Dill. 421. The common law of assignments is not a part of a state insolvent law, and is not suspended by the Bankrupt Law. Cook v. Rogers, 13 N. B. R. 97; Von Hein v. Elkns, 15 N. B. R. 194. A state law to prevent fraudulent assignments is not an insolvent law, and is not superseded by the Bankrupt Law. Ebersole v. Adams, 13 N. B. R. 141. Bankrupt laws do not divest state courts of jurisdiction over proceedings under their insolvent laws, pending at the time of the adoption of the Act of Congress. Lavender v. Gosnell, 12 N. B. R. 282. The effect is to *suspend*, *not repeal*, the state laws. When the act of Congress is repealed, the insolvent laws are again in force. Ibid.; Van Nostrand v. Carr, 30 Md. 128; Shryock v. Bashore, 13 N. B. R. 481. An assignee in an assignment under the state statute is not liable to the assignee in bankruptcy of the same debtor, for the value of the property assigned to him and disposed of in good faith under the orders of the state court. Cragin v. Thompson, 12 N. B. R. 81.

191. *Who Liable.*—This section, authorizing the assignee "to recover the property or the value of it from the person so receiving it, or so to be benefitted," does not create a qualification or limitation of power: There is no implication that the party paying is not also liable. Fox v. Gardner, 12 N. B. R. 137. A party who has accepted a draft with intent to enable the drawer to prefer the payee is not liable thereon. Ibid.

192. *United States Circuit Court* has jurisdiction of suit by an assignee to recover a preference. Flanders v. Abbey, 6 Biss. 16.

193. *Jurisdiction of State Courts.*—A state court may entertain a suit by an assignee for the enforcement of any right vested in him by the Bankrupt act, as for the recovery of a preference made. Jordan v. Downey, 12 N. B. R. 427; s. c., 40 Md. 401;

§§ 2129-5129a.]   Fraudulent Sales and Conveyances.   [Notes 193-195.

Claflin v. Houseman, 15 N. B. R. 49; s. c., 93 U. S. 130; Daubman v. White, 12 N. B. R. 438; s. c., 48 Cal. 439. *Contra*, Bromley v. Goodrich, 15 N. B. R. 289.

194. *Allegations and Proof.*—An assignee in suing need not allege his representative capacity in his petition. Daubman v. White, *supra*. It is not necessary to prove all the steps by which one has become assignee; a duly certified copy of the assignment is sufficient to prove title. Ibid. The petition must allege that defendant knew the sale was in fraud of the act. Crump v. Chapman, 15 N. B. R. 571.

195. *Miscellaneous Rulings.*—The *two months* limitation clause for *preferences* does not begin to run until the preference becomes an absolute payment. Haskill v. Frye, 14 N. B. R. 525. The change of the original act by inserting "knowing" is *remedial*. Singer v. Sloan, 12 N. B. R. 208; s. c., 3 Dill. 110. Knowing and reasonable cause to believe are not legal synonyms. Ibid. "In fraud of the provisions of this act" means anything which will give a preference to one creditor over another, and which will prevent an equal distribution of and participation in the assets of the bankrupt among his creditors. Boothe v. Brooks, 12 N. B. R. 398. The clauses of the Bankrupt Act giving the right to the assignee to recover illegal preferences are not penal. Tinker v. Van Dyke, 14 N. B. R. 112. *Contra*, Voorhees v. Frisbie, 8 N. B. R. 152; Brigham v. Claflin, 7 N. B. R. 412. The receipt of goods contrary to the provisions of this section is not tortious, but contingently valid. Schuman v. Fleckenstein, 15 N. B. R. 224.

IBID.; R. S. § 5129, AS AMENDED.—If any person, being insolvent, or in contemplation of insolvency or bankruptcy, within [three]¹ months before the filing of the petition by or against him, makes any payment, sale, assignment, transfer, conveyance, or other disposition of any part of his property to any person who then has reasonable cause to believe him to be insolvent, or to be acting in contemplation of insolvency, and [knowing]¹ that such payment, sale, assignment, transfer, or other conveyance is made with a view to prevent his property from coming to his assignee in bankruptcy, or to prevent the same from being distributed under this act, or to defeat the object of, or in any way impair, hinder, impede, or delay the operation and effect of, or to evade any of the provisions of this title, the sale, assignment, transfer, or conveyance shall be void, and the assignee may recover the property, or the value thereof, as assets of the bankrupt.² *Fraudulent transfers of property*

§ 5129a. AMENDMENT OF 1874.—That in cases of involuntary or compulsory bankruptcy, the period of four months mentioned in section thirty-five of the act to which this is an amendment is hereby changed to two months; but this provision shall not take effect until two months after the passage of this act. And in the cases aforesaid, the period of six months mentioned in said section thirty-five is hereby changed to three months; but this provision shall not take effect until three months after the passage of this act.³ *Changes periods of preceding section to two and three months.*

(1) So amended by Act of June 22, 1874, § 11. For the full section of the Act of 1874, by which the above amendments were interpolated, see post, § 5129b.
(2) This section and the preceding one are very nearly related to each other in their provisions, and the authorities under both are collected in the notes under the former.
(3) Act of June 22, 1874, § 10.

§§ 5129b–5132.] Fraudulent Transfers—Penalties against Bankrupt. [Notes 196–197.

196. *Not Retrospective.*—This amendment has no retrospective operation. Bradbury v. Galloway, 12 N. B. R. 299.

§ 5129b. ADDITIONAL AMENDMENT OF 1874.—That section thirty-five of said act be, and the same is hereby amended as follows: 1. After the word "and" in line eleven, insert the word "knowing;" 2. After the word "attachment" in the same line, insert the words "sequestration, scizure;" 3. After the word "and," in line twenty, insert the word "knowing." And nothing in said section thirty-five shall be construed to invalidate any loan of actual value, or the security therefor, made in good faith, upon a security taken in good faith on the occasion of the making of such loan.[1]

<small>Verbal changes in section thirty-five of original act.</small>

197. *Security taken in Good Faith.*—That portion of this amendatory act which provides that nothing contained in section 35 (§§ 5128 and 5129) shall be construed to invalidate any security taken in good faith at the time of making a loan, is merely declaratory of what the law was before the passage of the amendment. *Re* Montgomery, 12 N. B. R. 321.

IBID. § 35; R. S. § 5130.—The fact that such a payment, pledge, sale, assignment, transfer, conveyance, or other disposition of a debtor's property as is described in the two preceding sections, is not made in the usual and ordinary course of business of the debtor, shall be *prima facie* evidence of fraud.

<small>Presumptive evidence of fraud.</small>

198. *Construed* in Rison v. Knapp, 4 N. B. R. 349; Walbrun v. Babbitt, 16 Wall. 577.

IBID. § 35; R. S. § 5131.—Any contract, covenant, or security made or given by a bankrupt or other person with, or in trust for, any creditor, for securing the payment of any money as a consideration for or with intent to induce the creditor to forbear opposing the application for discharge of the bankrupt, shall be void; and any creditor who obtains any sum of money or other goods, chattels, or security from any person as an inducement for forbearing to oppose, or consenting to such application for discharge, shall forfeit all right to any share or dividend in the estate of the bankrupt, and shall also forfeit double the value or amount of such money, goods, chattels, or security so obtained, to be recovered by the assignee for the benefit of the estate.

<small>Fraudulent agreements: Penalty against creditors.</small>

IBID. § 44; R. S. § 5132.—Every person respecting whom proceedings in bankruptcy are commenced, either upon his own petition or upon that of a creditor: 1, who secretes or conceals any property belonging to his estate; or, 2, who parts with, conceals, destroys, alters, mutilates, or falsifies, or causes to be concealed, destroyed, altered, mutilated, or falsified, any book, deed, document, or writing relating thereto; or, 3, who removes or causes to be removed any such property or book, deed, document, or writing out of the district, or otherwise disposes of any part thereof, with intent to prevent it from coming into the posses-

<small>PENALTIES AGAINST BANKRUPT: For secreting property, mutilating books, frauds, etc.</small>

---

(1) Act of June 22, 1874, § 11.

§ 5132.]   Penalties against Bankrupt.   [Notes 199-203.

sion of the assignee in bankruptcy, or to hinder, impede, or delay him in recovering or receiving the same; or, 4, who makes any payment, gift, sale, assignment, transfer, or conveyance of any property belonging to his estate with the like intent; or, 5, who spends any property belonging to his estate in gaming; or, 6, who, with intent to defraud, willfully and fraudulently conceals from his assignee or omits from his inventory any property or effects required by this title to be described therein; or, 7, who, having reason to suspect that any other person has proved a false or fictitious debt against his estate, fails to disclose the same to his assignee within one month after coming to the knowledge or belief thereof; or, 8, who attempts to account for any of his property by fictitious losses or expenses; or, 9, who, within three months before the commencement of proceedings in bankruptcy, under the false color and pretense of carrying on business and dealing in the ordinary course of trade, obtains on credit from any person any goods or chattels with intent to defraud; or, 10, who, within three months next before the commencement of proceedings in bankruptcy, with intent to defraud his creditors, pawns, pledges, or disposes of, otherwise than by transactions made in good faith in the ordinary way of his trade, any of his goods or chattels which have been obtained on credit and remain unpaid for;—shall be punishable by imprisonment, with or without hard labor, for not more than three years.

199. *Constitutionality.*—This section is constitutional and valid. United States v. Pusey, 6 N. B. R. 284.

200. *Information.*—The bankrupt may be prosecuted by information. United States v. Block, 15 N. B. R. 325.

201. *As to Clause 6.*—The original act of 1867 read "if any debtor or bankrupt shall, after the commencement of proceedings in bankruptcy," etc. It was held that "omission of property from schedule of assets filed with a voluntary petition," was not qualified by this limitation, and that this clause required no limitation. United States v. Clark, 4 N. B. R. 59. In order to convict for concealing, it is not necessary to prove a demand by the assignee. United States v. Smith, 13 N. B. R. 61.

202. *As to Clause 9.*—To obtain a conviction under this clause, it must be shown: 1, that proceedings in bankruptcy were commenced against the defendant; 2, that he obtained on credit from the parties named in the indictment the goods therein described; 3, that he obtained them within three months before the commencement of proceedings in bankruptcy; 4, that he obtained them under pretense of carrying on business and dealing in the ordinary course of trade, and that the parties were induced to part with their goods by reason of this pretense, which pretense may have been by conduct as well as by words; 5, that such color and pretense were false; 6, that he obtained them with intent to defraud. United States v. Penn, 13 N. B. R. 464.

203. *As to Clause 10.*—In order to convict it must be shown: 1, that proceedings in bankruptcy were commenced against the defendant; 2, that he sold the goods in the indictment described; 3, that he sold them within three months next before the commencement of proceedings in bankruptcy; 4, that the goods were obtained on credit and were unpaid for; 5, that the sale was not made in good faith in the ordinary way of trade; 6, that the sale was made with the intent to defraud his creditors. This intent must be shown to have existed against the creditors in general. United Ntates v. Penn, *supra;* United States v. Clark, *supra;* United States v. Geary, 4 N. B. R. 535. It must appear that an adjudication has been had. United States v. Prescott, 4 N.

§ 5132a.]   Act of 1874—Effect on Revised Statutes.   [Notes 202-206.

B. R. 112. It is not necessary that goods which have been fraudulently disposed of shall have been obtained within three months prior to the commencement of proceedings in bankruptcy, in order to convict the party of fraudulent disposition thereof. United States v. Smith, 13 N. B. R. 61. A chattel mortgage is a disposition of property, out of the usual course of business. United States v. Bayer, 13 N. B. R. 88; s. c,, 3 Cent. L. J. 11. If a man commits an act, the natural consequences of which are to defraud his creditors, the law presumes that it is done with that intent. United States v. Smith, *supra*.

204. *Bankrupts are not competent witnesses* in criminal proceedings against them. United States v. Black, 12 N. B. R. 340. Section 8 of the act of June 22, 1874, relating to bankrupts being witnesses, applies to civil causes only. Ibid.

205. *Conspiracies.*—Other persons than the bankrupt can *conspire* with the latter to commit the acts made criminal under the seventh and tenth subdivisions of section 5132 and be indicted for the same. United States v. Bayer, 3 Cent. L. J. 11.

5132a. ACT OF 1874—GENERAL REPEALING CLAUSE.—That all acts and parts of acts inconsistent with the provisions of this act be, and the same are hereby repealed.[1]

206. *The Revised Statutes of the United States* must be regarded as passed on the 1st day of December, 1873; and all other acts of the same session of Congress passed subsequent to that date are to be treated as subsequent acts, repealing the Revised Statutes, so far as they are inconsistent therewith. *Re* Oregon Pub. Co. 14 N. B. R. 405; s. c., 3 Sawy. 614. See on this subject *Re* Leavenworth Bank, 14 N. B. R. 82, 92; *Re* First, 3 Cent. L. J. 51.

(1) Act of June 22, 1874, § 19.

Rules in Bankruptcy.

GENERAL ORDERS IN BANKRUPTCY,

ADOPTED APRIL 12, 1875.

SUPREME COURT OF THE UNITED STATES.

OCTOBER TERM, 1874.

ORDER
1. Clerk's duties; Note Time on Papers when filed; Keep Dockets and Minute Books.
2. Process, Summons and Subpœnas issued under Seal of Court and tested by the Clerk.
3. Proceedings may be conducted by Bankrupt, Creditor or Attorney; Orders granted to contain Name of Party or attorney obtaining them.
4. Bankruptcy Petitions to be referred to Register; Attendance of Bankrupt before him; Protection from Arrest.
5. Registers: Their Powers; Time and place of Acting; Submission of Bankrupt for Examination.
6. Dispatch of Business; what is day's sitting; Adjournments.
7. Right to examine and certify correctness of Bankrupt's Petition and Schedule; Papers filed, Part of the Record.
8. Orders to recite Notice to Adverse Party; Motions to be heard unless Objection is made; Review.
9. Assignee notified of his Appointment; no Public Assignee; Additional Assignees.

ORDER
10. Testimony: how Taken; no Power in Register to decide Competency, etc; Attendance of Witnesses.
11. Memoranda of Acts to be Filed with Clerk; Certifying Issue to District Judge.
12. Expense Account of Register and Marshal, how made.
13. Surrender of Property by Voluntary Bankrupt; Seizure in Involuntary Cases; Claim by Third Person of Property taken by Marshal; Contents of Notices sent by Marshal.
14. Petitions and Schedules; Requirements.
15. Cases of two or more Petitions being filed; which first heard, etc.
16. Petitions filed in different Districts against same Parties; Proceedings.
17. Redeeming Encumbered Property; Practice.
18. Practice in Cases of Co-partnership.
19. Assignee; His Duties; Exemptions; Monthly Report; Accounts.
20. Compounding Controversy by Agreement.

Order I.] Duties of Clerks of District Courts.

ORDER
21. Disposition of Property; Sales.
22. Sale in case of Perishable Property.
23. Notice of Meetings.
24. Discharge. of Bankrupt; Opposition thereto; Practice.
25. Second and Third Meetings of Creditors may be filed for same Day as Day for showing Cause against Discharge.
26. Appeals; Rules respecting same.
27. Imprisoned Debtor's presence procured at Examination, how.
28. Depositories of Money of Estates; Money, how drawn from the Depositories.
29. Security for Fees of Court's Officers.
30. Fees of Officers: Clerks, Registers, Marshal, Assignees, Witnessses, Jurors; Contempt for charging Excess.

ORDER
31. Costs in Contested Adjudications; paid Creditor when; paid Debtor when; Debtor to have Clerk to prepare Schedule.
32. What Forms are to be used in Bankruptcy Proceedings.
33. Omissions in Schedule to be Explained; Amendments how made.
34. Proof of Claim how made; to whom delivered; Request by Creditor as to how Notice to him is to be Addressed; Assigned Claims, Objection to Proof; Letter of Attorney Certifying Objections to Court.
35. Trial before Marshal of Issue on Involuntary Petition in Bankruptcy.
36. Proceedings for Composition with Creditors.
37. Reference of Orders to the Bankrupt Act.

It is hereby ordered by the Chief Justice and Associate Justices of the Supreme Court of the United States, in pursuance of the powers conferred upon them by the several acts of Congress in that behalf, that the general orders in bankruptcy heretofore established by the court, be, and they are hereby, amended so as to read as follows:

I. The clerks of the several district courts shall enter upon each petition in bankruptcy the day, and the hour of the day, upon which the same shall be filed, and shall also make a similar note upon every subsequent paper filed with them, except such papers as have been filed before the register, and so indorsed by him; and the papers in each case shall be kept in a file by themselves. No paper shall be taken from the files for any purpose except by order of the court. Every paper shall have indorsed upon it a brief statement of its character. The clerks shall keep a docket, in which the cases shall be entered and numbered in the order in which they are commenced; and the number of each case shall be indorsed on every paper. The docket shall be so arranged that a brief memorandum of every proceeding in each case shall be entered therein, in a manner convenient for reference, and shall at all times be open for public inspection. The clerks shall also keep separate minute-books for the record of proceedings in bankruptcy, in which shall be entered a minute of all the proceedings in each case, either of the court or of a register of the court, under their respective dates.

Duties of clerks of district courts; Filing papers, etc.

Keeping dockets and minute books.

II. All process, summons, and subpœnas shall issue out of the court

Orders II-V.] Process—Appearance—Commencement of Proceedings.

under the seal thereof, and be tested by the clerk; and blanks, with the signature of the clerk and seal of court, may upon application, be furnished to the registers. *Process: Blanks.*

III. Proceedings in bankruptcy may be conducted by the bankrupt in person in his own behalf, or by a petitioning or opposing creditor; but a creditor will only be allowed to manage before the court his individual interest. Either party may appear and conduct the proceedings by attorney, who shall be an attorney or counselor authorized to practice in the circuit or district court. The name of the attorney or counselor, with his place of residence and business, shall be entered upon the docket, with the date of the entry. All papers or proceedings offered by an attorney to be filed shall be endorsed as above required; and orders granted on motion shall contain the name of the party or attorney making the motion. Notices and orders which are not, by the act or by these rules, required to be served on the party personally, may be served upon his attorney. *Appearance: Attorneys: Filing papers: Orders: Notices.*

IV. Upon the filing of a petition in case of voluntary bankruptcy, or as soon as any adjudication of bankruptcy is made upon a petition filed in case of involuntary bankruptcy, the petition shall be referred to one of the registers in such manner as the district court shall direct, and the petitioner shall furnish the register with a copy of the papers in the case, and thereafter all the proceedings required by the act shall be had before him, except such as are required by the act to be had in the district court, or by special order of the district judge, unless some other register is directed to act in the case. The order designating the register to act upon any petition shall name a day upon which the bankrupt shall attend before the register, from which date he shall be subject to the orders of the court in all matters relating to his bankruptcy, and may receive from the register a protection against arrest, to continue until the final adjudication on his application for a discharge, unless suspended or vacated by order of the court. A copy of the order shall forthwith be sent by mail to the register, or be delivered to him personally, by the clerk or other officer of the court. *Commencement of Proceedings: Proceedings before register. Bankrupt to attend before register: Protected against arrest.*

V. The time when and the place where the registers shall act upon the matters arising under the several cases referred to them, shall be fixed by special order of the district court, or by the register acting under the authority of a general order, in each case, made by the district court; and at such times and places the registers may perform the acts which they are empowered to do by the act, and conduct proceedings in relation to the following matters, when uncontested, viz: making adjudication of bankruptcy on petition of the debtor; administering oaths; receiving the surrender of a bankrupt; granting protection thereon; giving re- *Registers: Time and place of acting: may perform what acts, etc.*

quisite direction for notices, advertisements, and other ministerial proceedings; taking proofs of claims; ordering payment of rates and taxes, and salary or wages of persons in the employment of the assignee; ordering amendments, or inspection, or copies, or extracts of any proceedings; taking accounts of proceeds of securities held by any creditor; taking evidence concerning expenses and charges against the bankrupt's estate; auditing and passing accounts of assignees; proceeding for the declaration and payment of dividends, and taxing costs in any of the proceedings; and generally dispatching all administrative business of the court in matters of bankruptcy, and making all requisite uncontested orders and directions therein, which are not, by the acts of Congress concerning bankruptcy, specifically required to be made, done, or performed by the district court itself; all of which shall be subject to the control and review of the said court: *Provided, however*, That by the surrender of a bankrupt mentioned and referred to in this order and in the act in that behalf, is intended and understood a personal submission of the bankrupt himself for full examination and disclosure in reference to his property and affairs, and not a surrender or delivery of the possession of his property.

<small>Surrender of bankrupt.</small>

VI. Every register, in performing the duties required of him under the act, and by these orders, or by orders of the district court, shall use all reasonable dispatch, and shall not adjourn the business but for good cause shown. Six hours' session shall constitute a day's sitting if the business requires; and when there is time to complete the proceedings in progress within the day, the party obtaining any adjournment or postponement thereof may be charged, if the court or register think proper, with all the costs incurred in consequence of the delay.

<small>DISPATCH OF BUSINESS; Adjournments: Six hours a day's sitting: Costs of adjournment.</small>

VII. It shall be the duty of the register to examine the bankrupt's petition and schedules filed therewith, and to certify whether the same are correct in form; or, if deficient, in what respect they are so; and the court may allow amendments to be made in the petition and schedules upon the application of the petitioner, upon proper cause shown at any time prior to the discharge of the bankrupt. The register shall indorse upon each paper filed with him the time of filing, and, at the close of the last examination of the bankrupt, the register having charge of the case, shall file all the papers relating thereto in the office of the clerk of the district court, and these papers, together with those on file in the clerk's office, and the entries in the minute-book, shall constitute the record in each case; and the clerk shall cause the papers in each case to be bound together.

<small>EXAMINATION AND FILING OF PAPERS: Register to examine: Amendments.</small>

<small>Filing, indorsing and preserving papers.</small>

VIII. Whenever an order is made by a register in any proceeding in

Orders VIII-X.]   Orders by Register—Assignee—Testimony.

which notice is required to be given to either party before the order can be made, the fact that the notice was given, and the substance of the evidence of the manner in which it was given, shall be recited in the preamble to the order, and the fact also stated that no adverse interest was represented at the time and place appointed for the hearing of the matter upon such notice; and whenever an order is made where adverse interests are represented before the register, the fact shall be stated that the opposing parties consented thereto, or that the adverse interest represented made no opposition to the granting of such order; provided, however, if any party interested adversely to such order shall not, before the hearing of the application therefor, give reasonable notice in writing to the register that he intends to contest the same, and objects to its being heard by the register, the same shall be heard by the register as by consent. But all such orders may be reviewed by the district court at the request of any party aggrieved, upon his paying the cost of certifying the matter to said court within ten days from the making of the order; which request and payment shall be entered by the register on his docket; and he shall thereupon forthwith certify the said matter to the court, and said court, upon making its decision, may make such order with regard to the costs as justice shall require.

Orders by the Register: Must recite what.

Motion heard as by consent, when.

Review by District Court: Costs.

IX. It shall be the duty of the register, immediately upon the appointment of an assignee, as prescribed in sections twelve and thirteen[1] of the act (should he not be present at such meeting), to notify him, by personal or mail service, of his appointment; and in such notification the assignee so appointed shall be required to give notice forthwith to the register of his acceptance or rejection of the trust. No official assignee shall be appointed by the court or judge; nor any general assignee to act in any class of cases. No additional assignee shall be appointed by the court or judge under section thirteen[2] of the act, except upon petition of one-fourth in number and value of the creditors who have proved their debts, and upon good and sufficient cause shown.

Notification to assignee of his appointment: Register to give.

Official, general and additional assignees.

X. The examination of witnesses before a register in bankruptcy may be conducted by the party in person or by his counsel or attorney, and the witnesses shall be subject to examination and cross-examination, which shall be had in conformity with the mode now adopted in courts of law. The depositions upon such examination shall be taken down in writing by or under the direction of the register in the form of narrative, unless he determines that the examination shall be by question and answer in special instances, and

Testimony: How taken.

(1) §§ 5083, 5084, R. S.
(2) § 5034, R. S.

when completed shall be read over to the witness and signed by him in the presence of the register. Any question or questions which may be objected to shall be noted by the register upon the deposition, but he shall not have power to decide on the competency, materiality or relevancy of the question; and the court shall have power to deal with the costs of incompetent, immaterial, or irrelevant depositions, or parts of them, as may be just. In case of refusal of a witness to attend, or to testify before a register, the same proceedings may be had as are now authorized with respect to witnesses to be produced on examination before an examiner of any of the courts of the United States on written interrogatories.

XI. A memorandum made of each act performed by a register shall be in suitable form, to be entered upon the minute-book of the court, and shall be forwarded to the clerk of the court not later than by mail the next day after the act has been performed. Whenever an issue is raised before the register in any proceedings, either of fact or law, he shall cause the same to be stated in writing in the manner required by the *fourth* and *sixth*[1] sections of the act, and certify the same forthwith to the district judge for his decision. The pendency of the issue undecided before a judge shall not necessarily suspend or delay other proceedings before the register or court in the case.

MINUTES BEFORE REGISTER: Filing, etc.

Certifying issue to judge: Other proceeding not delayed.

XII. Every register shall keep an accurate account of his traveling and incidental expenses, and those of any clerk or other officer attending him in the performance of his duties in any case or number of cases which may be referred to him; and shall make return of the same under oath, with proper vouchers (when vouchers can be procured), on the first Tuesday in each month; and the marshal shall make his return under oath, of his actual and necessary expenses in the service of every warrant addressed to him, and for custody of property, publication of notices, and other services, and other actual and necessary expenses paid by him, with vouchers therefor whenever practicable, and also with a statement that the amounts charged by him are just and reasonable.

ACCOUNTS FOR SERVICES OF REGISTER AND MARSHAL: To be returned under oath.

XIII. In cases of voluntary bankruptcy, the bankrupt, after being decreed such, and after the appointment of an assignee or trustee, and assignment duly made, shall, unless the court otherwise direct, deliver possession of all his property and assets (including evidences of debt and books of account) to said assignee or trustee, unless at or after such decree and before said assignment, the court, on application of any creditor or creditors, and upon good cause shown by affidavit, shall deem it necessary for the interest of the creditors that possession of such property

MARSHAL AS MESSENGER: Bankrupt to surrender property.

(1) §§ 5009, 5010, R. S.

Order XIII.   Duties of Marshal as Messenger.

and assets should be sooner delivered up; in which case, as in cases of involuntary bankruptcy, the court may order said property and assets to be taken possession of by the marshal as messenger, directions for which may be inserted, in pursuance of such order, in the original warrant in bankruptcy, or in a special warrant to be issued for that purpose.

It shall be the duty of the marshal as messenger to take possession of the property of the bankrupt when required thereto by warrant or order of the court, and to deliver the same to the assignee or trustee when appointed and assignment made as aforesaid. *Marshal to take possession.* The marshal, when taking possession, as aforesaid, shall make an inventory of the property and assets by him received, and deliver the same, with the said property and assets, to said assignee or trustee, who shall verify the same, and, if found correct and full, no further inventory shall be required: *Provided, however,* That if any goods or effects so taken into possession as the property of the bankrupt shall be claimed by or in behalf of any other person, the marshal shall forthwith notify the petitioning creditor, or assignee, if one be appointed, of such claim, and may, within five days after so giving notice of such claim, deliver them to the claimant or his agent, unless the petitioning creditor or party at whose instance possession is taken, shall, by bond with sufficient sureties, to be approved by the marshal, indemnify the marshal for the taking and detention of such goods and effects, and the expenses of defending against all claims thereto; and, in case of such indemnity, the marshal shall retain possession of such goods and effects, and proceed in relation thereto as if no such claim had been made: *And provided, further,* that in case the petitioning creditor claims, that any property not in possession of the bankrupt belongs to him, and should be taken by the marshal, the marshal shall not be bound to take possession of the same, unless indemnified in like manner. *Proceeding in case of goods adversely claimed.* He shall also, in case the bankrupt is absent or can not be found, prepare a schedule of the names and residences of his creditors, and the amount due to each, from the books or other papers of the bankrupt that may seized by him under his warrant, and from any other sources of information; but all statements upon which his return shall be made shall be in writing, and sworn to by the parties making them, before one of the registers in bankruptcy of the court, or a commissioner of the courts of the United States. *Marshal to prepare schedule.* In cases of voluntary bankruptcy, the marshal may appoint special deputies to act, as he may designate, in one or more cases, as messengers, for the purpose of causing the notices to be published and served as required in the eleventh [1] section of the act, and for no other purpose. *May appoint deputies.* In giving the notices required by the third subdivision of the eleventh [2] section of the act, it *Notice to creditors; Contents.*

(1) §§ 5019, 5032, R. S.
(2) § 5032, R. S.; Act 1874, § 5.

shall be sufficient to give the names, residences, and the amount of the debts (in figures) due the several creditors, so far as known, and no more.

XIV. All petitions, and the schedules filed therewith, shall be printed or written out plainly, and without abbreviation or interlineation, except where such abbreviation and interlineation may be for the purpose of reference; and whenever any amendments are allowed, they shall be written and signed by the petitioner on a separate paper, in the same manner as the original schedules were signed and verified; and if the amendments are made to different schedules, the amendments to each schedule shall be made separately with proper reference to the schedule proposed to be amended, and each amendment shall be verified by the oath of the petioner in the same manner as the original schedules.

<small>PETITIONS AND AMENDMENTS: How written out and verified.</small>

XV. Whenever two or more petitions shall be filed by creditors against a common debtor, alleging separate acts of bankruptcy committed by said debtor on different days within six months prior to the filing of said petitions, and the debtor shall appear and show cause against an adjudication of bankruptcy against him on the petitions, that petition shall be first heard and tried which alleges the commission of the earliest act of bankruptcy; and in case the several acts of bankruptcy are alleged in the different petitions to have been committed on the same day, the court before which the same are pending may order them to be consolidated, and proceed to a hearing as upon one petition; and if an adjudication of bankruptcy be made upon either petition, or for the commission of a single act of bankruptcy, it shall not be necessary to proceed to a hearing upon the remaining petitions, unless proceedings be taken by the debtor for the purpose of causing such adjudication to be annulled or vacated.

<small>PRIORITY OF ACTIONS (INVOLUNTARY BANKRUPTCY.)</small>

<small>Consolidation of actions.</small>

<small>Proceeding on one petition only.</small>

XVI. In case two or more petitions shall be filed against the same individual in different districts, the first hearing shall be had in the district in which the debtor has his domicile, and such petition may be amended by inserting an allegation of an act of bankruptcy committed at an earlier date than first alleged, if such earlier act is charged in either of the other petitions; and in case of two or more petitions against the same firm in different courts, each having jurisdiction over the case, the petition first filed shall be first heard, and may be amended by the insertion of an allegation of an earlier act of bankruptcy, than that first alleged, if such earlier act is charged in either of the other petitions, and in either case, the proceedings upon the other petitions may be stayed until an adjudication is made upon the petition first heard; and the court which makes

<small>PETITIONS IN DIFFERENT DISTRICTS: Where heard: Amendment.</small>

<small>Two or more Petitions against same Firm in different courts.</small>

Orders XVI–XVIII.] Redemptions of Property and Compounding Claims.

the first adjudication of bankruptcy shall retain jurisdiction over all proceedings therein until the same shall be closed. In case two or more petitions for adjudication of bankruptcy shall be filed in different districts by different members of the same copartnership, for an adjudication of the bankruptcy of said copartnership, the court in which the petition is first filed having jurisdiction, shall take and retain jurisdiction over all proceedings in such bankruptcy until the same shall be closed; and if such petition shall be filed in the same district, action shall be first had upon the one first filed. *By different members of same firm.*

XVII. Whenever it may be deemed for the benefit of the estate of a bankrupt to redeem and discharge any mortgage or other pledge, or deposit, or lien upon any property, real or personal, or to relieve said property from any conditional contract, and to tender performance of the conditions thereof, or to compound any debts or other claims or securities due or belonging to the estate of the bankrupt, the assignee, or the bankrupt, or any creditor who has proved his debt, may file his petition therefor in the office of the clerk of the district court; and thereupon the court shall appoint a suitable time and place for the hearing thereof, notice of which shall be given in some newspaper, to be designated by the court at least ten days before the hearing, so that all creditors and other persons interested may appear and show cause, if any they have, why an order should not be passed by the court upon the petition authorizing such act on the part of the assignee. *Redemptions of property and compounding claims: Petition. Appointment and notice of hearing.*

XVIII. In case one or more members of a copartnership refuse to join in a petition to have the firm declared bankrupt, the parties refusing shall be entitled to resist the prayer of the petition in the same manner as if the petition had been filed by a creditor of the partnership, and notice of the filing of the petition shall be given to him in the same manner as provided by law and by these rules in the case of a debtor petitioned against; and he shall have the right to appear at the time fixed by the court for the hearing of the petition, and to make proof, if he can, that the copartnership is not insolvent, or has not committed an act of bankruptcy, and to take all other defenses which any debtor proceeded against is entitled to take by the provisions of the act; and in case an adjudication of bankruptcy is made upon the petition, such copartner shall be required to furnish to the marshal, as messenger, a schedule of his debts and an inventory of his property, in the same manner as is required by the act in cases of debtors against whom adjudication of bankruptcy shall be made. *Proceedings in case of copartnerships: Partners declining to join in petition may resist: Must have notice. May appear and make what defences. Must furnish schedule and inventory.*

XIX. The assignee shall, immediately on entering upon his duties,

[Orders XIX-XX.] Duties of Assignee—Composition with Creditors.

DUTIES OF ASSIGNEE: To make inventory: Verify marshal's inventory, etc.
prepare a complete inventory of all the property of the bankrupt that comes into his possession, except where an inventory is furnished to him by the marshal; in which case, having verified the same, he shall add thereto a certificate that the same is correct, or that the same is correct as modified by a supplemental inventory to be annexed thereto; in which supplemental inventory he shall state any deficiency of assets named in the marshal's inventory, and shall add any property or assets not contained therein. The assignee shall

To report exemptions: Exceptions by creditors.
make report to the court within twenty days after receiving the deed of assignment, of the articles set off to the bankrupt by him, according to the provisions of the fourteenth section[1] of the act, with the estimated value of each article, and any creditor may take exceptions to the determination of the assignee within twenty days after the filing of the report. The register may require the exceptions to be argued before him, and shall certify them to the court for final determination at the request of either party. The substance of each monthly return of the assignee shall be sent by the

Creditor entitled to substance of monthly return.
register to any creditor who shall request it and pay the fee provided for notices to creditors. In case the assignee shall neglect to file any report or statement which it is made his duty to file or to make by the bankrupt act, or any general order in bankruptcy, within five days after the same

Assignee failing to report, removal.
shall be due, it shall be the duty of the register to make an order requiring the assignee to show cause before the court, at a time specified in the order, why he should not be removed from office. The register shall cause a copy of the

Accounts of assignees.
order to be served upon the assignee at least seven days before the time fixed for the hearing, and proof of the service thereof to be delivered to the clerk. All accounts of assignees are to be referred as of course to the register for audit unless otherwise specially ordered by the court.

XX. Whenever an assignee shall make application to the court for

COMPOSITION WITH CREDITORS: ARBITRATION: Reasons to be set forth in application.
authority to submit a controversy arising in the settlement of demands against the bankrupt's estate, or of debts due to it, to the determination of arbitrators, or for authority to compound and settle such controversy by agreement with the other party, the subject-matter of the controversy and the reasons why the assignee thinks it proper and most for the interest of the creditors that it should be settled by arbitration or otherwise, shall be set forth clearly and distinctly in the

Court may take testimony or direct notice to show cause.
application; and the court, upon examination of the same, may immediately proceed to take testimony and make an order thereon, or may direct the assignee to give notice of the application either by publication or by

(1) 5045, R. S.

mail, or both, to the creditors who have proved their claims to appear and show cause, on a day to be named in the order and notice, why the application should not be granted, and may make such order thereon as may be just and proper.

XXI. Upon application to the court, and for good cause shown, the assignee may be authorized to sell any specified portion of the bankrupt's estate at private sale; in which case he shall keep an accurate account of each article sold, and the price received therefor, and to whom sold; which account he shall file with his report at the first meeting of creditors after the sale. In making sale of the franchise of a corporation it may be offered in fractional parts, or in certain numbers of shares corresponding to the number of shares in the bankrupt corporation. *DISPOSAL OF PROPERTY BY ASSIGNEE: Sales: Accounts of sales: Sale of franchise of corporation.*

XXII. In all cases where goods or other articles come into possession of the messenger or assignee which are perishable, or liable to deterioration in value, the court may, upon application, in its discretion, order the same to be sold and the proceeds deposited in court. *PERISHABLE PROPERTY: Court may order sale of.*

XXIII. The notice provided by the eighteenth section[1] of the act shall be served by the marshal or his deputy, and notices to the creditors of the time and place of meeting provided by the [eighteenth] section[2] shall be given through the mail by letter, signed by the clerk of the court. Every envelope containing a notice sent by the clerk or messenger shall have printed on it a direction to the postmaster at the place to which it is sent to return the same within ten days unless called for. *SERVICE OF NOTICE: Printed directions to postmasters.*

XXIV. A creditor opposing the application of a bankrupt for discharge shall enter his appearance in opposition thereto on the day when the creditors are required to show cause, and shall file his specification of the grounds of his opposition in writing, within ten days thereafter, unless the time shall be enlarged by order of the district court in the case, and the court shall thereupon make an order as to the entry of said case for trial on the docket of the district court, and the time within which the same shall be heard and decided. *OPPOSITION TO DISCHARGE: Appearance of opposing creditor: Specifications, when filed: Order for hearing.*

XXV. Whenever any bankrupt shall apply for his discharge, within three months from the date of his being adjudged a bankrupt, under the provisions of the twenty-ninth section[3] of the act, the court may direct that the second and third meetings of creditors of said bankrupt, required by the twenty-seventh and twenty-eighth sections[4] of said act, shall be had on the day which may be fixed in the order of notice for the creditors to appear *SECOND AND THIRD MEETING OF CREDITORS: May be had on Day fixed for showing cause against discharge, when: Notice.*

---

(1) § 5089, R. S.
(2) §§ 5080, 5041, R. S
(3) 5108, R. S.
(4) §§ 5092, 5093, R. S.

and show cause why a discharge should not be granted such bankrupt; and the notices of such meeting shall be sufficient if it be added to the notice to show cause, that the second and third meetings of said creditors shall be had before the register upon the same day that cause may be shown against the discharge, or upon some previous days or day.

XXVI. Appeals in equity from the district to the circuit court, and from the circuit court to the Supreme Court of the United States, shall be regulated by the rules governing appeals in equity in the courts of the United States.

Appeals. By what rules governed: Notice of appeal.

Any supposed creditor who takes an appeal to the circuit court from the decision of the district court rejecting his claim, in whole or in part, according to the provisions of the eighth section[1] of the act, shall give notice of his intention to enter the appeal within ten days from the entry of the final decision of the district court upon his claim; and he shall file his appeal in the clerk's office of the circuit court within ten days thereafter, setting forth a statement in writing of his claim in the manner precribed by said section; and the assignee shall plead or answer thereto in like manner within ten days after the statement shall be filed. Every issue thereon shall be made up in the court, and the cause placed upon the docket thereof, and shall be heard and decided in the same manner as other actions at law.

Time of filing and answering.

Issue and Hearing.

XXVII. If at the time of preferring his petition the debtor shall be imprisoned, the court, upon his application, may order him to be produced upon *habeas corpus* by the jailor, or any officer in whose custody he may be, before the register, for the purpose of testifying in any matter relating to his bankruptcy; and if committed after the filing of his petition upon process in any civil action founded upon a claim provable in bankruptcy, the court may, upon like application, discharge him from such imprisonment. If the petitioner, during the pendency of the proceedings in bankruptcy, be arrested or imprisoned upon process in any civil action, the district court, upon his application, may issue a writ of *habeas corpus* to bring him before the court, to ascertain whether such process has been issued for the collection of any claim provable in bankruptcy, and, if so provable, he shall be discharged; if not, he shall be remanded to the custody in which he may lawfully be. Before granting the order for discharge, the court shall cause notice to be served upon the creditor, or his attorney, so as to give him an opportunity of appearing and being heard before the granting of the order.

Imprisoned Debtor: Habeas corpus.

Creditor to have notice.

XXVIII. The district court in each district shall designate certain

---

(1) §§ 4980, 4983, R. S.

Orders XXVIII-XXIX.] Deposits and Payments of Moneys—Fees.

national banks, if there are any within the judicial district, or if there are none, then some other safe depository, in which all moneys received by assignees are paid into court in the course of any proceedings in bankruptcy shall be deposited; and every assignee and the clerk of said court shall deposit all sums received by them, severally, on account of any bankrupt's estate, in one designated depository; and every clerk shall make a report to the court of the funds received by him, and of deposits made by him, on the first Monday of every month. On the first day of each month, the assignee shall file a report with the register, stating whether any collections, deposits, or payments have been made by him during the preceding month, and if any, he shall state the gross amount of each. The register shall enter such reports upon a book to be kept by him for that purpose, in which a separate account shall be kept with each estate; and he shall also enter therein the amount, the date, and the expressed purpose of each check countersigned by him. No moneys so deposited shall be drawn from such depository unless upon a check, or warrant, signed by the clerk of the court, or by an assignee, and countersigned by the judge of the court, or one of the registers designated for that purpose, stating the date, the sum, and the account for which it is drawn; and an entry of the substance of such check or warrant, with the date thereof, the sum drawn for, and the account for which it is drawn, shall be forthwith made in a book kept for that purpose by the assignee or the clerk; and all checks and drafts shall be entered in the order of time in which they are drawn, and shall be numbered in the case of each estate. A copy of this rule shall be furnished to the depository so designated, and also the name of any register authorized to countersign said checks.

Deposit and payment of moneys: Court to designate nate depositories.

Clerk and assignee to make report of funds.

Register to keep accounts.

Moneys, how drawn from depository.

XXIX. The fees of the register, marshal, and clerk shall be paid or secured in all cases before they shall be compelled to perform the duties required of them by the parties requiring such service; and in the case of witnesses their fees shall be tendered or paid at the time of the service of the summons or subpœna, and shall include their traveling expenses to and from the place at which they may be summoned to attend. The court may order the whole, or such portion of the fees and costs in each case to be paid out of the fund in court in such case as shall seem just. The funds deposited with the register, marshal, and clerk shall, in all cases where they come out of the bankrupt's estate, be considered as a part of such estate, and the assignee shall be charged therewith and shall not be allowed for any disbursements therefrom, except upon the production of proper vouchers from such officers, respectively, given after the due allowance of their respective bills.

Prepayment or security of fees.

When paid out of fund.

Assignee's disbursements.

Order XXX.] Fees and Costs—Clerks—Registers.

XXX. The fees of the clerk shall be the same as now allowed by law for similar services in the general fee-bill, section 828, Revised Statutes, except as herein provided; but no charge shall be made for filing any paper previously filed with the register. Also,

FEES AND COSTS: Clerks.

For entering memoranda or minutes of register, each folio........ $0 10
For sending notice to creditors by mail, each...................... 15
For inserting notice in newspaper 50
  (The necessary cost of advertising to be paid as an expense of the estate.)
For taxing the costs in each case................................ 1 00
—and for each folio of taxed bill................................ 10

Registers. The following and no other fees shall be allowed to the register:

For filing and entry of the general order of reference, and for office rent, stationary, and other incidental expenses of proceedings, conducted in the usual office of the register, to be allowed only once in any cause... 5 00
When the proceedings are not conducted in the usual office of the register, but in some other city or town, he shall be allowed for each day employed in going, attending, and returning............ 5 00
  Also, in such case, traveling and incidental expenses of himself and of any clerk or other officer attending him, which expenses and fees shall be appropriated among the cases, as provided in section 5 of the act, or section 5125 of the Revised Statutes.
For each day's service while actually employed under a special order of the court, a sum to be allowed by the court, not exceeding 5 00
  But only one *per diem* allowance to be made for a single day, and no duplication of such allowances to be made for different cases on the same day; and no other allowance shall be made for clerk hire except as above stated.
For every affidavit to any petition, schedule, or other proceeding in bankruptcy, except proof of debt by a creditor or his agent, for each oath, and certifying the same............................. 25
For examining petition and schedules and certifying to their correctness.. 3 00
For every warrant in bankruptcy, or other process, issued and directed to the marshal (not including warrants for payment of money or anything other than process)............................ 2 00
For each day in which a general meeting of creditors is held, and attending same... 3 00
For notification to assignee of his appointment.................... 50
For assignment of bankrupt's effects............................. 1 00
For every bond with sureties 1 00
For every application for a general meeting of creditors.......... 1 00

Order XXX.] Fees and Costs—Registers.

For every summons or subpœna requiring the attendance of a bankrupt, a bankrupt's wife, or a witness for examination, for each person summoned 10
For taking depositions, including proofs of debts, and examination of bankrupt or his wife, for each folio 20
For certifying proof of debt as satisfactory 25
For copies of depositions and other papers, each folio 10
For each notice which the register may be required to send to or serve on any creditor (which shall include for postage and stationery) 15
For mileage in making personal service, when necessary, the same as allowed by law to the marshal.
For inserting notice in newspaper when required 50
(Cost of advertising to be allowed as part of the expenses of the estate.)
For each order for a general dividend 3 00
For computation of dividends 3 00
In addition thereto, for each creditor 10
For every judicial order made by a register, necessary or proper to be made by him, and not herein otherwise specially provided for, and not including matters merely ministerial 1 00
For every discharge where there is no opposition 2 00
For auditing the accounts of assignees 1 00
—and for each additional hour necessarily employed therein, after the first hour 1 00
For every certificate of question to the district court or judge, under sections four and six of the act, or sections 5009 and 5010 of the revised statutes 1 00
For preparing such certificate, each folio 20
For each folio of memorandum sent to the clerk 10
For countersigning each check of assignee 10
For filing every paper not previously filed by the clerk, and marking and identifying every exhibit 10

Fees paid by creditors for establishing their debts shall be entitled to rank with other fees and costs in the case under section 5101, revised statutes. The deposit of fifty dollars required to be made as security for the fees of the register shall be delivered by the clerk to the register to whom the case is referred, and be by him accounted for at the termination of the case.

Marshal.

The fees of the marshal shall be the same as are allowed for similar services by the general fee-bill in section 829 of the revised statutes, as modified by section 5126, including additional fees allowed by the latter section for distinct services; but no allowances shall be made under the last clause of section 5126, commencing with the words " For cause shown."

Order XXX.| Fees and Costs—Assignees.

The marshal shall be allowed for each hour necessarily employed in making inventory of bankrupt's property.................... 1 00
—and for each folio of inventory................................ 20
For each hour actually and necessarily employed in personal attention in taking care of bankrupt's property..................... 1 00

No other allowance to be made for custody of property, except for actual disbursements, which shall in all cases be passed upon by the court.

The fees and allowances of assignees shall be as prescribed and provided for in sections 5099 and 5100 of the revised statutes; provided that, in addition to disbursements made, no allowance shall be made other than the commissions provided for in section 5100, except as hereinafter specified; and said commissions shall be calculated but once upon the amount of money received and paid, and not upon both the receipt and payment thereof. Besides which, there shall be allowed to the assignee as follows: *Assignees.*

For serving or sending notices to creditors, or publishing the same, when required to be done by the assignee, the same amount allowed to the register for like services.

For each hour necessarily employed in making inventory or supplemental inventory of bankrupt's property, or verifying marshal's inventory... 1 00

For each folio of inventory or supplemental inventory made by assignee.. 20

For all services in designating the exempt property of a bankrupt, and filing report thereon....................................... 5 00

For attending a general meeting of creditors..................... 3 00

For every deed for real estate sold............................. 2 00

For drawing and filing each monthly report...................... 1 00

For drawing and finding each quarterly report, not exceeding four, unless specially allowed.. 5 00

For each general account submitted to a creditors' meeting, not exceeding two, unless specially allowed 10 00

For all services in paying a general dividend, or executing an order of final distribution, and making report thereon, including all disbursements 5 00

In addition, for each creditor to whom a dividends is paid......... 25

[It being found that, in certain special cases requiring great care and exertion on the part of assignees in bankruptcy, the fees and allowances now provided are insufficient, it is therefore hereby

Ordered, That, in such cases as are above mentioned, the district judge be, and is hereby authorized, by and with the advice of the circuit justice or judge, to make such additional allowance to the assignee or trustee, or to both or either of them if there be more than one, as in his judgment shall be a fair and just compensation for his or their ser-

Orders XXX-XXXI.]   Fees and Costs.

vices, having regard to the amount of assets, the amount of labor required, and the special circumstances of the case; and that so much of General Order 30 as conflicts herewith be repealed.[1]

The fees of witnesses and jurors shall be the same as prescribed in the general fee-bill, in sections 848 and 852 of the Revised Statutes.   *Witnesses and jurors.*

No allowance shall be made against the estate of the bankrupt for fees of attorneys, solicitors, or counsel, except when necessarily employed by the assignee, when the same may be allowed as a disbursement; and no allowance shall be made to the assignee for custody of the bankrupt's property, except necessary disbursements in relation thereto. The necessity and reasonableness of disbursements shall in all cases be passed upon by the court.   *Attorneys: Disbursements of assignee.*

Any money received by either of the officers mentioned, in excess of lawful fees or compensation, shall be ordered by the judge to be paid into court, and such order may be enforced, if necessary, by attachment as for contempt. No bankrupt's discharge shall be refused or delayed by reason of the non-payment of any fees, except the fee for his certificate of discharge.   *Excess paid into Court: Contempt.*   *Bankrupt's discharge not delayed.*

Ten days before the day fixed for the consideration of the assignee's final account, or at any other time fixed by the court on its own motion, or on the application of any person interested, the clerk, marshal, and register, shall file with the clerk a statement of fees, including prospective fees for final distribution, which shall exhibit, by items, each service and the fee charged for it, and the amount received. Said clerk shall tax each fee-bill, allowing none but such as are provided for by these rules, which taxation shall be conclusive, reserving to any party interested exceptions to the bills as taxed, which shall be decided by the court. The office of auditor is hereby discontinued.   *Taxation of costs.*   *Auditors.*

XXXI. In cases of involuntary bankruptcy, where the debtor resists an adjudication, and the court, after hearing, shall adjudge the debtor a bankrupt, the petitioning creditor shall recover, to be paid out of the fund, the same costs that are allowed by law to a party recovering in a suit in equity; and in case the petition shall be dismissed, the debtor may recover like costs from the petitioner.   *Costs in contested adjudications.*

When a debtor shall be adjudged a bankrupt on the application of a creditor, and shall be required under the provisions of the act to furnish a schedule of his creditors, and an inventory and valuation of his estate, the court, if the estate is large and the required schedule and inventory are likely to be   *Debtor may have clerk, when.*

(1) So amended March 17, 1877.

[Orders XXXI–XXXIII.] Forms and Schedules—Omissions and Amendments.

voluminous or complicated, or other good reasons exist, may, on application of such debtor, allow him the services of a clerk or accountant to aid him therein, at such rate of compensation, not to exceed five dollars per day, as the court may deem reasonable.

XXXII. The several forms specified in the schedules annexed to the former general orders for the several purposes therein stated, shall be observed and used, with such alterations as may be necessary to suit the circumstances of any particular case. The tabular forms hereto annexed shall be used respectively by the several officers named in section nineteen of the amendatory act of June 22, 1874, in making the returns required by said section. In all cases where, by the provisions of the act, a special order is required to be made in any proceeding, or in any case instituted under the act in a district court of the United States, such order shall be framed by the court to suit the circumstances of the particular case; and the forms hereby prescribed shall be followed as nearly as may be, and so far as the same are applicable to the circumstances requiring such special order. In proceedings in equity, instituted for the purpose of carrying into effect the provisions of the act, or for enforcing the rights and remedies given by it, the rules of equity practice established by the Supreme Court of the United States shall be followed as nearly as may be. In proceedings at law, instituted for the same purpose, the rules of the circuit court regulating the practice and procedure in cases at law shall be followed as nearly as may be. But the court, as [or] judge thereof, may, by special rule in any case, vary the time allowed for return of process, for appearance and pleading, and for taking testimony and publication, and may otherwise modify the rules for the preparation of any particular case so as to facilitate a speedy hearing.

Forms and Schedules: Previous ones Continued.
Forms hereto annexed.
Special orders.
Rules in equity.
Rules at law.
Special rules: Modification of rules.

XXXIII. Whenever a debtor shall omit to state in the schedules annexed to his petition any of the facts required to be stated concerning his debts or his property, he shall state, either in its appropriate place in the schedules or in a separate affidavit to be filed with the petition, the reason for the omission, with such particularity as will enable the court to determine whether to admit the schedules as sufficient, or to require the debtor to make further efforts to complete the same according to the requirements of the law; and in making any application for amendment to the schedules, the debtor shall state under oath the substance of the matters proposed to be included in the amendment, and the reasons why the same had not been incorporated in his schedules as originally filed, or as previously amended. In like manner, he may correct any statement made during the course of his examination.

Omissions and Amendments: In debtors schedules.
In his examination.

Order XXXIV.]   Proof of Debts—Assignment of Claims.

XXXIV. Depositions to prove claims against a bankrupt's estate shall be correctly entitled in the court and in the cause. When made to prove a debt due to a co-partnership, it must appear on oath that the deponent is a member of the creditor firm; when made by an agent, the reason the deposition is not made by the claimant in person must be stated; and when made to prove a debt due to a corporation, and the corporation has no such officer as cashier or treasurer, the deposition may be made by the officer whose duties most nearly correspond to those of cashier or treasurer. Depositions, to prove debts existing in open account shall state when the debt became or will become due; and if it consists of items maturing at different dates, the average due date shall be stated; in default of which it shall not be necessary to compute interest upon it. All such depositions shall contain an averment that no note has been received for such account nor any judgment rendered thereon. Proofs of debt received by any assignee shall be delivered to the register to whom the cause is referred. The register may decline to file any deposition until the fee for filing the same is paid. When a proof of debt is sent by mail to the register, and it shall be accompanied by the fee for filing it, and the fee for sending a notice to a creditor, the register shall acknowlege the receipt of it, and state the amount at which he has entered it, and if it shall be insufficient or unsatisfactory to the register he shall state the reason. Any creditor may file with the register a request that all notices to which he may be entitled, shall be addressed to him at any place, to be designated by the post-office box or street number, as he may appoint, and thereafter, and until some other designation shall be made by such creditor, all notices shall be so addressed; and in other cases notices shall be addressed as specified in the proof of debt. Claims which have been assigned before proof, shall be supported by a deposition of the owner at the time of the commencement of proceedings, setting forth the true consideration of the debt, and that it is entirely unsecured, or, if secured, such deposition shall set forth the security, as is required in proving secured claims. Upon filing with the register satisfactory proof of the assignment of a claim proved and entered on the register's docket, the register shall immediately give notice by mail, to the original claimant, of the filing of such proof of assignment. And if no objection be entered within ten days, he shall make an order subrogating the assignee to the original claimant. If objection be made within the time specified, or within such further time as may be granted for that purpose, the register shall certify the objection into court for determination. The claims of persons contingently liable for the bankrupt may be proved in

Marginal notes: PROOF OF DEBTS: What deposition must state. — Delivered to register: His duties. — When sent by mail. — Notices to creditors, how addressed. — Claims assigned before proof. — Assignment of claims: Duty of register: Certifying objection.

Orders XXXIV-XXXV.] Proof of Debts—Trial before Marshal.

the name of the creditor, when known, by the party contingently liable.
Where creditor's name is unknown. When the name of the creditor is unknown, such claims may be proved in the name of the party contingently liable; but no dividend shall be paid upon such claim, except upon satisfactory proof that it will diminish, *pro tanto*, the original debt.
Acknowledgment of instruments. The execution of any letter of attorney to represent a creditor, or of an assignment of claim after proof, or of the consent of a creditor to a bankrupt's discharge, may be proved or acknowledged before a register in bankruptcy, or a United States Circuit Court commissioner.
On behalf of co-partnership. When executed on behalf of a co-partnership, or of a corporation, the person executing the instrument shall make oath that he is a member of the firm, or duly authorized officer of the corporation on whose behalf he acts.
Proof of identity. When the party executing is not personally known to the officer taking the proof or acknowledgment, his identity shall be established by satisfactory proof.
Re-examination of claims. When the assignee or any creditor shall desire the re-examination of any claim filed against the bankrupt's estate, he may apply by petition to the register to whom the cause is referred, for an order for such re-examination; and thereupon the register shall make an order fixing a time for hearing the petition, of which due notice shall be given by mail, addressed to the creditor. At the time appointed, the register shall take the examination of the creditor, and of any witnesses that may be called by either party; and if it shall appear from such examination that the claim ought to be expunged or diminished, the register, if no
Certifying objection to court. objection be made, may order accordingly. If objection be made, the register shall require the parties then, or within a time to be fixed for that purpose, to form an issue to be certified into court for determination. If the petitioner is in default in making up said issue, the petition shall be dismissed; if the creditor whose claim is re-examined is in default in making said issue, the claim may be diminished or expunged by the register. All orders thus made by the register may be reviewed by the court on special petition, and upon showing satisfactory cause for such review.

XXXV. If the debtor, under the provisions of section fourteen of the amendatory act relating to proceedings in bankruptcy,
Trial before Marshal. approved June 22, 1874, shall elect to have a trial of the facts before the marshal, he shall make such election in writing, and file the same with the clerk of the court; and thereupon the court, on application of the debtor, may award the *venire facias* in
Venire facias. said section prescribed, upon and by virtue of which the marshal shall summon twenty-four good and lawful men,

Orders XXXV-XXXVI.] Trial before Marshal—Composition with Creditors.

inhabitants of the vicinity of the place of trial, and indifferent between the parties, from whom to select a jury to try the said facts; and the names of the persons so summoned shall be drawn by lot to make the said jury, and each party shall be entitled to challenge four persons peremptorily; and if a sufficient number of jurors unchallenged and free from exception shall not appear to make the full panel of twelve men (or such less number as the parties may agree upon) to try the said cause, the marshal shall complete the number by forthwith summoning other proper persons for the purpose. And any person summoned by the marshal to sit on said jury, and failing to appear without sufficient excuse, shall be returned by the marshal and subject to be fined by the court. The petitioning creditor shall be deemed the actor, give due notice of trial, and have the opening and close before the jury. Subpœnas may be issued to witnesses, and objections to evidence shall be decided by the marshal presiding at the trial, subject to review by the court. The trial shall be had upon the petition to have the debtor declared a bankrupt, and no other pleadings shall be necessary. The debtor may, on his part, prove any fact or state of facts which will entitle him to have the case dismissed. The jury, if desired, shall find a special verdict upon any point or question of fact stated for that purpose in writing by either party before the case shall have been submitted to them. The verdict shall be signed by the foreman of the jury and countersigned by the marshal, who shall immediately return the same to the court with the venire, and any points or questions raised and decided by him at the trial. The court, for good and legal cause shown, may set aside the verdict and award a new venire as often as occasion shall require.

Mode of selecting jury.

Penalty for failing to sever.

Notice and conduct of trial: Witnesses: Evidence.

Verdict.

Venire de novo.

XXXVI. If at any time after the filing of a petition for an adjudication in bankruptcy, a petition duly verified be filed by the debtor or bankrupt, or by any creditor of such debtor or bankrupt, setting forth that a composition had been proposed by such debtor or bankrupt, and that he verily believes that such proposed composition would be accepted by a majority in number and three-fourths in value of the creditors of such debtor or bankrupt, in satisfaction of the debts due from such debtor or bankrupt, the court shall forthwith order a meeting of the creditors to be called to consider of the said proposition as provided in the 17th section of said amendatory act, whereupon such proceedings shall be had as are therein directed. The register acting in the case, or, if no register has been assigned, a register to be designated by the court, shall at the time and place specified in the notice for holding such meeting, hold and preside at the same, and report to the

Composition with creditors: Meeting of creditors.

Duty of Register.

court the proceedings thereof, with his opinion thereon; upon filing of which, the clerk shall give the notices to creditors required by said section, and the court shall at the time therein fixed, proceed to hear and determine the matter as is in said section is prescribed. In like manner, additional meetings in relation to such proposed composition, or any modification thereof, may, upon like application, be called and held, and the proceedings returned in like manner.

Notice and final hearing.

Additional meetings.

XXXVII. All orders referring specifically to any section or sections of the original bankrupt act, shall be deemed and construed to refer to the corresponding sections, respectively, in the Revised Statutes of the United States; for example, order IX, in referring to sections 12 and 13 of the act, shall be construed to refer to sections 5033 and 5034, respectively, of the Revised Statutes; and so of the rest. And all forms heretofore prescribed shall be adapted to any modification of the law, or of these orders.

Reference to sections of act, etc.

Forms.

BANKRUPT LAW. 113

Forms and Schedules.

FORMS AND SCHEDULES.

Annual report of , marshal of the district of for the year ending June 30, 18 , required by the 19th section of the amendatory act of Congress, relating to matters of bankruptcy, approved June 22, 1874.   REPORTS OF MARSHAL.

Number of cases in bankruptcy in which warrants were received.
Number of warrants returned during year............................
Fees for service of warrants so returned............................
Fees for serving creditors with notice..............................
Mileage thereon...
Expenses of publication thereon.....................................
Expenses of postage thereon...
Other expenses thereon, such as for.................................
  Other fees, costs, expenses, and emoluments, namely:
For service-fees for serving writs and process......................
For mileage thereon...
For serving notices...
For mileage thereon...
Expenses of publication thereon.....................................
Expenses of postage thereon...
For making inventories of property..................................
For taking care of property...
Expenses and disbursements thereon..................................
  All other fees and emoluments, such as for:
  All other expenses and disbursements, such as for:

SUMMARY OF FEES, COSTS, EMOLUMENTS, EXCLUSIVE OF ACTUAL DISBURSEMENTS.

Service fees..
Mileage...
Making inventories..
Care of property..
Other fees and emoluments in bankruptcy.............................

    SUMMARY OF ACTUAL DISBURSEMENTS.

For publications..
For postage...
For custody of property...
For traveling expenses..
For other expenses, such as...

Form of Schedule.

REPORT OF CLERK. No. 1.

Annual statement of   , clerk of the district court of the United States for the district of   , for the year ending June 30, 18 , in pursuance of section 19 of the amendatory act relating to proceedings in bankruptcy, approved June 22, 1874, of all cases of bankruptcy pending, etc.

Cases pending at beginning of year. Names of bankrupts.	Whether Disposed of.	Amount of dividends.	Number of reports of Assignee.	Disposition of case.	Number of assignee's account filed and settled.
Cases begun during year.					

REPORT OF CLERK. No. 2.

Names and residences of all marshals, registers, and assignees who have failed to make and file reports, as required by section 19 of amendatory act relating to proceedings in bankruptcy, for the year ending June 30, 18 , furnished in pursuance of said section.

MARSHAL.

[Here insert names and residences of delinquents.]

REGISTERS.

[Here insert names and residences of delinquents.]

ASSIGNEES.

[Here insert names and residences of delinquents.]

Form of Schedule.

Annual report of , clerk of the district court of the United States for the district of , for the year ending June 30, 18 , of all his fees, charges, costs, and emolument earned or accrued in bankruptcy cases during said year; and also of all moneys paid into and disbursed out of court in bankruptcy, and the balance in hand or on deposit, made in pursuance of section 19 of the amendatory act relating to proceedings in bankruptcy, approved June 22, 1874.

REPORT OF CLERK, No. 3.

Services.   Amount.

For performing all ordinary duties of clerk, such as issuing process, filing and entering papers, orders, rules, etc., in bankruptcy cases..
For entering memoranda or minutes of registers................
For giving notice to creditors by mail or publication (exclusive of postage and costs of publication)..............................
For taxing costs..
For receiving, keeping, and paying out money...................
For taking examinations ....
For preparing and certifying papers on appeal to circuit court....

Moneys received in court in cases of bankruptcy................
Balance on hand at beginning of year ....
Moneys paid out of court in cases in bankruptcy................
Balance on hand at end of year ....
Balance on deposit at end of year ....

Form of Schedule.

<small>REPORT OF REGISTER.</small> Annual report of , register in bankruptcy in and for the district of the state and district of , for the year ending June 30, 18 , in pursuance of section 19 of the amendatory act relating to proceedings in bankruptcy, approved June 22, 1874.

Number of cases of voluntary bankruptcy referred...............
Amount of assets of the bankrupts therein........................
Amount of liabilities of the bankrupts therein...................
Amount of dividends declared therein............................
Average rate per cent. of dividends declared therein.............
Number of cases in which discharge granted.....................
Number in which discharge not granted.........................
Number of compulsory cases referred...........................
Amount of assets of the bankrupts therein......................
Amount of liabilities of the bankrupts therein...................
Amount of dividends declared therein..........................
Average rate per cent. of dividends declared therein.............
Number of cases in which discharge granted....................
Number in which discharge not granted........................
Amount of fees, costs, etc., received or earned in cases of voluntary bankruptcy ....
Amount of fees, costs, etc., received or earned in cases of Involuntary bankruptcy...

Form of Schedule.

Annual report of　　　, of the　　　, in the state of　　　, assignee in bankruptcy, for the year ending June 30, 18　, in pursuance of section 19 of the amendatory act relating to proceedings in bankruptcy, approved June 22, 1874.

REPORT OF ASSIGNEE.

Name and number of bankrupts	Assets.	Liabilities.	Receipts.	Disbursements.	Dividends.	Rate per cent.	Fees, charges, and emoluments earned or received.	Expenses for legal proceedings and counsel fees.	Discharged or not discharged.
VOLUNTARY.									
INVOLUNTARY.									

INDEX.

ABATEMENT AND REVIVAL,
of suits in which assignee is party. R. S. § 5048, p. 39.
proceedings do no not abate on death of bankrupt. R. S. § 5090, p. 54.

ACCOUNTS,
of assignee; audited how. R. S. § 4998, cl. 8, p. 11; § 5096, p. 56.
of assignee; subject to inspection of creditors. R. S. § 5065b, p. 44.
assignee to account for interest, benefits, etc. R. S. § 5065b, p. 44.
of assignee, examination of. R. S. § 5065b, p. 44.
of mutual debts, set-off, etc. R. S. § 5073, p. 47.
of assignee submitted to meeting of creditors. R. S. § 5092, p. 55.
of expenses of register and marshal. O. XII, p. 96.

ACKNOWLEDGEMENTS,
of letters of attorney and other instruments. O. XXXIV, p. 109.
by members of firm; oath. O. XXXIV, p. 109.
proof of identity. O. XXXIV, p. 109.

ACT OF BANKRUPTCY,
what shall be considered an. R. S. § 5021, p. 19.
a person of unsound mind can not commit an. u. 30, p. 21.
a lunatic may be proceeded against in bankruptcy. n. 30, p. 21.
appointment of receivers for a corporation deemed an. n. 30, p. 21.
an assignment for benefit of creditors valid under state law is an. u. 32, p. 21.
if the assignment is invalid not an. n. 32, p. 22.
suspension of payment of commercial paper an. n. 32, p. 22.
unlawful preference can not be alleged as an, by whom. n. 32, p. 22.
committed since March 2, 1867, may be foundation of involuntary proceedings. R. S. § 5022, p. 24.

ACTION. (SEE SUITS.)

ADJUDICATION,
who may oppose. n. 58, p. 27.
set aside when. n. 59, p. 27.
is conclusive. n. 61, p. 28.
to be had when. R. S. § 5028, p. 28.
of corporations, a proceeding *in rem*. n. 179, p. 77.

ADJOURNMENT,
of trial of petition for cause shown. R. S. § 5026, p. 26.
of proceedings for want of legal notice. R. S. § 5033, n. 64, p. 32.
of proceedings before register. O. VI, p. 94.
cost of. O. VI, p. 94.

ADVERTISING,
cost of. O. XXX, p. 104.

AFFIDAVIT, (SEE OATH, PERJURY.)
evidence may be taken in form of. R. S. § 5003, p. 12.
defective may be amended. n. 38, p. 22.
of assignee, to settlement. R. S. § 5065b, p. 44.

AFFIRMATION, (SEE OATH.)
the word "oath" includes "affirmation." R. S. § 5013, p. 14.

AGREED CASES,
may be submitted to court; judgment final unless appeal provided for; may provide for what; may provide for costs. R. S. § 5011, p. 13.

AMENDMENTS,
of 1874, are they retroactive? u. 45, p. 24.
of allegation of sufficiency in number. n. 33, p. 22.
of schedule by bankrupt. R. S. § 5020, n. 29, p. 17.
to petition and schedules. O. VII, p. 94.
how written out and signed and verified. O. XIV, p. 98.
where petitions are filed in different courts. O. XVI, p. 98.
of schedule. O. XXXIII, p. 108.

APPEAL,

from the district court, allowed to whom and when, R. S. § 4980, p. 6. Instances —n. 9. p. 6. Conditions; within what time; notice, to whom given; bond. R. S. § 4981, p. 7; dismissed, unless law is complied with, n. 11, p. 7.

waiver of; effect of waiver, R. S. § 4983, p. 7.

proceedings under, R. S. § 4984, n. 14, p. 7.

judgment of circuit court in, conclusive, R. S. § 4985, p. 8.

costs of, R. S. § 4985, p. 8.

no appeal from circuit court in the exercise of its power of superintendance, n. 19, p. 9; but it does lie from it in the exercise of its concurrent jurisdiction, n. 19, p. 9.

in equity, by what rules governed. O, XXVI, p. 102.

appeal from rejection of claim; notice of. O. XXVI, p. 102.

filing answer and hearing. O. XXVI, p. 103.

APPEARANCE,

may be in person or by attorney. O. III. p. 93.

name of counsel to be entered on docket, etc. O. III, p. 93.

ARRANGEMENT,

(SEE TRUSTEES; COMPOSITION WITH CREDITORS.)

ARREST,

of debtor when ordered. R. S. § 5024, p. 25.

of debtor is for appearance, and can not be after adjudication. n. 51, p. 25.

bankrupt protected from, on civil process. R. S. § 5107, p. 66.

of debtor, made prior to bankruptcy proceedings, n. 151, p. 66.

bankrupt protected against. O. IV, p. 93.

ARBITRATION,

application of assignee for authority to arbitrate, to set forth facts distinctly. O. XX, p. 100.

proceedings thereon. O. XX, p. 100.

ASSIGNEE,

may be sued in trover in state court, n. 5, p. 4.

shall recover money and property fraudulently conveyed. R. S. § 5021, p. 21.

how chosen. R. S. § 5034, p. 32; n. 65, p. 33.

ASSIGNEE, (Continued.)

shall accept trust in writing. R. S. § 5034, p. 32.

eligibility for, and who may vote for, n. 65, p. 33.

no preferred creditor to vote for, R. S. § 5035, p. 33.

ineligibility of, not to effect title to property conveyed by him. R. S. § 5035, p. 33.

required to give bond. R. S. § 5036, p. 33.

failing to give bond removed. R. S. § 5036, p. 33.

liable for contempt for neglect and disobedience. R. S. § 5037, p. 33.

resignation of. R. S. § 5038, p. 34.

removal of. R. S. § 5039, p. 34.

removal of, "in the discretion," n. 66, p. 34.

effect of resignation or removal of. R. S. § 5040, p. 34.

vacancies in the office of, how filled. R. S. § 5041, p. 34.

in cases of vacancies, estate vests in remaining assignee or in successors. R. S. § 5042, p. 34.

former assignee to make conveyances, etc., to new assignee. R. S. § 5043, p. 34.

assignment to new assignee relates back. n. 67, p. 35.

what vests in by adjudication and assignment. R. S. § 5044, p. 34.

unacknowledged assignment good as against whom, n. 67, p. 35.

assignee's title relates back to adjudication. n. 67, p. 35.

represents creditors as well as debtors. n. 68, p. 35.

acquires no title to exempt property. n. 68, p. 35; n. 71, p. 37.

accountable for unauthorized exemption of real estate. n. 72, p. 37.

takes what interests under assignment. R. S. § 5046, n. 79, p. 38.

may recover in his own name, be admitted to prosecute or defend pending suits, etc. R. S. § 5047, p. 38.

rights of. n. 80, p. 39.

must give notice of his appointment, etc. R. S. § 5054, p. 40.

must demand and receive estate. R. S. § 5055, p. 41.

not to be sued without previous notice. R. S. § 5056, p. 41.

exceptions to this rule. n. 85, p. 41.

to deposit money and keep effects how. R. S. § 5059, p. 41.

INDEX. 121

ASSIGNEE, (Continued.)
may settle controversies and submit disputes to arbitration. R. S. § 5061, p. 42.
this power construed. n. 87, p. 42.
may carry on business under order of court. R. S. § 5061a, p. 42.
sale of, soliciter for, cannot bid at. n. 88, p. 42.
to keep accounts and make reports of, etc. R. S. § 5065b, p. 44.
penalties against. R. S. § 5065b, p. 44.
may, under order of court, discharge liens, perform contracts, etc. R. S. § 5066, p. 45.
occupation of leased premises by. n. 96, p. 47.
to keep account of claims proved. R. S. § 5080, p. 51.
statement of, at second meeting of creditors. R. S. § 5092, p. 55.
to give notice of meeting of creditors. R. S. § 5094, p. 56.
settlement of accounts and discharge of. R. S. § 5096, p. 56.
allowance to, and fees of. R. S. § 5099, p. 56, n. 123, 124, 125, p. 57.
commissions allowed to. R. S. § 5100, p. 57.
need not proceed without funds. R. S. § 5100, p. 57.
to be removed upon appointment of trustees. n. 129, p. 59.
in partnership cases chosen by creditors of company. R. S. § 5121, p. 74.
accounts of, in partnership cases. R. S. § 5121, p. 74.
reports of, to contain what, penalties. R. S. §§ 5127d, 5127f, p. 82.
register to notify, of appointment. O. IX, p. 95.
assignee to notify register of acceptance or rejection. O. IX, p. 95.
no official or general assignees appointed. O. IX, p. 95.
nor additional assignees except, etc. O. IX, p. 95.
surrender of bankrupt's property, when made to, O. XIII, p. 96.
marshal to deliver property to, when. O. XIII, p. 96.
to make inventory, verify that of marshal and make supplemental inventory, etc. O. XIX, p. 99.
to report exempt articles set off to bankrupt. O. XIX, p. 99.
neglecting duties, proceedings for removal. O. XIX, p. 99.
accounts of, audited by register. O. XIX, p. 99.

ASSIGNEE, (Continued.)
application by, to arbitrate or compound claims. O. XX, p. 100.
may sell at private sale, when. O. XXI, p. 101.
accounts of sales. O. XXI, p. 101.
sale of franchise of corporation. O. XXI. p. 101.
of perishable property. O. XXII, p. 101.
to deposit in designated depository. O. XXVIII, p. 102.
to make monthly report. O. XXVIII, p. 102.
disbursements in payment of costs; vouchers, etc. O. XXIX, p. 103.
to deliver proof of debts to register. O. XXXIV, p. 109.
form of annual report of. p. 117.
ASSIGNMENT,
in bankruptcy, vests what in assignee. R. S. § 5046, n. 79, p. 38.
intended to give preference, void. n. 79, p. 38.
fraudulent by debtor a bar to discharge. R. S. § 5110, cl. 9, p. 68.
of property giving preference, an act of bankruptcy. n. 190, p. 86.
assigned claims, how proved. O. XXXIV, p. 109.
proceedings to subrogate assignee. O. XXXIV, p. 109.
ATTACHMENTS,
issued less than four months prior to bankruptcy proceedings are thereby dissolved *ipso facto*. R. S. § 5044, p. 34; n. 69, p. 35.
not dissolved if realized upon prior to filing petition. n. 69, p. 35.
issued more than four months prior may be enforced, how. n. 69, p. 35.
of exempt property, not dissolved. n. 69, p. 35.
obligation of bond for production of attached property superseded and surety released. n. 69, p. 35.
state laws govern rights of assignee under. n. 69, p. 35.
of firm property not dissolved by bankruptcy proceedings against partner individually. n. 69, p. 35.
not dissolved by composition proceedings. n. 140, p. 63.
fraudulent to prefer creditor, a bar to discharge. R. S. § 5110, cl. 3 p. 67.
ATTORNEY,
creditor's petition may be verified by R. S, § 5021, p. 21.
creditor may act by, at meetings. R. S. § 5095, p. 56.

ATTORNEY, (Continued.)
powers of. n. 122, p. 56.
of assignee, fees. n. 123, p. 57.
fees of. u. 127, p. 57.
parties may appear by. O. III, p. 93.
must be attorney of the court. O. III, p. 93.
name of, to be entered on docket, etc. O. III, p. 93.
papers offered by, to be filed, etc. O. III, p. 93.
name of, must appear in orders granted on motion. O. III, p. 93.
what notices may be sued upon. O. III, p. 93.
may conduct examination of witnesses before register. O. IX, p. 95.
fees of, when allowed out of bankrupt's estate. O. XXX, p. 104.

AUDITING,
of assignee's accounts by register. R. S. § 4996, p. 11.
of assignee's accounts by court. R. S. § 5006, p. 56.

BAIL,
arrested debtor admitted to, when. R. S. § 5024, p. 25.
claim of, when provable. R. S. § 5070, p. 46.
when entitled to dividend. R. S. § 5091, p. 54.
not released by discharge of principal. R. S. § 5118, p. 71.

B

BANKRUPT,
duty of, to bring suit for protection of property. u. 2, p. 3.
may correct schedule. R. S. § 5020, u. 29, p. 17.
can not file a second petition while first is pending. n. 27, p. 15.
may be arrested when. R. S. § 5024, p. 25.
to execute necessary instruments, etc. R. S. § 5051, p. 40.
may move the expunging of a claim. n 113a, p. 52.
may be examined. R. S. § 5086, p. 53.
examination of, restrictions. n. 117, p. 53.
competent as witness. R. S. § 5087a, p. 54.
examination of wife of; failure of her attendance a bar to discharge, when. R. S. § 5088, p. 54.
examination of, when imprisoned, absent, etc. R. S. § 5089, p. 54.
death of, not to abate proceedings. R. S. § 5090, p. 54.

BANKRUPT, (Continued.)
to convey and deliver to trustees under oath. R. S. § 5103, p. 58.
subject to order of court; punishable, etc. R. S. § 5104, p. 65.
protected against suits. R. S. §§ 5105, 5106, p. 65; n. 130, p. 66.
not liable to arrest in civil action. R. S. § 5107, p. 66.
as to arrest of, prior to bankruptcy. n. 151, p. 66.
application for discharge of. R. S. § 5108, p. 66.
penalties against. R. S. § 5132, p. 88.
not competent witness in criminal proceedings against himself. n. 204, p. 90.
to attend before register. O. IV, p. 93.
protected against arrest. O. IV, p. 93.
subject to order of court from what time to what time. O. IV, p. 93.
surrender of, to be deemed a personal submission. O. V, p. 93.

BANKRUPT ACT,
who may have benefit of; what steps thereto. R. S. § 5014, p. 15.
a lunatic may have benefit of. u. 27, p. 15.
repeal of conflicting laws. R. S. § 5132a, p. 90.
Revised Statutes to be considered as passed on Dec. 1st, 1873. n. 206, p. 90.
references to, to be deemed to apply to corresponding sections of revised statutes. O. XXXVII, p. 112.

BLANKS,
for writs, furnished register, signed. O. II, p. 92.

BOND,
for appeal or writ of error. R. S. § 4981, p. 7.
of register. R. S. § 4995, p. 10.
of assignee, when required, conditioned how, approval, etc. R. S. § 5036, p. 33.
liability of surety on bond of assignee not affected by his resignation or removal. R. S. § 5040, p. 34.

BOOKS AND PAPERS,
production of, before register. R. S. § 5002, p. 12.
production of, generally. R. S. § 5003, p. 12.
no one may withhold books or papers of bankrupt or claim a lien on them. R. S. § 5050, p. 40.
falsification, mutilation or destruction of, by bankrupt bar to discharge. R. S. § 5111, cl. 4, p. 68.

BOOKS AND PAPERS, (Continued.)
failure to keep, by bankrupt, merchant or tradesman, a bar to discharge. R. S. § 5111, cl. 7, n. 156, 157, p. 68.
penalties for mutilation, destruction or concealment of. R. S. § 5132, p. 88

BRIBES,
taking, by judge or other officer, how punished. R. S. § 5012, p. 13.

C

CASE STATED.
to be submitted to judge by certificate of register. R. S. § 5010, n. 25, p. 13.

CERTIFICATE,
f judge's opinion, how taken. R. S. § 5010, p. 13.
of discharge. R. S. § 5114, p. 70.
of discharge, form of. R. S. § 5115, p 70.
of discharge, conclusive evidence. R. S. § 5119, p. 72.

CHOSES IN ACTION,
arising out of contract or injuries to property of bankrupt, vest in assignee by virtue of assignment. R. S. § 5046, p. 38.
may be sold by assignee under order of court. R. S. § 5064, p. 43.

CIRCUIT JUDGE,
to act in place of district judge, when.. R. S. § 4976, p. 5.

CIRCUIT COURT. (SEE COURTS OF BANKRUPTCY.)

CLERK,
wages due to, up to $50, have priority. R. S. § 5101, cl. 4, p. 57.
who considered a. n. 127, p. 57.

CLERKS OF COURTS,
clerk of district court to keep minute-book of memoranda transmitted by register. R. S. § 5000, p. 11.
to file all depositions and written acts tranemitted by register. R. S. § 5004, p. 12.
penalty against, for taking gratuity. R. S. § 5012, p. 13.
not to be of counsel nor otherwise interested in the estate. R. S. § 5127a, p. 81.
annual report of, to attorney general. R. S. § 5127e, p. 82.
penalties for failure to report, etc. R. S. 5127f, p. 82.
duty as to indorsing, filing and docketing papers. O. I, p. 92; O. III, p. 93; O. VII, p. 94.
to keep minute-book. O. I, p. 92.

CLERKS OF COURTS, (Continued.)
order designating register to act, how delivered to him. O. IV, p. 93.
to deposit money in designated depository. O. XXVIII, p. 102.
to make monthly report of funds. O. XXVIII, p. 102.
fees of, to be paid or tendered in advance. O. XXIX, p. 104.
schedule of clerk's fees. O. XXX, p. 104.
form of annual statement of (No. 1). p. 114.
form clerk's report of delinquent officers (No. 2). p. 114.
form of clerk's annual report (No. 3). p. 115.

COMMENCEMENT OF PROCEEDINGS
the filing of the petition to be considered. n. 30, p. 39.

COMMERCIAL PAPER.
supension of payment of, an act of bankruptcy. n. 32, p. 22.
what is considered. n. 32, p. 23.
how described in debtor's statement. when composition is proposed. R. S. § 5103a, p. 61.

COMMISSIONERS OF CIRCUIT COURTS.
evidence may be taken before. R. S. § 5003, p. 12.
voluntary petition may be verified before. R. S. § 5017, n. 28, p. 15.
proof of claims may be made before, subject to revision of and forwarded to register. R. S. § 5076 n. 107. p. 50.

COMMITTEE,
of creditors to overlook trustees. R. S. § 5103, p. 58.

COMPOSITION WITH CREDITORS,
composition proceedings. R. S. § 5103a. p. 60.
resolution to be passed by what proportion in number and value of creditors. R. S. § 5103a, p. 60.
resolution to, approved by court. R. S. § 5103a, p. 60.
terms of, may be afterwards varied, how. R. S. § 5103a, p. 61.
binding upon what creditors. R. S. § 5103a, p. 61.
outstanding commercial paper, how described in debtor's statement. R. S. § 5103a, p. 61.
unsecured debts to be paid *pro rata*. R. S. § 5103a, p. 61.
how enforced. R. S. § 5103a, p. 61.
may be set aside for cause by court.

COMPOSITION WITH CREDITORS.
(Continued.)
R. S. § 5103a, p. 61.
constitutionality of, n. 130, p. 62.
resolution, passage of, confirmation of, number and value of creditors voting for, terms of, n. 131, 132, 136, 138, p. 62.
oath not required of creditor voting on, n. 133, p. 62.
on unliquidated claims, proceedings, n. 135, p. 62.
debtor should be present at meeting, n. 137, p. 62.
recording resolution. n. 138, p. 62.
all creditors with provable claims bound. n. 139, p. 63.
does not dissolve attachments. n. 140 p. 63.
a second meeting for, may be held. n. 141, p. 63.
conclusive on state courts. n. 142, p. 63.
adjudication and discharge not necessary. n. 143, p. 63.
does not release co-obligees. n. 144, p. 63.
confines a secured creditor to his security. n. 145, p. 63.
procured by fraud, invalid. n. 146, p. 63.
provisions for, apply to corporations. n. 147, p. 63.
in partnership cases, individual or firm creditors may demand separate vote. n. 148, p. 63.
petition for composition and meeting. O. XXXVI, p. 111.
final hearing by court and additional meetings. O. XXXVI, p. 111.

COMPOUNDING CLAIMS,
by assignee. R. S. 5061, n. 87, p. 42.
notice of hearing of petition to compound claim, etc., and proceedings. O. XVII, p. 99.
application by assignee for authority to compound, to set forth facts distinctly. O. XX, p. 100.
proceedings thereon. O. XX, p. 100.

COMPUTATION OF TIME,
under this act. R. S. § 5013, p. 14.
in a suit to recover a preference. n. 26, p. 14.

CONCEALMENT,
of person or property an act of bankruptcy. R. S. § 5021, p. 19.
of books, effects, etc., by bankrupt, a bar to discharge. R. S. § 5110, cl. 2. p. 67.

CONCEALMENT, (Continued.)
of books, effects, etc., by bankrupt, punishable how. R. S. § 5132, n. 211, p. 89.

CONSOLIDATION OF ACTIONS,
when authorized. O. XV, p. 98.

CONSPIRACY,
conspiracy of other person with the bankrupt to defraud. n. 205, p. 90.

CONSTITUTIONAL LAW,
bankrupt act constitutional. n. 78, p. 38.
penal § 5182, constitutional. n. 199. p. 89.

CONTEMPT,
district judge may compel obedience by process of. R. S. § 4975, p. 4.
register has no power to commit for. R. S. § 4999, p. 11.
register to refer matters of, to district judge. R. S. § 5006, p. 12.
bankrupt's wife punishable for. n. 22, p. 12.
assignee refusing or neglecting to execute instruments or disobeying order of court punishable for. R. S. § 5087, p. 33.
bankrupt punishable for, when. R. S. § 5104, p. 65.
in refusing to pay money into court. O. XXX. p. 104.

CONTINGENT DEBTS,
how allowed as claims. R. S. § 5068, p. 46.
what considered as. n. 93, p. 46.

CORPORATIONS,
claims of, to be proved by officers. R. S. 5078, n. 110, p. 51.
act providing for composition proceedings applies to. n. 145, p. 63.
what, subject to bankrupt law. R. S. § 5122, p. 76; n. 181. 182, p. 77.
distribution of assets of bankrupt. R. S. § 5122, p. 77.
adjudication of, a proceeding *in rem.* n. 179, p. 77.
not discharged. n. 180, p. 77.
fraudulent representations of officers of, to purchaser of stock no defense against assignee. n. 180, p. 77.
number and value of creditors of. n. 183, p. 77.
prior proceedings in state courts against insolvent, deemed valid. R. S. § 5123, p. 77.
act not applicable to Union Pacific Railway Company. R. S. § 5123a, p. 78.

INDEX. 125

CONVERSION OF CHATTELS,
 demand growing out of, proveable claims. R. S. § 5067, p. 45.
COSTS, (SEE FEES.)
 to have priority in distribution. R. S. § 5124, p. 79.
 petitioner to deposit $50 to secure. R. S. § 5124, n. 184, p. 79.
COURTS OF BANKRUPTCY,
 DISTRICT COURTS,
 jurisdiction of, as. R. S. § 4972, p. 2; n. 1, 2, p. 3.
 jurisdiction of, exclusive of state courts. u. 3, p. 3, n. 4, 5, p. 4.
 always open as. R. S. § 4973, p. 4.
 power of judge of, in chambers. R. S. § 4973, p. 4.
 may sit anywhere in district, notice of session. R. S. § 4974, p. 4.
 powers of, to enforce their decrees. R. S. § 4975, p. 4.
 circuit judge to act in case of absence, disability, etc., of district judge. R. S. § 4976, p. 5.
 has jurisdiction to restrain chattel mortgagee from selling. n. 6, p. 6.
 CIRCUIT COURTS,
 judge of, to act in absence, disability, etc., of district judge. R. S. § 4976, p. 5.
 have concurrent jurisdiction with district courts in all suits to which assignee is a party. R. S. § 4979, p. 5.
 controversies to be cognizable under concurrent jurisdiction must concern property or rights of bankrupt. u. 6, p. 6.
 has concurrent jurisdiction whether assignee appointed in that district or another. n. 6, p. 6.
 concurrent jurisdiction of, not restricted by amendatory act of June 8, 1872. u. 7, p. 6.
 jurisdiction of, arising from the citizenship of the parties. n. 8, p. 6.
 appellate jurisdiction of. R. S. § 4980, p. 6.
 appeal to; writ of error. n. 9, 10, p. 6.
 appellate jurisdiction of, final. R. S. § 4985, p. 8.
 general superintendence and jurisdiction of. R. S. § 4986, p. 8.
 general superintendence distinct from appellate jurisdiction. n. 16, p. 8.
 general superintendence and jurisdiction, final. u. 17, p. 8.
 judge of, has power in chambers though without the district; practice. n. 18, p. 8.

COURTS OF BANKRUPTCY, (Contin'd)
 STATE COURTS,
 certain assets collectible in. R. S. § 4979, p. 2.
 SUPREME COURT OF DISTRICT OF COLUMBIA,
 has powers of district courts in bankruptcy. R. S. § 4977, p. 5.
 TERRITORIAL DISTRICT COURTS,
 have powers of district courts in bankruptcy. R. S. § 4978, p. 5.
CREDITORS. (SEE MEETINGS OF CREDITORS.)
 may appeal from decision of district court. R. S. § 4980, p. 6.
 number and amount joining in petition in involuntary proceedings. R. S. § 5021, p. 19.
 having signed petition not to withdraw. n. 35, p. 22.
 number and amount of, how computed. R. S. § 5021, p. 20, 21; n. 37, p. 23.
 secured, not reckoned. n. 39, p. 23.
 secured, joining in petition surrender security. u. 39, p. 23.
 if partially secured, how computed. n. 39, p. 23.
 attaching, not reckoned. n. 42, p. 23.
 sufficiency in number of, signing petition. n. 36, p. 23.
 right of, to elect assignee. R. S. § 5034, p. 32.
 majority of, may apply for removal of. R. S. § 5039, p. 34.
 rights of, when holding an order on a fund. n. 68, p. 35.
 majority of, to consent before assignee may carry on business of bankrupt. R. S. § 5061a, p. 42.
 to have access to assignee's accounts. R. S. § 5080, p. 51.
 fraudulently preferred must surrender preference. R. S. § 5084, p. 52, u. 115, 116, p. 53.
 majority in value of, to decide whether there shall be a dividend. R. S. § 5092 p. 55.
 may act at meetings by attorney. R. S. § 5095, u. 122, p. 56.
 what proportion of, must consent to appointment of trustees. R. S. § 5103, p 58.
 need not prove claims in case of appointment of trustees. n. 129, p. 59.
 what proportion, must consent to composition. R. S. § 5103a, p. 60.
 what, bound by composition. R. S. § 5103a, p. 61, n. 139, p. 63.
 what, may vote at composition proceedings. u. 134, p. 62.

CREDITORS, (Continued.)
secured, are confined to security by composition proceedings. n. 145, p. 63.
what proportion of, must assent to discharge of bankrupt whose estate does not pay thirty per cent. of the debts proved. R. S. §§ 5112, 5112a, p. 69; n. 161, p. 70.
what proportion must assent to discharge of bankrupt in the second bankruptcy. R. S. § 5116, p. 71.
penalties against for fraudulent agreements. R. S. § 5131, p. 88.

D

DEBTS AND PROOF OF CLAIMS,
what debts may be proved against bankrupt estate. R. S. § 5067, p. 45.
debts due the United States. n. 90, p. 45.
debts barred by limitation not proveable. n. 91, p. 45.
what are proveable debts? n. 92, p. 45.
contingent debts proveable, how. R. S. § 5068, n. 93, p. 46.
liability on commercial paper when fixed proveable. R. S. § 5069, n. 94, p. 46.
a person liable as surety, guarantor, etc., having paid the debt may prove his claim. R. S. § 5070, p. 46; n. 95, p. 47.
debts, falling due at stated periods, may be proved proportionately. R. S. § 5071, p. 47.
no debts proveable, except those enumerated. R. S. § 5072, p. 47.
in case of mutual debts balance only proveable. R. S. § 5073, p. 47.
proof of debt where bankrupt is liable in two or more capacities, as individual and as member of firm. R. S. § 5074, p. 48.
secured debts, how and when proved. R. S. § 5075, p. 48; n. 100, 101, 102, p. 49.
a creditor holding a security not the debtor's may prove the whole of his claim. n. 105, p. 50.
proof of claims may be had before what officers. R. S. §§ 5076, 5076a, n. 107, 108, p. 50.
deposition in support of claim to contain what. R. S. §. 5077, p. 50; n. 109, p. 51.
to be sworn to by whom. R. S. § 5078, n. 110, p. 51.
deposition in support of claim to be sent to register by mail. R. S. § 5079, p. 51.

DEBTS AND PROOF OF CLAIMS, (Continued.)
deposition in support of claim to be forwarded by register to assignee and a memorandum made of it in his book. R. S. § 5080, p. 51.
withdrawal of proof of claim. n. 111, p. 51.
quantum of proof. n. 112, p. 52.
court may examine into proof of claim. R. S. § 5081, n. 113, 113a, p. 52.
proof of claim may be postponed if there is doubt of its validity. R. S. § 5083, n. 114, p. 52.
a fraudulently preferred creditor may not prove his claim without surrender of the preference. R. S. § 5084, p. 52, n. 115, 116, p. 53.
claims duly proved to be allowed and listed. R. S. § 5085, p. 53.
proof of claim deemed a waiver of right to sue. R. S. § 5105, n. 149, p. 65.
certain debts not released by discharge, though prevable. R. S. § 5117, n. 164, p. 71.

DEEDS,
former assignee to execute, to successor. R. S. § 5043, p. 34.
debtor to execute, at request of assignee. R. S. § 5051. p. 40.
secured creditor to execute, with assignee, when. R. S. § 5075, p. 48.

DEFALCATION,
debts created by, provable, but not discharged. R. S. § 5117, n. 164, p. 71.

DEFENCES,
what, may be made by member of a firm where co-partners file petition against firm. O. XVIII, p. 99.

DELAY,
rules for preventing. O. VI, p. 94; XI, p. 96.

DEPOSIT OF MONEYS,
court to designate depository, and assignee and clerk to deposit therein, O. XXVIII, p. 102.
moneys, how drawn from depository. O. XXVIII, p. 102.

DEPOSITIONS,
taken by register to be filed in clerk's office. R. S. § 5002, p. 12.
when defective, supplemental ones may be filed. n. 33, p. 22.
to acts of bankruptcy must be of personal knowledge. n. 33, p. 22.
in support of claims to contain what. R. S. § 5077, p. 50.
in support of claim to be made by whom. R. S. § 5078, p. 51.

DEPOSITIONS, (Continued.)
in support of claim may be taken before whom. R. S. § 5079, p, 51.
in support of claim to be sent to assignee. R. S. § 5080, p. 51.
how taken, in proceedings before register. O. X, p. 95.
how entitled. O. XXXIV, p. 109.
depositions to prove claims, must state what. O. XXXIV, p. 109.
DEPUTIES,
marshal may appoint special, when and for what purpose. O. XIII, p. 96.
DISCHARGE OF BANKRUPT,
a legal voluntary assignment without preference not to be a bar to. R. S. § 5021, p. 20.
bankrupt not entitled to retain money to pay costs of. n. 68, p. 35.
may be withheld upon failure of bankrupt's wife to attend. R. S. § 5088, p. 54.
in case of appointment of trustees. R. S. § 5103, p. 59.
composition proceedings operate as a. n. 142, p. 63.
when, may be applied for. R. S. § 5108, p. 66, n. 152, p. 67.
notice of application for. R. S. § 5109, p. 67.
not granted, or if granted not valid, when. R. S. § 5110. n. 153, 154, p. 67; n. 155, 156, 157, 158, p. 68; n. 159, p. 69.
may be opposed by creditor; proceedings. R. S. § 5111, n. 160, p. 69.
when assets are less than fifty per cent of the debts proved. R. S. § 5112, p. 69.
in involuntary proceedings assent of creditors to, not required. R. S. § 5112a, p. 69.
when assets are less than thirty per cent. of the debts proved. R. S. § 5112a, p. 69.
final oath of bankrupt before. R. S. § 5113, p. 70.
final oath necessary. n. 162, p. 70.
certificate of. R. S. § 5114, p. 70.
form of certificate of. R. S. § 5115, p. 70.
in case of second bankruptcy. R. S. § 5116, n. 163, p. 71.
certain debts not released by. R. S. § 5117, n. 164, p. 71, n. 167, p. 72.
persons co-liable with bankrupt not released by. R. S. § 5118, p. 71.
is a release from provable debts. R. S. § 5119, n. 167, p. 72.
how pleaded, evidence, etc. R. S. § 5119, n. 168, 169, p. 72.

DISCHARGE OF BANKRUPT, (Cont'd)
application for, governed by. § 5109, n. 165, p. 72.
set aside for fraudulent omission. n. 166, p. 72.
proceedings to annul. R. S. § 5120, n. 170, 171, 171a, p. 73.
in partnership cases. R. S. § 5121, p. 75; n. 177, p. 76.
not granted to corporation. n. 180, p. 77.
fraudulent agreement in regard to. R. S. § 5131, p. 88.
specifications against and proceedings thereon. O. XXIV, p. 101.
DISPUTED PROPERTY,
in possession of assignee may be ordered sold by the court and the proceeds held to abide the result of the proceeding. R. S. § 5063, p. 43.
in possession of claimant can not be sold. n. 89, p. 43.
DISTRIBUTION OF BANKRUPT'S ESTATE,
to be pro rata among the creditors proving their claims. R. S. § 5091, p. 54.
rights of preferred creditors in. n. 119, p. 55.
a majority of the creditors present at meeting to determine what dividend, if any, to be had. R. S. § 5092, p. 55.
all creditors who have proved claims to participate in. n. 121, p. 56.
no dividend to be disturbed on account of subsequently proved debts. R. S. § 5097, p. 56.
priorities and order of payment in. R. S. 5101. n. 127, p. 57; n. 128, p. 58.
in case of composition proceedings. R. S. § 5103a, p. 61.
in partnership cases. R. S. § 5121, p. 74; n. 175, p. 75.
in case of corporations. R. S. § 5122, p. 77.
DISTRICT COURT. (SEE COURTS OF BANKRUPTCY.)
DISTRICT JUDGE,
may exercise powers of circuit judge in certain districts. R. S. § 4988, p. 9.
DISTRICT OF COLUMBIA,
supreme court of, a court of bankruptcy. R. S. § 4977, p. 5.
DIVIDENDS,
a majority of creditors may eclare a, at second meeting. R. S. § 5092, n. 120, p. 55.
a majority of creditors may declare further, at third meeting. R. S. § 5093, p. 55.

DIVIDENDS, (Continued,)
all who have claims proved may participate in. n. 121, p. 56.
final, upon settlement of assignee's accounts. R. S. § 5096, p. 56.
not to be disturbed by debts subsequently proved. R. S. § 5097, p. 56.
priorities in payment of. R. S. § 5101, n. 127. p. 57. n. 128, p. 58.
notice of, to each creditor. R. S. § 5102, p. 58.
to be deemed payment *pro tanto* of certain debts not discharged. R. S. § 5117, n. 164, p. 71.

DOCKETS,
or short memoranda of proceedings to be kept in clerk's office. R. S. § 4992, p. 10.

DRAWER OF BILLS,
claim against bankrupt as when proveable. R. S. § 5069, n. 94, p. 46.
not released by discharge of acceptor. R. S. § 5118, p. 71.

E

EMBEZZLEMENT,
debts created by, proveable, but not released by discharge. R. S. § 5117, n. 164, p. 71.

EVIDENCE,
certified copies of memoranda filed in clerk's office to be presumptive. R. S. § 4992, p. 10.
may be taken in form of affidavit. R. S. § 5003, p. 12.
may be taken before what officers. R. S. § 5003, p. 12.
in involuntary proceedings the burden of proof is on the creditor. n. 44, p. 24.
what is, of insolvency. n. 44, p. 24.
a defense which has been stricken out may be put in evidence as an admission. n. 44, p. 24.
what is, of an intent to prefer. n. 44, p. 24.
certified copy of assignment conclusive evidence of assignee's rights. R. S. § 5049, p. 39; n. 194, p. 87.
certified copy of a portion of the record is. n. 81, p. 40.
instrument, an evidence of debt may be withdrawn from files when. R. S. § 5082, p. 52.
of bankrupt and parties interested, competent. R. S. § 5087a, p. 54.
of bankrupt's wife may be taken. R. S. § 5088, p. 54.
may be taken in aid of trustees. R. S. § 5103, p. 59.

EVIDENCE, (Continued.)
certificate of discharge conclusive. R. S. § 5119, p. 72.
under application to annul discharge. R. S. § 5120, n. 171, 171a, p. 73.
what is, of fraudulent intent in preferences. n. 189. p. 85.
what is *prima facie*, of fraud in conveyances. R. S. § 5130, p. 88.
of bankrupt not competent in criminal proceedings against himself. n. 204, p. 90.
testimony, how taken in proceedings before register. O. X, p. 95.
proof of claims against bankrupt. O. XXXIV, p. 109.

EXAMINATION,
of witnesses to be before register. O. X, p. 95.
of bankrupt, may correct statements. O. XXXIII, p. 108.

EXCEPTIONS,
register may not decide on competency, materiality or relevancy of testimony. O. X, p. 95.
to assignee's report or exempt property. O. XIX, p. 100.

EXEMPTIONS,
no title to exempted property acquired by assignee. n. 68, p. 35; n. 71, p. 37.
liens on exempt property existing prior to bankruptcy, preserved. n. 68, p. 35.
money for immediate necessities not exceeding with other property exemption allowed by law may be retained by bankrupt. n. 68, p. 35.
what property exempted from the operation of the assignment. R. S. § 5045, p. 36.
what is exempted as "articles or necessaries." n. 70, p. 37.
court to see exempt property secured to debtor. n. 71, p. 37.
assignee to set exempt property apart, creditors may contest exemptions. n. 72, p. 37.
extend to what property. n. 73, p. 37.
homestead purchased in fraud of creditors. n. 74, p. 37.
physical character of homestead. n. 75, p. 38.
partners not entitled to, from partnership estate. n. 76, p. 38.
state laws in force in 1871 control. n. 77, p. 38.
when operating against partnership debts. n. 176, p. 76.

F

FAILURE TO KEEP BOOKS,
by bankrupt trader, bar to discharge.
R. S. § 5110, cl. 7, n. 156, p. 68.

FALSIFYING BOOKS,
falsification or mutilation of books, documents, papers, etc., by bankrupt a bar to discharge. R. S. § 5110, cl. 4, p. 68.

FEES, COMMISSIONS, ETC.,
register not to be interested in certain. R. S. § 4306, p. 11.
of register; to be paid by parties to whom services are rendered. R. S. § 5008, n. 23, p. 13.
and allowances of assignee. R. S. § 5099, p. 50, n. 123, 124, 125; p. 57.
order of payment, in distribution. R. S. § 5101, n. 127, p. 57.
of register, priority of payment. R. S. § 5124, n. 184, p. 79.
traveling or incidental expenses of register. R. S. § 5125, p. 80.
and allowance of marshal. R. S. § 5126, p. 80.
supreme court may alter. R. S. § 5127, p. 80.
to be reduced one-half until fixed by new rules. R. S. § 5127a, p. 80.
costs of adjournments before register. O. VI, p. 94.
of review of registers' orders by district court. O. VIII, p. 94.
of incompetent, immaterial or irrelevant depositions. O. IX, p. 95.
fees of register, marshal and clerk, to be paid or secured. O. XXIX, p. 103.
of witnesses and expenses, to be tendered. O. XXIX, p. 103.
costs when paid out of fund. O. XXIX, p. 103.
disbursements of costs by assignee; vouchers. O. XXIX, p. 103.
fees of clerk. O. XXX, p. 104.
fees and expenses of register. O. XXX, p. 104.
fees paid by creditors in establishing their debts to rank with other fees and costs. O. XXX, p. 104.
fees and allowances of marshals. O. XXX, p. 104.
of witnesses and jurors. O. XXX, p. 104.
fees of attorneys. O. XXX, p. 104.
disbursements for care and custody of property. O. XXX, p. 104.
excess over lawful costs paid into court; contempt. O. XXX, p. 104.

FEES, COMMISSIONS, ETC., (Contin'd)
discharge of bankrupt not delayed by non-payment of fees, etc. O. XXX, p. 104.
mode of claiming and taxing costs. O. XXX, p. 104.
office of auditor discontinued. O. XXX, p. 104.
costs in contested adjudications. O. XXXI, p. 107.
when debtor may have clerk or accountant. O. XXXI, p. 107.
fee for filing proof of debt paid in advance. O. XXXIV, p. 109.

FICTITIOUS DEBTS,
bankrupt's undisclosed knowledge of, a bar to discharge. R. S. § 5110, cl. 6, p. 68.
bankrupt's undisclosed knowledge of, penalty for. R. S. § 5132, p. 89.

FIDUCIARY DEBTS,
provable but not released by discharge. R. S. § 5117, n. 164, p. 71.

FORMS,
of certificate of discharge. R. S. § 5115, p. 70.
what ones to be used. O. XXXII, p. 108.
special orders, how framed. O. XXXII, p. 108.
forms heretofore prescribed adapted to modification of law or of orders. O. XXXVII, p. 112.
report of marshal. p. 112.
of register. p. 116.
of assignee. p. 117.
of clerk (No. 1). p. 114.
of clerk (No. 2). p. 114.
of clerk (No. 3). p. 115.

FRAUD,
debtor's co-operation with petitioning creditors no evidence of collusion. n. 56, p. 28.
on part of bankrupt a bar to discharge. R. S. 5110, cl. 2, p. 67.
debts created by, provable but not released by discharge. R. S. § 5117, n. 16, p. 71.
prima facie evidence of. R. S. § 5130, p. 86.
of bankrupt, penalty for. R. S. § 5132, n. 202, 203, p. 89.

FRAUDULENT CONVEYANCES,
creditor knowingly receiving a fraudulent preference shall not be permitted to prove more than half his claim. R. S. § 5021, p. 21.
what is deemed a. n. 32, p. 22.

FRAUDULENT CONVEYANCES, (Continued.)
a conveyance to be an act of bankruptcy must be shown to be made with a fraudulent intent. n. 33, p. 22.
does not change identity of property. n. 68, p. 35.
property conveyed in fraud of creditors vests in assignee. R. S. § 5046, n. 79, p. 38.
by bankrupt is a bar to discharge. R. S. § 5110, cl. 2, 5, 9, p. 67.
what deemed a. R. S. § 5128, p. 83; n.. 187, p. 84; n. 188, p. 85.
a conveyance made within three months prior to filing petition construed as. R. S. §§ 5129, 5129a, p. 87.
security taken in good faith not considered. R. S. § 5129b, n. 196, p. 88.
within time prescribed *prima facie* a. R. S. § 5130, n. 198, p. 88.
penalties for, against creditor. R. S. § 5132, p. 88.

FUNDS,
how deposited and drawn out of depository. O. XXVIII, p. 102.
copy of rule furnished depository. O. XXVIII, p. 102.

G

GAMING,
dissipation of property in, by bankrupt a bar to discharge. R. S. § 5110, cl. 5, p. 68.
penalties for, against bankrupt. R. S. § 5132, p. 88.

GENERAL ORDERS IN BANKRUPTCY
of supreme court; variation; rescission, etc. R. S. § 4990, p. 9.

GUARANTORS,
claims of, proveable when. R. S. §§ 5069, 5070, n. 94, p. 46.
entitle to dividend when. R. S. § 5091, p. 54.
not released by discharge of principal. R. S. § 5118, p. 71.

H

HABEAS CORPUS,
in case of imprisoned debtor. O. XXVII, p. 102.

HOLIDAYS,
what excluded in computation of time. R. S. § 5013, p. 14.

HOUSE SERVANT,
wages due to, have a priority in distribution. R. S. § 5101, p. 57.

I

IMPRISONED DEBTOR,
may be produced to testify on *habeas corpus*. O. XXVII, p. 120.

IMPRISONED DEBTOR. (Continued.)
and discharged in what case. O. XXVII, p. 102.
but creditor to have notice and be heard. O. XXVII, p. 102.

INDEMNIFYING BOND,
unless given, marshal to surrender goods adversely claimed. O. XIII, p. 96.
to be given when property is not in possession of bankrupt. O. XIII, p. 96.

INDORSER,
bankrupt's liability as, when a provable debt. R. S. § 5069, n. 94, p. 46.
claim of, when provable. R. S. § 5070 p. 46.
when entitled to dividend. R. S. § 5091, p. 54.
not released by discharge of co-obligee. R. S. § 5118, p. 71.

INFORMATION,
bankrupt may be prosecuted by. n. 200, p. 89.

INJUNCTION,
court may enjoin debtor from disposing of property, when. R. S. § 5024, p. 25.
restraining any person from interfering with debtor's property. n. 50, p. 25.
supposed fraudulent conveyee may be restrained from selling. n. 51, p. 25.

INSOLVENCY,
defined. n. 44, p. 24.

INTEREST,
stops at date of filing petition. n. 43, p. 23.
to be accounted for by assignee. R. S. § 5065b, p. 44.

INVENTORY OF ESTATE,
petitioner in voluntary proceedings must file an. R. S. § 5014, p. 15.
must contain what. R. S. § 5016, p. 16.
to be verified, how. R. S. § 5017, p. 16.
in involuntary proceedings debtor ordered to file. R. S. § 5050, p. 28.
to be prepared and filed by messenger and assignee, when. R. S. § 5031, p. 28.
fraudulent omission in, by bankrupt, penalties. R. S. § 5132, p. 89.
of bankrupt's property seized, marshal to prepare and deliver. O. XIII, p. 93.
to be furnished by opposing partner, where co-partner files petition against firm. O. XVIII, p. 99.
to be made by assignee. O. XIX, p. 99.

INVENTORY OF ESTATE, (Continued)
assignee to verify, correct or note deficiencies in marshal's inventory. O. XIX, p. 99.
to make supplemental inventory when. O. XIX, p. 99.

INVOLUNTARY BANKRUPTCY,.
what proportion in value and number of creditors must join in petition. R. S. § 5021, p. 20.
where petition must be brought. R. S. § 5021, p. 20.
if debtor deny the facts set up in the petition the issue shall be tried, how. R. S. § 5021, p. 20.
debtor may be adjudged bankrupt on petition of creditors when. R. S. § 5021, p. 21.
petition to be filed when. n. 31, p. 21.
adjudication and warrant in. R. S. § 5026, p. 28.
proceedings on warrant. R. S. § 5029, p. 28.
petitioners must prove facts alleged. n. 63, p. 28.
discharge of bankrupt in. R. S. § 5112, p. 69; n. 161, p. 70.
of partnership. n. 174, p. 75.

ISSUE,
what is of law and what of fact. u. 24, p. 13.
certified by register to judge for decision O. XI, p. 96.
pendency of issues not to delay proceedings. O. XI, p. 96.

J

JOINT LIABILITIES,
not released by discharge of co-obligee. R. S. § 5118, p. 71.

JURISDICTION, (SEE COURTS OF BANKRUPTCY.)
of district courts at law and in equity as courts of bankruptcy. n. 2, p. 3.
of district courts as courts of bankruptcy. R. S. § 4972, p. 2; n. 6, 7, p. 6.
of district courts as courts of bankruptcy, original. n. 1, p. 3.
of district and circuit courts exclusive of jurisdiction of state courts in suits to which assignee is a party. u. 3, p. 3; n. 4, p. 4.
of district and circuit courts not exclusive in some cases of jurisdiction of state courts, in suits against assignee. n. 5, p. 4.
of Supreme Court of District of Columbia as a court of bankruptcy. R. S. § 4977, p. 5.

JURISDICTION, (Continued.)
of territorial district courts; subject to superintendence of circuit courts. R. S. § 4973, p. 5.
of circuit and district courts arising from citizenship. n. 8, p. 8.
of circuit courts on appeals and writs of error. R. S. § 4980, n. 9, 10, p. 6.
and general superintendence of circuit court. R. S. § 4986, u. 18, p. 8. judgment final. n. 17, p. 8. practice in chambers. n. 18, p. 8.
sufficiency of number and value of petitioning creditors a jurisdictional fact. n. 46, p. 24.
of district court in adjustment of priorities and marshalling of assets. R. S. § 4972, p. 2.
in partnership cases where partners reside in different districts. R. S. § 5121, p. 75.
of circuit courts in actions to recover preference. n. 192, p. 86.
of state courts in actions to recover preference. u. 193, p. 86.

JURORS.
fees of. O. XXX, p. 104.

JURY TRIAL,
debtor may demand in writing a, the fact of bankruptcy. R. S. § 5026, p. 26.
demand for must be made when. n. 57, p. 27.
of specification against discharge. R. S. § 5111, n. 160, p 69.

JUSTICES OF SUPREME COURT,
shall have power to make general rules and orders in bankruptcy. R. S. § 5127a, p. 80.

L

LIENS,
upon exempted property preserved. n. 68, p. 35.
certain, preserved. R. S. § 5052, u. 82, p. 40.
may be discharged by assignee under order of the court. R. S. § 5066, p. 45.
landlord's lien for rent preserved. n. 96, p. 47.
who are lien creditors. n. 101, p. 49.
upon realty sold before bankruptcy proceedings not released by discharge. n. 167, (3) p. 72.

LIMITATIONS,
within which creditors' petition must be brought after act of bankruptcy. R. S. § 5021, p. 20.
debts barred by statute of, disregarded. n. 41, p. 23.
of all actions by or against assignee. R. S. § 5057, n. 86, p. 41.

M

MARSHAL,
penalties against, for certain offenses.
R. S. § 5012, p. 13.
warrant to be directed to. R. S. § 5019,
p. 16; § 5024, p. 24.
may seize property fraudulently conveyed under warrant of seizure. n.
53, p. 25.
fees and allowances of. R. S. §§ 5126,
5127a, p. 60.
reports of, to contain what; penalties.
R. S. § 5127b, p. 61; § 5127f, p. 62.
to make return of expenses on oath,
with vouchers. O. XII, p. 96.
when to take possession of bankrupts'
property. O. XII, p. 96.
and deliver to assignee or trustee. O.
XIII, p. 96.
and make and deliver inventory. O.
XIII, p. 96.
may redeliver goods adversely claimed, on notice, etc., unless indemnifying bond be given. O. XIII, p. 96.
may demand indemnifying bond before seizing property not in bankrupt's possession. O. XIII, p. 96.
o prepare schedule, but only on written statements under oath, when.
O. XIII, p. 96.
may appoint special deputies, when.
O. XIII, p. 96.
requisites of notices to creditors. O.
XIII, p. 96.
fees of, to be paid or secured in advance. O. XXIX, p. 103.
schedule of fees and allowances of.
O. XXX, p. 104.

MARSHALLING OF ASSETS,
in case of a creditor holding two
classes or kinds of security. n. 104, p.
49.

MEETINGS OF CREDITORS,
creditor may act at all, by attorney.
R. S. § 5095, n. 122, p. 56.

FIRST MEETING,
notice of, to creditors; contents. R.
S. § 5082, p. 32.
register to preside; marshal to make
return of adjournment. R. S. § 5033
n. 64, p. 32.
assignee to be elected at. R. S. § 5084,
p. 32, n. 65, p. 33.

SECOND MEETING,
when to be called; assignee's report;
dividend. R. S. § 5092. n. 120, p. 55.

THIRD MEETING,
when to be called. R. S. § 5093, p. 55.

MEETINGS OF CREDITORS, (Contin'd)
OTHER MEETINGS,
second and third need not be called by
assignee unless he has funds in his
hands. n. 120, p. 55.
omission of assignee, to call, others to
be held on order of court. R. S. §
5098, p. 56.
no second or third meetings held in
case of appointment of trustees. n.
129, p. 59.
meeting to consider [proposition for
composition. R. S. § 5103a, p. 60.
second and third, may be had on day
fixed for showing cause against discharge, when. O. XXV. p. 101.
notice of such meeting. O. XXV, p.
101.

MESSENGER,
marshal to act as. R. S. § 5019, p. 16.

MINUTE BOOKS,
of all acts done by register to be kept
in clerk's office. R. S. § 4992, p. 10.
how kept by clerk. O. I, p. 92.

MISDEMEANOR,
conviction of, a bar to discharge. R. S.
§ 5110, cl. 10, p. 69.

MONEYS,
how deposited and drawn from depository. O. XXVIII, p. 102.
copy of rule furnished depository. R.
XXVIII, p. 102.

MORTGAGES,
assignee in possession of mortgaged
property entitled to rents until claimed. n. 68, p. 35.
of certain chattels not invalidated by
assignment in bankruptcy. R. S. §
5052, p. 46.
of chattels not recorded, valid, if
valid by the laws of the state. n. 82,
p. 40.
assignee may discharge lien of. R. S.
§ 5066, p. 45.
ien of a mortgagee failing to prove his
claim not lost. n. 102, p. 49.

MULTIPLICITY OF ACTIONS,
in involuntary bankruptcy, where several petitions are filed, what to have
priority. O. XV, p. 98.
may be consolidated, when. O. XV, p.
98.

N

NEGLIGENCE,
of bankrupt a bar to discharge. R. S.
§ 5110, cl. 2, p. 67.

NOTARY PUBLIC,
  may administer oath in verification of schedule. n. 28, p. 16.
  may take proof of claims. R. S. § 5078a, n. 108, p. 50.
NOTICE,
  of bankruptcy how served and on whom. R. S. § 5019, p. 16.
  to bankrupt of adjudication in involuntary proceedings. R. S. § 5031, p. 28.
  to creditors, of bankruptcy, shall state what. R. S. § 5032, p. 32.
  of his appointment to be given by assignee. R. S. § 5054, p. 40.
  assignee to receive before suit. R. S. § 5056, p. 41. Exception. n. 86, p. 41.
  of assignee's sales, how published, etc. R. S. § 5065a, p. 43.
  of meetings of creditors. R. S. § 5094, p. 56.
  of assignees' settlements. R. S. § 5096, p. 56.
  of application for discharge. R. S. § 5109, p. 67.
  of application to annul discharge. R. S. § 5120, p. 73.
  to creditors, requisites of. O. XIII, p. 98.
  of hearing of petition to redeem, perform contract, compound claim, etc. O. XVII, p. 99.
  partner refusing to join in petition against firm entitled to. O. XVIII, p. 99.
  to assignee to show cause against removal. O. XIX, p. 99.
  notices under § 18, how served or sent. O. XXIII, p. 101.
  envelope to contain printed direction to return, etc. O. XXIII, p. 101.
  of second and third meetings on day fixed for showing cause against discharge. O. XXV, p. 101.
  of meeting to consider composition. O. XXXVI, p. 102.

O

OATH
  of office by register. R. S. 4995, p. 10.
  includes "affirmation." R. S. § 5013, p. 14.
  to schedule by petitioner, before what officer. R. S. § 5017, n. 28, p. 16.
  of allegiance by petitioner in voluntary proceedings necessary. R. S. § 5018, p. 16.
  to petition in involuntary proceedings, by whom. R. S. § 5021, p. 21, n. 35, p. 22.

OATH, (Continued.)
  in support of claim, may be administered by what officers. R. S. § 5076a, n. 108, p. 50, § 5079, p. 51.
  in support of claim, to be made by whom. R. S. § 5078, n. 110, p. 51.
  false on part of bankrupt a bar to discharge. R. S. § 5110, n. 158, p. 67.
  final, of bankrupt before discharge. R. S. § 5113, n. 162, p. 70.
OFFICERS,
  penalties against. R. S. § 5012, p. 13.
  of corporations to make proof in support of claim. R. S. § 5078, n. 110, p. 51.
  of bankrupt corporations, duties. R. S. § 5122, p. 76.
  to have no interest in estate. R. S. § 5127a, p. 81.
  fees and emoluments of. R. S. § 5124, p. 79; §§ 5125, 5126, 5127, 5127a, p. 80.
  reports of to contain what; penalties. R. S. §§ 5127b, 5127c, p. 81; §§ 5127d, 5127f, p. 82.
OPERATIVE,
  wages up to $50 have priority in distribution. R. S. § 5101, p. 57.
OPINION OF DISTRICT JUDGE,
  may be taken, on point submitted, when and how. R. S. § 5019, p. 13.
  must be on point actually arising. n. 25, p. 13.
ORDERS,
  granted on motion, to show name of attorney. O. III, p. 93.
  order designating register to act, to be delivered to him how. O. IV, p. 93.

P

PAPERS,
  filing and indorsing. O. I. p. 92; O. III, p. 93.
  removing from files. O. I, p. 92.
  to be bound together by clerk, and to constitute record. O. VII, p. 94.
PARTNERSHIP,
  debts are counted in computing number and value of creditors in involuntary proceedings. n. 38, p. 23.
  in composition proceedings either individual or partnership creditors may demand separate vote. n. 148, p. 68.
  a partner is not released from partnership liabilities by discharge of his co-partner. R. S. § 5118, p. 71.
  proceedings in bankruptcy of. R. S. § 5121, p. 74; n. 172, p. 75.

PARTNERSHIP, (Continued.)
distribution of the estate and the discharge of the. R. S. § 5121, p. 74.
when there are several petition against the, first takes precedence. n. 178, p. 76.
proceedings when two or more petitions are filed against the same firm in different courts. O. XVI, p. 98.
or in different districts against same firm by different member thereof. O. XVI, p. 98.
partners declining to join in petitions against the firm may resist. O. XVIII, p. 99.
must have notice. O. XVIII, p. 99.
may appear and make what defenses. O. XVIII, p. 99.
must furnish schedule and inventory. O. XVIII, p. 99.

PAYMENT OF DEBTS,
to be *pro rata;* priorities. R. S. § 5101, p. 57.
in composition proceedings. R. S. § 5103a, p. 61.

PARTY,
may conduct proceedings in person. O. III, p. 93.
and also examination of witnesses before register. O. IX, p. 95.

PENALTIES,
for taking illegal fees. R. S. § 5012, p. 13.
against assignee; co-conspirators. R. S. § 5085b, p. 44.
against officers for failure to report. R. S. § 5127f, p 82.
against creditor for fraudulent agreement. R. S. § 5131, p. 88.
against bankrupt for concealment of property, mutilation of books, etc. R. S. § 5132, p. 88.

PERISHABLE PROPERTY,
may be ordered sold by the court. R. S. § 5085a, p. 43; O. XXII, p. 101.

PERJURY,
of assignee; penalties for. R. S. § 6065b, p. 44.
of bankrupt a bar to discharge. R. S § 5110, cl. 1, n. 153, p. 67.

PERSON,
includes "corporation." R. S. § 5013, p. 14.

PETITION,
in voluntary proceedings shall contain what. R. S. § 5014, p. 15.
in involuntary proceedings to contain what; to be brought within what time. R. S. § 5021, p. 19.

PETITION, (Continued.)
to be filed where. R. S. § 5014, p. 15, n. 31; p. 21.
not to be dismissed because of defective depositions. n. 33, p. 22.
register to note deficiencies in. O. VII, p. 94.
when amendments allowed to. O. VII, p. 94.
to be written out plainly, etc. O. XIV, p. 98.

PLEADING,
a charge in the alternative that a debtor is in contemplation of bankruptcy or insolvent is insufficient. n. 33, p. 22.
petition in involuntary proceedings need not contain detailed statement of demand; should show it to be provable. n. 33, p. 22.
general stoppage of payment of commercial paper or a particular instance may be alleged. n. 33, p. 22.
discharge, how pleaded. R. S. § 5119a. n. 168, p. 72.
in an action to recover preference what are necessary allegations. n. 194, p. 87.
assignee in suing need not allege representative capacity. n. 194, p. 87.

PRACTICE,
filing of petition to be deemed commencement of proceedings. R. S. § 4991, n. 20, p. 10.
if petition is signed by an insufficiency in number or value of creditors, others may join. R. S. § 5021, p. 20.
if sufficiency join matter to proceed, otherwise to be dismissed. R. S. § 5021, p. 21.
verification of creditor's petition. R. S. § 5021, p. 21.
an order to show cause granted on an insufficient showing set aside; alias issued. n. 83, p. 22.
debtor's denial of facts stated in petition must be verified. n. 47, p. 24.
list of creditors filed in involuntary proceedings to be verified. n. 47, p. 24.
debtor ordered to show cause; enjoined; arrested. R. S. § 5024, p. 24.
grounds for injunction; arrest; seizure. n. 48, p. 25.
warrant for arrest, seizure, etc., to be prayed for in a separate petition. n. 54, p. 25.
service of petition and order to show cause. R. S. § 5025, p. 26.

INDEX. 135

PRACTICE, (Continued.)
  upon return of petition and order proceedings dismissed, when. R. S. § 5025, p. 26.
  "if the debtor cannot be found," means within the jurisdiction; corporation in hands of receiver. n. 55, p. 26.
  finding of the court as to number and amount, final. n. 56, p. 26.
  trial of petition. R. S. § 5026, p. 26.
  debtor failing to appear in involuntary proceedings adjudicated bankrupt by default. R. S. § 5026, p. 27.
  appearance waives irregularities of service. n. 58, p. 27.
  evidence of debt may be withdrawn from files, when. R. S. § 5082, p. 52.
  under application to annul discharge. R. S. § 5120, p. 73.

PREFERENCE,
  fraudulent, an act of bankruptcy. n. 32 (3), p. 22.
  making a fraudulent, by bankrupt a bar to discharge. R. S. § 5110, cl. 4, 9, pp. 68, 69.
  fraudulent, by corporations. R. S. § 5122, p. 76.
  fraudulent defined; void. R. S. § 5128, p. 83; n. 185, 186, 187, p. 84, n. 188, 189, p. 85, 190, p. 88.
  amendments of June 22, 1874. n. 186, p. 84.
  may be recovered from person other than the one benefitted. n. 191, p. 86.
  actions to recover; jurisdiction. n. 192, 193, p. 86.
  miscellaneous rulings on. p. 195, p. 87.
  fraudulent by bankrupt, how punished. R. S. § 5132, p. 88; n. 200, 202, p. 89.

PRIORITIES, (SEE DISTRIBUTION.)
  policy of the law to preserve. n. 88, p. 35.

PRIORITY OF ACTIONS,
  in involuntary bankruptcy; what petition shall be first heard. O. XV, p. 98.
  when court may order consolidation. O. XV, p. 98.
  when petition may be amended. O. XVI, p. 98.
  petition against firm, what one first heard. O. XVI, p. 98.
  what may be amended. O. XVI, p. 98.

PROCESS,
  how issued and treated. O. II, p. 92.
  signed blanks furnished to register. O. II, p. 92.

PROOF OF DEBTS,
  (SEE DEBTS AND PROOF OF CLAIMS.)
  may be made before what officers; to be sent to register; revision. R. S. §§ 5078, 5078a, n. 107, 108, p. 50; R. S. § 5079, p. 51.
  may be made by whom; in case of corporations. R. S. § 5078, n. 110, p. 51.
  register's duty with reference to; to be sent to assignee. R. S. § 5080, p. 51.
  withdrawal of. n. 111, p. 51.
  depositions, how entitled. O. XXXIV, p. 109.
  contents of. O. XXXIV, p. 109.
  delivered to register; his duties. O. XXXIV, p. 109.
  notices to creditors, how addressed. O. XXXIV, p. 109.
  depositions when claim is assigned before proof. O. XXXIV, p. 109.
  proceeding in case of the assignment of claims. O. XXXIV, p. 109.
  proof of claims of persons contingently liable, and allowance. O. XXXIV, p. 109.
  re-examination of claims; proceedings before register. O. XXXIV, p. 109.
  certifying issue to court; dismissal of issue. O. XXXIV, p. 109.

PUBLICATION,
  of notice to creditors, of first meeting. R. S. § 5019, p. 16.
  service of order to show cause, by. R. S. § 5025, p. 26.
  of notice of assignee's appointment. R. S. § 5054, p. 40.
  of notice of assignee's sales. R. S. § 5065a, p. 43.
  of notice of application for discharge. R. S. § 5109, p. 67.

PURCHASE,
  of claim in good faith in order to join petition, valid. n. 34, p. 22.
  if void for fraud, assignee deemed owner. n. 34, p. 22.

PURCHASING ASSENT OF CREDITOR, by bankrupt a bar to discharge. R. S. § 5110, cl. 8. n. 158, p. 68.

R

REBATE OF INTEREST,
  allowed when debt is not due. R. S. § 5067, p. 45.

RECEIVER. (SEE ASSIGNEE.)
  may be appointed by court when and for what purpose. n. 2, p. 3.
  should be appointed when. n. 52, p. 25.
  may carry on business under order of the court. R. S. § 5061a, p. 42.

RECORD, (SEE DOCKETS.)
how kept; open for public inspection; certified copies *prima facie* evidence, R. S. § 4992, p. 10.
what shall constitute record in each case. O. VII, p. 94.

REDEMPTION,
assignee may exercise the right of, or sell it, subject to order of court. R. S. § 5066, p. 45.
assignee may release bankrupt's right of. R. S. § 5075, p. 48.
by bankrupt, assignee or creditor, may may be had upon what proceedings, etc. O. XVII, p. 99.

RE-EXAMINATION OF CLAIMS,
proceedings before register; issue to court; view, etc. O. XXXIV, p. 109.

REFERENCE,
may be made to register, to take evidence. R. S. § 5003, p. 12.
in these rules to sections of original law, or to corresponding sections of revised statutes. O. XXXVII, p. 112.

REGISTERS IN BANKRUPTCY,
by whom appointed. R. S. § 4993, p. 10.
who eligible for. R. S. § 4994, p. 10.
bond and official oath. R. S. § 4995, p. 10.
restrictions upon. R. S. § 4996, p. 11.
removal of, by district judge. R. S. § 4997, p. 11.
powers of, R. S. § 4998, n. 21, p. 11.
limitations of powers of. R. S. § 4999, p. 11.
to make memoranda of his proceedings and to file copies in the clerk's office. R. S. § 5000, p. 11.
to attend at any place in the district under order of the court for certain purposes. R. S. § 5001, p. 12.
to have powers of court, except commitment when so attending. R. S. § 5002, p. 12.
evidence taken before. R. S. § 5003, p. 12.
all evidence and proceedings before, to be reduced to writing and filed in clerk's office; oath administered by. R. S. § 5004, p. 12.
may compel attendance of witnesses. R. S. § 5005, p. 12.
contempt before, to be referred to district judge and punished how. R. S. § 5006, p. 12.
contempt before, by bankrupt's wife punishable. n. 22, p. 13.
in the same district may act for each other. R. S. § 5007, p. 13.

REGISTERS IN BANKRUPTCY. (Continued.)
fees of, how established; paid by whom. R. S. § 5008, n. 23, p. 13.
issues of law or fact arising before, to be adjourned into court for decision. R. S. § 5009, n. 24, p. 13.
to certify a point or matter arising before him to district judge for decision. R. S. § 5010, n. 25, p. 13.
penalties against, for taking illegal fees. R. S. § 5012, p. 13.
to issue warrant on voluntary petition, when. R. S. § 5019, p. 16.
to preside at meeting of creditors. R. S. § 5033, n. 64, p. 32.
to appoint assignee, when. R. S. § 5034, p. 32; n. 65, p. 33.
to pass upon proof of claim and forward it to assignee. R. S. 5080, p. 51.
fees of, have a priority. R. S. § 5124, n. 184, p. 79.
travelling and incidental expenses of. R. S. § 5125, p. 80.
justices of supreme court may prescribe a tariff of fees of. R. S. § 5127, p. 80.
fees of, reduced; must not be interested in the estate. R. S. § 5127a, p. 80.
reports of, to clerk of supreme court. R. S. § 5127c, p. 81.
penalties against. R. S. § 5127f, p. 82.
papers referred to, when. O. IV, p. 93.
what proceedings had before. O. IV, p. 93.
order to name day of bankrupt's attendance. O. IV, p. 93.
register to protect bankrupt from arrest. O. IV, p. 93.
order, how delivered to register. O. IV, p. 93.
time and place of acting. O. V, p. 93.
may perform what acts. O. V, p. 93.
to proceed with dispatch; not to adjourn, but for cause. O. VI, p. 94.
six hours a day's sitting. O. VI, p. 94.
to examine petition and schedules and note deficiencies. O. VII, 94.
duty of, as to endorsing, filing and preserving papers. O. VII, p. 94.
orders made by, must recite what. O. VIII, p. 94.
motions heard as by consent, when. O. VIII, p. 94.
orders, how reviewed before district court; costs of review. O. VIII, p. 94.
to notify assignee of appointment. O. IX, p. 95.

INDEX. 137

REGISTERS IN BANKRUPTCY, (Continued.)
  mode of taking testimony in proceedings before. O. X, p. 95.
  memoranda of acts of register forwarded to clerk. O. XI, p. 96.
  to certify issues to judge for decision. O. XI, p. 96.
  pendency of issues not to delay proceedings. O. XI, p. 96.
  to keep accounts of expenses. O. XII, p. 96.
  and make returns on oath. O. XII, p. 96.
  to hear exceptions to assignee's report, setting off exempt property. O. XIX, p. 99.
  to furnish creditor with substance of assignee's monthly return. O. XIX, p. 99.
  to notify assignee of proceedings for removal. O. XIX, p. 99.
  to audit account of assignees. O. XIX, p. 99.
  to keep accounts with clerk and assignee. O. XXVIII, p. 102.
  to keep register of checks. O. XXVIII, p. 102.
  to countersign checks. O. XXVIII, p. 102.
  fees of, to be paid or received in advance. O. XXIX, p. 103.
  schedule of fees and allowances of. O. XXX, p. 104.
  proofs of debts delivered to. O. XXXIV, p. 109.
  fee paid in advance. O. XXXIV, p 109.
  duty when proof of debt is received by mail. O. XXXIV, p. 109.
  how to address notices to creditors. O. XXXIV, p. 109.
  duty in case of assigned claims; notice and subrogation. O. XXXIV, p. 109.
  proceedings before, as to re-examination of claims. O. XXXIV, p. 109.
  to preside at meeting called to consider composition. O. XXXV, p. 110.
  form of annual report of. p. 118.
REMOVAL OF OFFICERS,
  of registers. R. S. § 4997, p. 11.
  of assignees. R. S. § 5036, p. 38; § 5039, n. 66, p. 134.
REMOVAL OF PROPERTY,
  by bankrupt a bar to discharge. R. S. § 5110, cl. 4, p. 68.
  by bankrupt, penalty for. R. S. § 5132, cl. 8, p. 88.

RENT,
  falling due at stated periods, how proved. R. S. § 5071, p. 47.
  landlord's lien for. n. 96, p. 47.
  assignee liable for, when. n. 97, p. 47.
REPORTS OF OFFICERS,
  of assignee, to contain what, made when. R. S. § 5065b, p. 44.
  of marshal, annual. R. S. § 5127b, p. 81.
  of register, annual. R. S. § 5127c, p. 81.
  of assignee, annual. R. S. § 5127d, [p. 82.
  of clerk, annual. R. S. § 5127e, p. 82.
  penalties for failure. R. S. § 5124f, p. 82.
  forms of. p. 113.
RESIGNATION,
  of assignee. R. S. § 5038, p. 34.
REVIEW,
  by district court of orders of register. O. VIII, p. 94; O. XI, p. 96; O. XXXIV, p. 109.
  costs of same. O. VIII, p. 94.
REVISED STATUTES,
  references to bankrupt act to be deemed to correspond to original section of revised statutes. O. XXXVII, p. 112.
RULES,
  to be made by supreme court. R. S. § 4990, p. 9; § 5127a, p. 80.
  of practice in equity to govern, etc. O. XXXII, p. 108.
  at law. O. XXXII, p. 108.
  special rules; modification of rules. O. XXXII. p. 108.

S

SALE,
  assignee to sell incumbered estate subject to order of court. R. S. § 5062, p. 42.
  creditors, applying for a resale must fulfill offer to bid. n. 88, p. 42.
  of disputed property. R. S. § 5063, p. 43.
  disputed property in hands of claimant can not be sold. n. 89, p. 42.
  of uncollectible assets. R. S. § 5064, p. 43.
  of perishable property. R. S. § 5065, p. 43.
  of assignee, to be at auction; notice of. R. S. § 5065, p. 43.
  of incumbered property. n. 102, p. 49.
  secured creditor may apply for, of security. p. 104, p. 49.

SALE, (Continued.)
by assignee at private sale, O. XXI, p. 101.
of franchise of corporation. O. XXI, p. 101.
of perishable property, by order of court. O. XXII, p. 101.

SCHEDULES,
of petitioner in voluntary proceedings. R. S, § 5015, p, 15.
may be corrected. R. S. § 5020, p. 17.
corrections of, not allowed after first meeting of creditors. n. 29, p. 17.
and inventory to be verified. R. S. § 5017, n. 28, p. 16.
and inventory in involuntary proceedings. R. S. § 5030, p. 28.
prepared by marshal and assignee, when. R. S. § 5031. p. 28.
false verification of, a bar to discharge, R. S. § 5110, cl. 1, p. 67.
omission of creditor's name from, with creditor's consent not fraudulent. n. 153, p, 67.
of bankrupt's debt, when and how to be prepared by marshal. O. XIII, p. 96.
to be furnished by opposing partner, when co-partner files petition against firm. O. XVIII, p. 99.
debtor to explain omissions in; amendments to. O. XXXIII, p. 108.

SECOND BANKRUPTCY,
debtor not entitled to discharge unless assets pay 70 per cent. of debts proved. R. S. § 5116, n. 163, p. 71.

SEIZURE,
warrant of, when issued. R. S. § 5024, p. 24, n. 53; p. 25.

SERVANT,
wages up to $50 have priority. R. S. § 5101, cl, 4, p. 57.

SET-OFF,
claim against bankrupt can not be set-off against goods purchased of assignee. n. 88, p. 42.
what are allowed in. R. S. § 5073, p. 47.
claim of stockholder; of bailee. n. 98, p. 48.
of transferred claims. n. 99, p. 48.

STATE COURTS,
jurisdiction of, not divested by adjudication in bankruptcy. n. 3, p. 4.
jurisdiction of, to recover fraudulently conveyed property. n. 4, p. 4.
can not grant injunction restraining person from applying for benefit of bankrupt law. n. 5, p. 4.

STATE COURTS, (Continued.
jurisdiction not divested by filing petition in involuntary proceedings. n. 49, p. 25.
suits in, do not abate on adjudication n. 80, p. 39.
action in, to enforce lien stayed. n. 106, p. 50.
composition proceedings conclusive upon. n. 141, p. 63.
judgment by default against bankrupts in. n. 169, p. 72.
proceedings in, against corporations. R. S. § 5128, p. 77.
jurisdiction of, in actions to recover preference. n. 193, p. 86.

STATEMENT OF DEBTOR,
to be presented at composition meeting. R. S. § 5103a, p. 60.

STAYS,
of suits against debtor in state court. R. S. § 5106, p. 65; n. 150, p. 66.

SURETIES,
not released by composition proceedings. n. 143, p. 63.
not released by discharge of principal. R. S. § 5118, p. 71.

T

TAXES,
on estate in hands of assignee to the state. n. 125, p. 57.
due United States. R. S. § 5101, p. 57.

TEMPORARY INVESTMENTS,
court may order, of money in hands of assignee. R. S. § 5060; p. 41.

TERRITORIAL COURTS, (SEE COURTS OF BANKRUPTCY.

TESTIMONY, (SEE EVIDENCE.)
how taken in proceedings before register. O. X, p. 95.
objections to, on trial of fact of bankruptcy before marshal. O. XXXV, p. 110.

TIME,
computation of. R. S. § 5013, n. 26, p. 14.

TITLE,
of property conveyed by assignee not affected by his ineligibility, R. S. § 5035, p. 33.
vest in remaining assignee or successor in case of vacancy. R. S. § 5042, p. 34.
of assignee relates back to the commencement of proceedings. n. 67. p. 35.
assignee takes only such as debtor had n. 68, p. 35,
of trustees. R. S. § 5103, p. 59.

TRANSFER OF PROPERTY,
  fraudulent, deemed void. R. S. § 5129, p. 87.
TRIAL,
  of creditor's petition, summary; debtor may demand jury. R. S. § 5026, p. 26; n. 57, p. 27.
TRIAL BEFORE MARSHAL,
  trial of fact of bankruptcy before marshal; mode of selecting jury; challenges. O. XXXV, p. 110.
  penalty for juror failing to serve. O. XXXV, p. 110.
  notice and conduct of trial; subpœnas to witnesses; objections to testimony; pleadings; evidence: *venire de novo*. O. XXXV, p. 110.
TRUSTEE,
  appointed to take charge of the estate. R. S. § 5103, p. 58.
  conveyances to; duty and powers of. R. S. § 5103, p. 59.
  if resolution is not approved. R. S. § 5103, p. 59.
  no meetings of creditors necessary. u. 129, p. 59.
  surrender of bankrupt's property, when made to marshal. O. XIII, p. 96.
  marshal to deliver to, when. O. XIII, p. 96.
TRUST PROPERTY,
  a devise in trust free from claims of creditors does not pass to assignee. n. 63, p. 35.
  held by bankrupt does not pass to assignee. R. S. 5053, p. 40.
  identity of. n. 83, p. 40.

U

UNION PACIFIC RAILROAD COMPANY,
  bankrupt act not applicable to. R. S. § 5123a, p. 78.
UNITED STATES.
  debts and taxes due to. R. S. § 5101, n. 127, p. 57.
  debts due to, not released by discharge. u. 187, cl. (1), p. 72.

V

VACANCY,
  in office of district judge. R. S. § 4977, p. 5.
  in office of assignee, how filled. R. S. § 5041, p. 34.
VENUE,
  petitions filed in different districts, where heard. O. XVI, p. 98.

VOLUNTARY BANKRUPTCY,
  unopposed adjudication in, by register. R. S. § 5001, p. 12.
  a lunatic may file petition by his guardian. n. 30, p. 21.
  discharge of bankrupt in. R. S. § 5112a, p. 89; n. 161, p. 70.
  of partnership. n. 173, p. 75.

W

WAGES,
  due certain employees up to $50 have priority. R. S. § 5101, p. 57.
WARRANT IN BANKRUPTCY,
  issued when; to whom directed; to contain what. R. S. § 5019, p. 16.
  of seizure, issued when. R. S. § 5028, p. 28.
  what property subject to seizure under. u. 62, p. 28.
  may direct property to be surrendered to marshal, when. O. XIII, p. 96.
  special, may be issued. O. XIII, p. 96.
WASTE,
  of estate by bankrupt a bar to discharge, R. S. § 5110, cl. 2, p. 67.
WIFE OF BANKRUPT,
  punishable for contempt. n. 22, p. 12.
  may be examined. R. S. § 5088, p. 54.
WITNESSES,
  attendance of, before register. R. S. § 5003, p. 12.
  before register; contempt. R. S. § 5005, p. 12.
  contumacy before register. R. S. § 5006, p. 12.
  competent to prove claims. R. S. § 5078, n. 110, p. 51.
  attendance of. R. S. § 5087, p. 53.
  privileges of; assignee may be subpœnaed. n. 118, p. 54.
  examination of, before register. O. X, p. 95.
  proceedings in case of refusal of, to attend or testify. O. X, p. 95.
  fees and expenses of, to be tendered. O. XXIX, p. 103.
  what fees allowed. O. XXX, p. 104.
WORDS,
  meaning of. R. S. § 5013, p. 14.
WRIT OF ERROR,
  from district court when allowed and to whom. R. S. § 4980, p. 8.
  not allowed in cases tried without jury. n. 10, p. 8.
  conditions of. R. S. § 4981, p. 7.
  no question of fact re-examined on. u. 12, p. 7.

www.ingramcontent.com/pod-product-compliance
Lightning Source LLC
Chambersburg PA
CBHW030334170426
43202CB00010B/1118